Software,
Copyright,
and
Competition

Software, Copyright, and Competition

THE "LOOK AND FEEL" OF THE LAW

Anthony Lawrence Clapes

Illustrations by LISA CLAPES

QUORUM BOOKS

New York
Westport, Connecticut
London

Library of Congress Cataloging-in-Publication Data

Clapes, Anthony Lawrence.
  Software, copyright, and competition: the "look and feel" of the
law / Anthony Lawrence Clapes ; illustrations by Lisa Clapes.
    p. cm.
  Includes index.
  ISBN 0–89930–507–5 (lib. bdg. : alk. paper)
  1. Copyright—Computer programs—United States. 2. Competition,
Unfair—United States. I. Title.
KF3024.C6C55   1989
346.7304′82—dc20
[347.306482]   89–10477

British Library Cataloguing in Publication Data is available.

Library of Congress Catalog Card Number: 89–10477
ISBN: 0–89930–507–5

First published in 1989 by Quorum Books

Greenwood Press, Inc.
88 Post Road West, Westport, Connecticut 06881

Printed in the United States of America

∞

The paper used in this book complies with the
Permanent Paper Standard issued by the National
Information Standards Organization (Z39.48–1984).

10 9 8 7 6 5 4 3

Copyright Acknowledgments

Grateful acknowledgment is given for permission to use the following excerpts:

Pages 186–197 from Susan Lammers, "Programmers at Work," *PC World* (September 1986).
Reprinted by permission of Microsoft Press. Copyright © 1986 by Microsoft Press. All
rights reserved.

From Alan Kay, "Computer Software," *Scientific American* (September 1984). Copyright ©
1984 by Scientific American, Inc. All rights reserved.

For Jill

Contents

Acknowledgments

This book had its genesis in a law review article that in turn grew out of a lawsuit in which a collision occurred between the world of the law and the world of computer programming. My co-counsel in the lawsuit and co-authors of the article were Pat Lynch and Mark Steinberg of the law firm of O'Melveny and Myers. Although the present work is a major departure from the work that we did jointly, and although the views expressed in these pages are entirely my own, the intellectual and inspirational debt that I owe to my colleagues Lynch and Steinberg is manifest. For those interested, the article, "Silicon Epics and Binary Bards: Determining the Proper Scope of Copyright Protection for Computer Programs," can be found in volume 34 of the *UCLA Law Review* at page 1493.

Volume 34 of the *UCLA Law Review* is a special edition dedicated to the memory of Melville B. Nimmer, until his death the nation's foremost authority on copyright law. Anyone writing in that area of the law must acknowledge reliance on Mel Nimmer's monumental treatise. The three general-purpose litigators (later the authors of "Silicon Epics") who engaged Professor Nimmer in 1984 to aid them in understanding and explaining to a federal judge the work of the government commission whose recommendations led to the 1980 software-related revisions to the Copyright Act, however, have even greater cause to acknowledge the influence of Mel Nimmer on their thinking. Again, I claim full responsibility for what you are about to read, and wish only to indicate that my opinions in this region of the law have been shaped by Mel Nimmer's reflections on how the copyright law should apply to computer programs. A succinct version of those reflections may be found in the appendix to "Silicon Epics."

Others have had significant influence, directly or indirectly, on the evolution of my views on the copyright law. Although they did not contribute to the expression in these pages, their ideas and perspectives have informed my own, and for that they deserve thanks. They also deserve a disclaimer: The blame for any shortcomings in the ideas, perspectives, and the expression thereof that follow should be laid at the feet of the author, not the named individuals. I have learned much from Morton David Goldberg, of Schwab Goldberg Price and Dannay; Jon Baumgarten, formerly general counsel to the Copyright Office and now partner in the Proskauer firm's Washington, D.C., office; and Gunter Hauptman, formerly of IBM and now at the Kay, Scholer firm in New York. I also wish to express my appreciation to Nick Katzenbach, whose patience I feel I tried sorely when he was general counsel at IBM as I struggled toward a balanced view of copyright protection for software; Dan Evangelista, currently IBM's general counsel, who gave me the ability to remain active in this area of law; and Bob Townsend, Roger Smith, Dave Cartenuto, and Vic Siber of IBM, who have been willing sounding boards over the years. It must be said that this book does not purport to be a statement of the opinions of the listed individuals, nor does it represent the views of the International Business Machines Corporation.

On the technical side, the following people have helped me understand what computer programs are and how they are written. Again, they did not contribute directly to this book, and are not responsible for the synthesis I have made of their teachings. They are thanked here for their tutelage in the various contexts in which it occurred: Professor Bernard Galler of the University of Michigan; the late Jon Wilson of Evergreen Consulting; Marilyn Bohl, formerly of IBM and now at RTI; and from IBM, Ellen Hancock, Dick Case, Bill McPhee, Jim McInerney, Jim Grey, and Gerry Young, among a large number of computer scientists, software executives, and programmers to whom I have had access.

Working with Quorum Books has been a pleasure. I have benefitted enormously from the sage counsel and gentle persuasiveness of Eric Valentine, Executive Editor, and the care and attention of Lynn Flint, Production Editor.

Finally, there are several people whose views are quite different from mine, and whom the vagaries of life have thrust into the role of critic, not (so far) of this book but of earlier expressions of my opinions, either in litigation or otherwise. Their criticisms have caused me to smooth the jagged edges off my viewpoints, shore up or abandon analyses they demonstrated to be weak or otherwise flawed, and generally to be more precise in my exposition. Chief among these are Ken Liebman of Irell and Manella; Ray Fitzsimons and Rob Clarke of the NCR Corporation; Michael Jacobs, Preston Moore, and others at Morrison and Foerster; and computer consultant Ronald Alepin. *Qui habet aures audiendi, audiat.*

Introduction

The computer industry is in turmoil over the copyright law. The latest uproar is over the phenomenon that the industry calls "look and feel." The "look and feel" issue is exemplified by the reaction to Apple Computer, Inc.'s 1988 lawsuit against the software supplier Microsoft and the computer manufacturer Hewlett-Packard. The suit was widely seen as a kind of gauntlet thrown down before competitors who would like their computers to present "user-friendly" screen interfaces similar to those of the Apple Macintosh. As soon as the lawsuit was filed, the trade press ignited with speculation as to whether the Macintosh trashcan icon could really be monopolized by Apple, and whether the use of screen-border scroll bars could be precluded to anyone other than Apple. Despite the fact that those questions are not really posed by the Apple suits, inquiring minds around the industry still want to know the answers to them, and to the very similar questions raised by Ashton-Tate's suit against database clone Fox Software and by Lotus Development Corporation's suits against two spreadsheet clones, Paperback Software and Mosaic Software.

Not long before the Apple suit was filed, the Massachusetts Software Council had held a seminar moderated by the reynardine Ed Stead, then vice president and general counsel of Cullinet Software Corporation and now—by pure coincidence—vice president and general counsel at Apple. Ed had orchestrated the Massachusetts event around just such questions, and matched audience and speakers so as to achieve high drama. On the dais were eminent experts in copyright law and veteran software-case litigators, most notable among the latter being the indefatigable Jack

Brown, dean of the high-tech bar. Jack is the lawyer who led Apple to victory in *Apple Computer, Inc. v. Franklin Computer Corp.*, the foundational software copyright case and the fount from which just about all software copyright jurisprudence has sprung. He has continued to make history by virtue of his representation of Apple in its suit against Microsoft and Hewlett Packard.

In the audience that day were a hundred or so programmers and programming executives, and about the same feverish, swirling emotion as one would have experienced in the old days at Ebbetts Field in the last inning of the seventh game of the World Series, with the Brooklyn Dodgers down to the Yankees three to two. The subject that the panel had been asked to address that morning was the subject at the heart of the latest Apple lawsuit: "look and feel." "Look and feel" is a vaguely salacious-sounding topic that has split the programming community into two camps as diametrically opposed as the North and South Poles. My ultimate goal in these pages is to deal definitively with look and feel. For now, I only wish to observe—because it illustrates my immediate point—-that when the symposium was over a programmer strode up to me with his jaw set and seethed, "I disagree with everything you said." The reaction took me aback. I had just finished giving what I thought was a completely dispassionate and objective review of the state of copyright law as it applied to computer programs, a review with which an experienced copyright lawyer might quibble here and there, but that should not have made anyone as irate as this fellow was. It is not the fact of his displeasure on which I mean to focus your attention, though, but the particular turn taken by his displeasure. He might have said, but did not, "Gee, I'm very disappointed in the way the law has developed." He might also have said, but did not, "It appears that judges do not understand the nature of programming." Either reaction would have been appropriate from someone who had no prior knowledge of the law but substantial prior knowledge of software. What he said, though, was "I disagree with everything you said," as though by taking vigorous enough issue with the law, he could cause it to change course by an act of will.

The reaction of that unsettled speaker of alphanumeric languages is by no means isolated. Both from others in that audience and from computer science acquaintances generally I have encountered the view that force of logic not only ought to prevail but should be taken as having prevailed over the rule of law. A Really Big Name in microcomputer program development once patiently explained to me that the problem with the copyright law was that it didn't take account of the way programmers behaved. Programmers, he said, naturally refrained from copying the code of one another's programs (a highly questionable assertion in itself, as we shall see), but they routinely copied other programs' display-screen format and content from one another. The law, by his lights, should codify not behavior as it ought to be but behavior as it is.

Similarly, I have seen cases, sometimes as the plaintiff's lawyer, sometimes as the defendant's lawyer, in which the author of a program flatly refused to accept the notion that the copyright in his or her program protected only the expression in the program, not the ideas it contained. Even though it is as settled a rule of law as the rule that unmarried persons under the age of sixty-five with no dependents and no infirmities are entitled to only one exemption on their tax returns, the principle that one's precious and hard-won ideas, once published, are not protected from copying collides with the creative but orderly mind's sense of justice, and is rejected time and time again.

In fairness, the other side of the psychological coin is no more satisfying to the eye. If, as a rule, programmers don't understand the law, it is also true that lawyers, as a rule, don't understand programming. Most lawyers who encounter the programming community regard it as a strange and slightly madcap world in which people think and speak in code rather than in plain English. As a rule, in fact, lawyers who represent clients in connection with software issues fall very neatly into one of four categories:

Lawyers who haven't got time to learn what programming is all about, and don't;

Lawyers who decide not to take the time to learn because (they assume) judges and juries will never figure it out either, and don't;

Lawyers who—Luddites at heart—are constitutionally incapable of learning about programming, and don't; and

Lawyers who think they understand programming, but don't.

There is a fifth category, to wit, those lawyers who do understand programming and perhaps are even capable of actually writing programs, but the small proportion of lawyers in this category, like platypuses, occupy such a modest and singular niche in the lineage that they do not bear consideration in a work of general scope such as this one.

If all this begins to sound like a vague recapitulation of the theme of C. P. Snow's *The Two Cultures and the Scientific Revolution*, it is with good reason. Software is, after all, not poetry as we have heretofore known that art form. Software causes computers to do useful work, and is consequently thought of as appurtaining to the scientific culture. Copyright, on the other hand, is simply a branch of the law itself, and the law itself is a creature of the nonscientific culture. Issues of software copyright, then, are boundary issues; to use a term from the scientific side, they are issues at the interface between the world of the technologically literate and the world of those who are literate in the formalized structure of society.

We are going to explore herein what some regard as interesting questions relating to other types of interfaces: program interfaces, those points at which communication can occur between a program and something else (e.g., another program, a human being, a hardware device). We might also ask ourselves, though, whether at the interface between the software world and the legal world it is reasonable to expect that communication of any meaningful sort can occur.

There is ample cause for doubt. In the first place, the languages are different. Sometimes the words are the same, but the meanings are quite disparate. For example, to a computer scientist, "executable" refers to lines of text in a program, each of which will cause the processor hardware of the computer to perform an elementary operation. To a lawyer, "executable" connotes either an inmate on death row who has exhausted all his appeals or a will that is ready to be signed. Often, however, the words are completely different and have meanings not at all obvious to anyone unschooled in the trade. Common terms used daily by cognoscenti—such as, in the case of programming, *subroutine*, *data declaration*, or *macro*, and, in the case of the law, *certiorari*, *privity*, or *deficiency judgment*—convey no information at all to those not indoctrinated in one or the other profession.

Moreover, there are differences not just in the way programmers and lawyers talk, but in the way they think. Programmers are logical. Perfectly logical. Computer circuitry cannot understand instructions that are not perfectly logical. Successful programmers are therefore people whose minds easily imbed conceptual problems in inexorable webs of logical solutions. Lawyers' minds don't work that way. In the practice of law, logical reasoning is an important tool, but it is only one of many tools that lawyers use, and the successful lawyer knows when to use it and when to use other tools, such as rhetoric, fact gathering, surprise, or force of personality. "The life of the law," said Justice Holmes, "is not logic but experience."

The difference in thought process between programmers and lawyers was brought home to me not long ago at the end of a business dinner in a Silicon Valley restaurant. The establishment, Casa Isabella, is a small, family-owned restaurant that does not accept plastic in lieu of real money. That policy having been disclosed to the mixed table of programmers and lawyers at the end of the meal, it was decided to tax each diner equally. Legal tender in a variety of denominations was thrown on the table, and the lawyer who was acting as banker began to total up the wadge of bills in the random order in which he had scooped them into his hand: "20, 30, 31, 32, 37, 47," and so on. Under the influence of Mexican beer, seafood enchiladas, and the general post-prandial jesting taking place at the table, the lawyer stumbled in his count and had to start over.

At that point there came a roar of protest from the programmers, on the ground that the lawyer was following an unthinkable processing algorithm. "No programmer would count money that way," they explained, and insisted that the lawyer reorganize the bills in descending order of value. That was done, with all the twenties first, then the tens, then fives, then ones. Now the lawyer commenced again, but in a way that gave him the last laugh precisely because of the difference between the way programmers think and the way lawyers think: "20, 40, 60, 80, 81, 82, 87, 92 . . . " The programmers were confounded for a few seconds, their expectations of neatness disrupted. The lawyer had changed the algorithm in mid-processing, by beginning at the top of the stack and then switching to the bottom. When they realized that while their "program" was completely logical, the "processor" was not, the "techies" threw their hands heavenward in resignation and the table dissolved in laughter.

Despite the existence of considerable obstacles to communication between computer scientists and lawyers, however, it must be admitted that a communication of sorts is occurring. Whether that communication is often, or ever, effective is open to debate, judging in particular by both the scholarly and the popular writings of lawyers on topics at the interface. This book aims at improving that communication, in an area of substantial controversy in both the programming community and the legal community.

Computer law is a "hot" specialty at the moment. The clique of lawyers fondest of advertising that they practice this specialty would readily admit in private that computer law is only a marketing concept. It is not a separate area of law but rather a pastiche—an amalgam of various parts of contract law, criminal law, intellectual property law, banking law, and so forth—that, advertised as a specialty, can attract clients. Even so, the impact of the computer phenomenon on the substance of the law has thrown off, like meteors after the collision of two planets, massive amounts of commentary; commentary that attempts to parse the meager though growing body of caselaw and to offer up rules for anticipated problems that might or might not materialize in the real world. These scintillations, although spun casually off into the universe of legal discourse, can have in aggregate a profound effect on the direction taken by the caselaw and legislation that actually does come to affect the development of the computer industry. Given the importance of that industry, the need for effective communication between those who make the products and those who make the rules is critical. If this book can provide a base of common understanding between the computer programming community and the legal and judicial community, it will have served its purpose.

Everyone active in this field has biases on the subject of look and feel. I am no exception. Contrary to what some readers might think, my biases do not arise from my employment at IBM. If the knowledgeable executives and employees at IBM could vote on the issue of whether a computer program's look and feel should be protected by copyright, I have no idea how they would vote. I do know that IBM and other established software suppliers have no interest either in overprotection or in underprotection for computer programs, because they can find themselves defending copyright actions as often as prosecuting them. My own biases arise, rather, from my exposure to program authors, the way they work, and the material they produce. I am convinced that most computer programs are works of imagination, entitled to the full copyright protection accorded to other works of imagination. Software, the epic poetry of the information age, cannot be compared to the *Aeneid* in an aesthetic sense, of course, but that is not what is important. What is important is that the program author sitting down before an empty pad or a blank screen typically has broad expressive discretion. The task I have have undertaken in this book is to demonstrate the basis for my opinions, the fact that the developing caselaw reflects similar opinions, and the consequences of those opinions for the industry and for society.

Finally, a brief word on scholarship. Many years ago at Yale Law School, there was a teacher named Fred Rodell. One of Professor Rodell's major contributions to the education of Yale lawyers was to reduce their natural propensities to pepper their writings with footnotes. From him, I learned that rigorous exposition and academic integrity do not require the constant interruption of the reader's train of thought with asides printed in small type below the main text on the page. After years of practicing law, I've also learned that the presentation of footnotes to support a point made in the text is absolutely no guaranty either of rigor in exposition or integrity in assertion. An author without integrity or the discipline to present a rigorous exposition can be as spurious, sloppy, or misleading in footnotes as in the main text. This book is written for a broad audience, including not only lawyers, law teachers, law students, and judges, but also programmers, executives of companies supplying software, customers of those companies, and interested bystanders to the dispute over software look and feel. Footnotes do not intrude on the text. Instead, the sources for the material presented in each chapter are cited at the end of the book, with an indication of the textual point to which each source relates. No new thoughts, elaborations on textual materials, or qualifications of points made in the text appear in these endnotes. Professor Rodell would be pleased, and I trust the reader will also.

Part I

Setting the Stage

1

Learning from the Past

If we forget the scientific culture, then the rest of western intellectuals have never tried, wanted, or been able to understand the Industrial Revolution, much less accept it. Intellectuals, in particular literary intellectuals, are natural Luddites.

C. P. Snow, *The Two Cultures and the Scientific Revolution* (1959)

It is unlikely that the Founding Fathers knew anything about software. Although both Franklin and Jefferson had been to France, there is no reason to believe that, as the Founders sweltered through their debates in Philadelphia's Independence Hall in the summer of 1788, either traveller described to his colleagues the invention of a young Lyonnais named Joseph-Marie Jacquard, an invention that was soon to be put aside while Jacquard took up the cause of the French Revolution. It was not, in fact, until 1797 that the first programmable machine in history was clique-claquing away on the *vieux continent*. The Jacquard Loom, one of the great technological innovations of the Industrial Revolution, soon transformed the task of weaving tapestries from a handwork process of casting weft across warp in accordance with an artist's instructions into an automated process in which the artist's instructions were transformed into a pattern of holes in pasteboard cards. The cards were inserted into the loom, and, as the loom operated, hooks were thrust through the prepunched holes. The hooks caught particular threads in the loom's warp, and pulled them down so that when the shuttle passed through it would go over certain threads and under others, thereby weaving the chosen pattern. Changing the cards changed the pattern. The "loomware" of the Jacquard machine is a distant progenitor of the

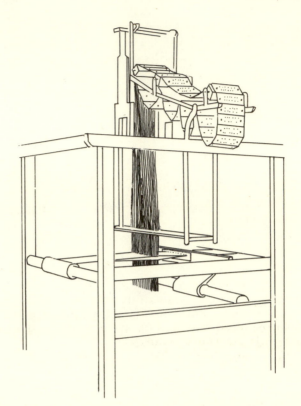

software of today, but by the time that loomware was put into service in France, the United States Constitution had already been adopted.

Thus we can't really assume that the Framers had specifically in mind the protection of software when they decreed in Article I, Section 8, Clause 8, of that august document (in the singular capitalization conventions of eighteenth-century America) that "The Congress shall have power . . . To promote the Progress of Science and the useful Arts, by securing for limited Times to authors and inventors the exclusive Right to their respective Writings and Discoveries."

Are we to conclude from this history that the copyright laws enacted by Congress pursuant to the powers granted in Article I, Section 8, Clause 8, cannot constitutionally extend copyright protection to computer programs? The question brings to mind the notion of "original intent," a philosophical approach to constitutional interpretation introduced to the general public during the controversy over the nomination of Judge Robert Bork to the Supreme Court. Proponents of the original intent philosophy urge that judges faced with the task of interpreting provisions of the Constitution somehow try to reconstruct what the collective intent of the Framers was in adopting those provisions, and then to confine their decisions within the boundaries of that reconstructed intent. The question is, then, if the original intent of the Framers cannot specifically have been to include computer programs among the categories of things that they termed "Writings," is the Congress powerless to protect computer programs by "securing" ... the exclusive right" (i.e., the copyright) in such works to their authors?

It may seem to the reader somewhat perverse to have started a discussion of a dynamic and rapidly evolving area of human endeavor and intellectual conflict with a question that is, if not off-putting because of its academic ring, then perhaps off-putting because it signals its own answer. We begin with that question, however, precisely because of its telegraphic quality. The question is a metaphor for the inquiry undertaken between these covers. In more generalized form, the question may be restated as follows: "Should a given set of new societal circumstances be governed by a given set of old societal rules?" That question is what was at the bottom of the debate at the Massachusetts Software Council seminar. That question is also what underlies the controversy over the "look and feel" cases.

The computer industry has certainly been a cause of new societal circumstances. It can fairly be said that, as much as anything else that it does, the computer is a generator of new circumstances. Today's students "input" their homework on word processors instead of typing or handwriting, and check their spelling with the push of a button rather than a dictionary. Banking can now be done by "interfacing" with a machine that is open long after the live tellers have gone home. On the stock market floor, the computer is proving to be a more aggressive and volatile trader than any human ever was. On the factory floor, assembly processes that were once the province of the human worker are now handled by apparatuses of infinite patience, blinding speed, and artificial intelligence: "machines of loving grace," in the biting words of the poet Richard Brautigan. Some readers no doubt rejoice at the myriad changes wrought by the computer revolution; others no doubt despair. All, however, will recognize the breadth of the societal transformations that have come about since the computer industry was born in the early 1950s.

The old societal rules consist of two centuries of American copyright law, shaped to provide protection to books, music, plays, movies, paintings, and other "works of authorship." Although many other legal norms have been touched by the computer revolution, it is most interesting to focus our attention on copyright law because, as the Congressional Office of Technology Assessment puts it:

First, since copyright is concerned primarily with the use and flow of information and information-based products and services, it is the area of intellectual prop-

erty law that will be most affected by advances in communications and information technologies. Second, it is to copyright rather than to other provisions
that the creators, developers, producers and distributors of new information
technologies are looking in their efforts to gain legislative protection for their
works.

To state the point a little more directly, the pressures placed on copyright
law by the new technologies are a special instance of the pressures that
technological change places on societal norms in general. By studying
the special case we may learn a good deal about the general.

Because technology has forced adaptation of the copyright laws many
times over the course of history, it is useful to begin our study by tracing
briefly the evolution of American copyright law, starting—as with so
many areas of American law—on the other side of the Atlantic.

England may legitimately lay claim to the honor of having had the
first copyright legislation known to Western civilization. The Statute of
Anne, enacted in 1710, provided authors with an exclusive transcription
right and a mechanism for enforcing that right against those who might
seek to reproduce the copyright owner's work without authorization.
Prior to that time, authors enjoyed a kind of copyright under the common
law, but the first legislation to spring up in post-Gutenberg Europe had
ignored writers and focused instead on the owners of printing presses.
Both as a way of increasing revenues and as a way of controlling the
power of the press, a practice evolved, beginning in the late fifteenth
century, of issuing royal privileges granting monopolies to print particular books, in exchange for a fee and for submission of the work to the
Crown for approval. The censorship potential inherent in that practice
attained its ultimate potential under the repressive influence of the in-
famous Star Chamber. In reaction to the excesses of that body, and to
the generally unhealthy consequences of the royal licensing practice,
the monopoly printing grant was abolished in England in 1649. The
immediate result was that book piracy flourished.

The Statute of Anne corrected that problem, but did so by the then-
novel, now-conventional means of providing exclusive rights to authors,
rather than printers, and by limiting the period of exclusivity. Statutory
protection was provided for a period of twenty-eight years, which may
tell us something about life expectancy during the reign of the last Stuart
monarch. The Statute of Anne was the basis for all subsequent copyright
legislation, and even though the nascent American nation had just ended
a bitter war with England, the principle of exclusive rights to authors
was sufficiently compelling to survive the trip across the ocean. It was
incorporated in the Constitution crafted in Philadelphia, along with other
basic powers, rights, and obligations thought to be essential to an effective democratic government. So compelling was the principle, in fact,

that Article I, Section 8, Clause 8, quoted above, was adopted without debate.

Shortly thereafter, in May 1790, the first Congress adopted the first copyright statute. It protected only maps, charts, and books. That was a beginning, but it was plainly not enough. Twelve years later, print-makers and graphic artists were gratified to learn that Congress had extended that protection to those who "shall invent and design, engrave, etch or work . . . any historical or other print or prints." In 1831, musical compositions were added to the list of protected subject matter, and in 1865—at a time when Matthew Brady was attaining fame for his tintype prints of the Civil War—photographs and photographic negatives were included. Only five years elapsed before passage of the next amendment, which added paintings, drawings, chromos, statuettes, statuary, and models or designs of fine art.

Then, in 1909, not well pleased with the hodgepodge of accretions and appendages it had engrafted onto the original copyright statute, and yet aware that even more amendment was necessary to take into account new media of expression, Congress adopted a major consolidation and update to the copyright laws. It may be that the lawmakers had thought thereby to settle copyright matters for all time or for a long time at least, but this was not to be. Only three years later, a new amendment was needed in order to bring another technologically new expressive form, motion pictures, within the ambit of the law. That done, the Congress was indeed able to rest. It was not until 1971 that a new medium of expression was added to the protected list. The medium was sound recordings, and the reason, once again, was technological change. Specifically, with the advent of audio tape and the audio tape recorder, piracy of sound recordings had become a problem of frightening proportions for the music industry.

In 1976, another general revision of the federal copyright law was enacted. At the time, another technology of expression, the one that interests us, had begun to intrude on the order of things. The medium called computer programs was so new and different that the lawmakers did not know what amendment to the statute would be appropriate. Accordingly, in a backhanded and tentative way, Congress merely gave recognition to the fact that computer programs were protected subject matter. Specifically, the 1976 act provided that computer programs should have no greater protection than they had enjoyed under prior law. Since the principal problem for program authors in 1976 was that the nature of the protection afforded software under the old 1909 law was completely unclear, this equivocation on the part of Congress can be seen as merely a temporizing gesture. It cannot be said, in other words, that the 1976 act was particularly comforting to those active in the software industry.

Obviously, the Congress was not unaware in 1976 of the need for illumination on this murky topic. In fact, two years earlier it had created a blue-ribbon commission to study the ways in which copyright law should be applied to computer programs and other new media of expression. The National Commission on New Technological Uses of Copyrighted Works, known colloquially as CONTU, held hearings and deliberated for several years, and ultimately recommended only modest changes in the 1976 act. These were, first, to add a definition of "computer program"; second, to provide that the owner of a copy of a copyrighted program did not infringe that copyright by using the program in a computer or by making an archival copy; and finally, to delete the "prior law" limitation of the 1976 act. These recommendations were accepted by Congress and enacted into law in 1980. Although the changes were modest, they were sufficient to make it clear that software was protectable by copyright. Except for unrelated amendments necessary to meet international treaty requirements, matters still stand thus, legislatively, as of this writing.

What this march of history shows is that since its inception, American copyright law has consistently flexed and expanded to embrace new technologies in which works of authorship have been embodied. That flexibility has been an important source of assurance to those who have taken the time and made the personal or corporate investment necessary to create works of authorship in technologically advanced media of expression. Why is this so? We'll consider the question more fully in Chapter 14, but in a nutshell the reason is this: The adaptability of copyright law has meant that the risk-takers—those willing to invest in the new media—could rely on a well-understood, long-standing body of law to protect their investments. The law does not guaranty a return on those investments, of course, but it does guaranty that the investments will not simply be appropriated by others. Software authors, like other authors, have been able to take comfort from the belief that most people both behave in accordance with the law and understand that, under the law, copyrighted works may not be copied.

The second of those beliefs is not a universal truth, however. Laws are not the same everywhere in the world, and copyright laws are no exception. Some countries have no copyright laws whatsoever. Not surprisingly, in those countries one does not find robust domestic industries built around the creation of works of authorship. One finds instead robust domestic industries built around the creation of works of piracy, as in the case of England at the end of the seventeenth century. Rather than encouraging creativity and discouraging plagiarism, such countries encourage plagiarism of foreign authors and discourage the creativity of indigenous authors. (Lest U.S. readers grow self-righteous in contemplation of this contrast, I would point out that for most of its history, the United States tried to have the best of both worlds by protecting domestic works of authorship under the copyright law but not imported works.)

As one would expect, though, the countries that don't provide copyright protection for software are the less-developed countries. These countries are not "where the action is" in terms of revenue and profit to program authors and so, although their copy shop activities have program authors fuming, it's fair to say that the number of programs written in the hope that they will attract a substantial following in those countries is not great. The United States, Europe, Japan, and the more heavily industrialized countries of the Pacific Rim are still the source of greatest demand for computer programs, and in those countries the copyright laws have been enhanced to make clear that program authors have exclusive rights in their writings.

Change engenders tension, however. The tension in the room at the Massachusetts Software Council seminar reflected a growing tension in the copyright law as it stood then and as it stands now. As the heaving, breathing shell of the law expanded to embrace the new medium of expression that is software, activities that had been undertaken by programmers in what they may have thought was a norm-free vacuum were suddenly discovered instead to be unlawful. Prestigious individuals in the field of computer programming found that they were at risk of being labelled as, and liable as, copyright infringers. We have already hinted at the loudly voiced opinion that it is the law that is wrong in such cases, not the programmers' practices. Those opinions, as well as the opposing opinions of others who support full copyright protection for software, have begun to feed into the legal process in two principal ways. First, program authors are suing one another for copyright infringement, and testimony in support of or in defense against such lawsuits helps inform judges and juries of the nature of the programming art and the meaning of copyright infringement in the software context. Better-informed decisions result from this testimony, and those decisions build on one another to create a body of caselaw that is increasingly reflective of commercial realities. Second, individual software authors, software companies, and trade associations have actively begun to speak at seminars, write articles, and even lobby members of Congress for— and against—legislation that would affect the scope of copyright protection for computer programs. Through these processes, society develops a better feel for the software phenomenon and the rules that should govern it.

In order to assess whether all the activity in the courtroom, in the auditorium, in the press, and in the capitol building is resulting in a desirable balancing of interests, we need to develop our own perspective on the software phenomenon and on the nature of program writing as a creative activity. We need also to examine the clash between the two cultures that occurred when program authors began to copyright their works. By alternating our reflections on the writing of programs with excursions into the courtroom, we will hopefully climb a ladder of understanding to a height from which we can simultaneously have an encompassing view of the landscape below and come to some constructive conclusions about what we are seeing. In part, we will be seeing an industry unlike any other.

2

The Business of Writing Software

Fifty years ago, there were no computer programs. Today, a multibillion dollar industry based on computer programs spans the globe, providing millions of users with products and services, and thereby satisfying a broad range of needs that pre–World War II society didn't even know it had. The customers fill the spectrum from the world's largest governments and corporations to individuals with personal computers in their homes. In the United States alone, there are over 14,000 enterprises writing programs for commercial distribution. Again, some of these enterprises are large corporations and some are individuals sitting at home in front of personal computers. While there may not yet be more lines of computer programming written today than there are lines of fictional narrative or music, there is doubtless more money made from the former activity than from the latter activities. Moreover, since computer programs are the "software" intended to be run through the "hardware" player (the computer), the demand for programs stimulates the demand for hardware, thereby supporting an industry that from mainframes to micros realizes sales well in excess of one hundred billion dollars per year. All of the major industrialized nations have recognized that the business of writing software is critical to the competitiveness of their economies. From today into the foreseeable future, it is obvious that the success of a country's computer industry on the world market will depend in large measure on the vitality of the software segment of that industry. Just as true, though, and just as clearly recognized by the governments of the industrialized nations, is the fact that the success of other industries—particularly service industries such as banking and brokerage—will depend on the quality and the efficiency of the software that controls their computerized facilities. As a result, now that economies based on manufacturing are considered *declassé*, having a strong domestic software sector is a mark of high fashion.

The stakes in the debate over whether an original software work of authorship may be copied for commercial advantage are, therefore, exceedingly high. Without programs, there would be no computer industry. On its own, the hardware can provide heat and a little light, but no information. It is the computer programs, which control the operation of the hardware and adapt it to the performance of a wide variety of tasks, that give life and meaning to the industry. Slide a diskette into the drive on your personal computer and it becomes a word processor. Eject that diskette, slide in another and the machine becomes an adventure game, an accounting system or a drafting system. What is on the diskette is what makes the device an electronic chameleon.

Not surprisingly, given this magical quality, software suppliers, in the aggregate, have realized growth rates that cause hearts to soar on Wall Street. By anyone's measure the software industry is burgeoning. Software revenues in the United States have increased at rates exceeding 30 percent per annum in recent years, to a level of more than $8 billion. The art of writing programs has fostered a market that is clearly as vital and valuable as the market spawned by the art of writing novels, plays, or music; perhaps more valuable, in fact, because the social benefits and economic efficiencies that derive from the availability of high-quality computer programs can commonly exceed the revenues of the programs themselves by several orders of magnitude. What I mean by this is that at the heart of each air traffic control system, bank clearing system, and payroll system, and at the heart of each of the countless other computer-based systems around which our very lives are increasingly organized, we find a silicon epic: a long, complex work in blank verse, the authors of which had imagined something that the chameleon machine could be, and then written down what was in their imagination. Because software plays the pivotal role in expanding the demand for computer systems, the extent to which society realizes the potential social and economic benefits of electronic data processing depends to a very large measure on the means that society uses to encourage the production of the works of authorship that adapt the computer to the conquest of ever more challenging tasks.

It is meaningful, then, to ask what sorts of encouragement are appropriate to that purpose. The reader will recognize that question as a recasting of the question posed in Chapter 1. To answer it requires that we take the pulse of the programming business and analyze what makes it beat.

When we apply our analytical instruments to that task, we find that first and foremost among the factors behind the beat of the industry is the fact that the products in question derive entirely from the creative activities of authors practicing a craft.

On seeing programming described as a craft, preachers in and adherents to the secular religion known as CASE, or Computer-Assisted Software Engineering, will no doubt cross themselves against what they view as heresy. Programming, to these believers, is not a craft or an art but a science, which can be made more productive by mechanization. We'll consider in Chapter 12 whether the availability and use of CASE methods differentiate programs from other kinds of literary works in ways that are socially meaningful. For now, I will readily grant that program authors are usually writing in an industrial context rather than a purely aesthetic context, and grant that the works of authorship they create are not necessarily written to enhance the learning, well-being, emotional experience, or morality of other readers. That said, however, it must also be said that neither concession changes the fact that programmers are authors.

That notion may be difficult for many readers to accept at face value. It is a critical point, however. If programmers should not be considered authors, then it might have been improper—or inconsistent with the constitutional empowerment—for Congress to have extended copyright protection to their handiwork. If, on the other hand, programming is properly considered a kind of authorship, then one can at least say that it was consistent with the Constitution to have protected it. Whether or not it was proper to do so is, one might suggest, a second question. It is a fair question, however, since the Constitution says that Congress has the power to protect works of authorship, but not that Congress in all cases must do so. In fact, there is yet a third question that—as we refine our inquiry—we are going to address: whether the two hundred years of constitutional interpretation in the form of legislation and judicial decisions that have fleshed out the skeleton left to us by the Framers have given us a corpus of law that produces reasonable and desirable results when applied to computer programs, or whether that bicentennial legal history simply fails to translate well into the new technological context. A substantial portion of this book is devoted to considering whether computer programs exhibit the characteristics typical of literary works, and to considering the kinds of results that have eventuated when the courts have sought to apply traditional copyright principles to computer programs. Readers who cannot for the moment accept at face value the notion that writing computer programs is a kind of authorship are invited to skip ahead—or, in computerese, to branch—to Chapters 7 through 10, and to return here after reading those chapters.

The fact that the enterprise of programming is at bottom based on authorship tells us to expect the software industry to have certain attributes typical of industries based on authorship. Prominent among those attributes are the following:

—Low capital requirements to enter the industry, which means lots of competition;

—High reliance on skilled intellectual labor to create new products, which means that creativity is what triggers progress;

—Great variability in the skill levels of people active in the profession, which means there will be leaders and followers; and

—A shortage of people who know how to write at all well, and a severe shortage of very good writers, which means there will be many more followers than leaders.

These are indeed the attributes that fuel the action in the software industry today. Because the cost of entering the business is so low, and because skilled individuals can have access to a large market with few economic inputs other than their own time and energy, we find large numbers of enterprises and individuals engaged in programming for profit. We also find that programs written by a single author or a small group of authors can become extraordinarily successful, and that garage-shop operators have suddenly found themselves major forces in the industry. As we shall see, the leader-follower syndrome is endemic.

Another important attribute that software shares with other types of literary works is that its value may be enhanced by translation. Specifically, its benefits as intellectual property may be realized on many different brands of computers, including hardware with a variety of different logical architectures. That is not to say that the same magnetic

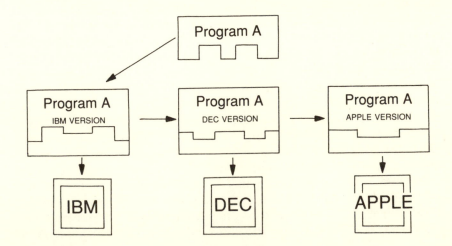

tape or diskette can be mounted on or in an IBM, DEC, or Apple computer and that the program on it will run successfully, any more than a videotape in VHS format can be mounted on a Beta player or Super–8 projecter and run successfully. Rather, a program written for one type of computer can be adapted or translated so as to be able to run on a different type of computer, particularly if the program is written from the outset with that possibility in mind. For the program author, adaptation rights can be of equivalent value to the rights to adapt a novel to the screen or to translate it into French: The adaptation to a new hardware environment can substantially increase demand for the program. Furthermore, for the program user, the availability of adaptations provides flexibility in choosing hardware suppliers and configuring computer installations. Under most copyright laws, adaptation and translation are exclusive rights granted to the copyright owner.

Finally, it is true of both computer programs and other kinds of works traditionally protected by copyright that the intangible content of the delivered product is high, while the cost of the physical medium of the delivered product is low. Software reaches its customers on magnetic tape or diskette, inside a computer chip, or as listings on paper (or indeed across a phone line, so that there is essentially no physical medium of delivery at all). The *softcopy* (magnetic) forms of programs can easily be duplicated, just as an audiotape can easily be duplicated. Their *hardcopy* (paper) forms can easily be duplicated on a photocopier, or typed into a computer, from which they can be stored on tape, disk, or diskette. Their chip-resident forms can be printed out in hardcopy by the computer in which the chips reside; or, if the program is physically *burned* into the logic of the chip, the chip can be shaved layer by layer and the program deduced.

It is Friday night. You take your spouse or significant other to the movies. On the screen, the Oscar-winning images of Bertolucci's *The Last Emperor* dance before your eyes. Sitting in the plush seats in the dark, you are the passive beneficiary of an investment of tens of millions of dollars, for which benefit you have made an investment of only a fistful of dollars. In effect, you are assimilating the "executive summary" of a project requiring the efforts of thousands of people, entailing delicate international negotiations, and necessitating substantial research, flowcharting, writing, and testing. The filmstock that carries the images and sound into your consciousness costs less than a tank of gasoline, and yet it provides you with intangible experiences that—were we not all jaded by years of moviegoing—we would have to count as priceless.

Monday morning arrives. You are at your desk, suffused in the greenish glow from your workstation. You need information. You want to know which of your customers in the Boston area have increased their orders by more than 25 percent in the past six months for any one of three different product lines who did not also do so in the same period last year. You plan to target those customers for special attention, both to thank them for their business and to encourage them to even greater heights of spending. By composing a simple search argument and asking the computer to execute it, you are able to obtain the information instantaneously. You promptly ask the computer to list the names and phone numbers of the sales representatives servicing those customers and then ask for the sales reps' compensation history for the year. In less than a minute, you have the information you need to make important revisions to both your marketing plan and your sales bonus plan.

The user of a large data base program, such as IBM's DB2, Cullinet's IDMS, or Software AG's ADABAS has the experience of organizing, storing, and retrieving vast amounts of information at electronic speeds. Like *The Last Emperor*, the program that provides those experiences was a project years in the making and involving large numbers of people, but was delivered to the customer on a medium—a reel of tape—that is not intrinsically valuable. In addition, the user pays only a small fraction of the eight- or nine-figure development cost of the program for the privilege of having those experiences. The high-value, low-cost character of computer programs makes them, like most copyrighted works, tempting targets for intellectual property buccaneers and underscores the need for legal protection.

In sum, the business of computer programming has much in common with other branches of the business of writing. The products of the programming business are the products of human activity, the nature of which, as we will shortly see, is authorship. The fact that programmers will never hear shouts of "Author! Author!" from their audiences, and that programs are generally written in languages not euphoneous or even intelligible to most of us, does not deprive programmers of the right to be called authors and programs to be called works of authorship. The fact that these works are computer programs, as opposed to movies, musical scores, or college textbooks, does, however, add an important dimension of competitive urgency to their authors' motivation because of the dynamics of the computer industry.

The dynamics of competition in the computer industry in general are familiar to students of contemporary commerce. They are difficult to summarize in terms that are not breathtaking—if the reader will allow that any aspect of industrial history can be breathtaking. Since its birth in the 1950s, the computer industry has done nothing but break its own records year after year. According to the Congressional Office of Technology Assessment, in 1952 it cost about $300 to do a million processing operations. Thirty years later, the cost of a million processing operations was a thousandth of a cent. Computation speed was a billion times faster in 1980 than it was in 1950, and is expected to be a million times faster again by the 1990s. The amount of information a computer could

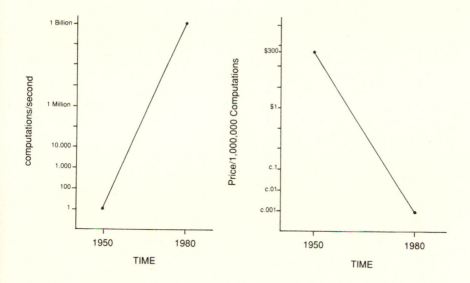

store in its main memory was on the order of 40,000 characters in 1952. Today, it is on the order of one hundred million characters, and the amount of information available in on-line storage for a large processor is measured in trillions of characters. The litany of incredibles could continue for many pages, but the point is adequately made already: The industry's research and development facilities are hyperactive. Product improvements resulting from technical advance tumble after one another in blinding succession.

The computer industry, in other words, is characterized by competition on the basis of price-performance and functional capability. Price-performance is a fancy way of referring to what used to be called "bang for the buck." It is the ratio of a product's price to its (quantitatively measured) primary capabilities. The cost of a million processing operations, for example, is a price-performance measure. Functional capability simply refers to the services that a particular product offers. Competition on the basis of price-performance and functional capability, which I will call innovational competition, is far different from simple price competition. In the case of the computer industry, innovational competition has resulted in consumer benefits on a scale unequaled in American economic history.

The process of innovational competition manifestly requires that firms develop new products. Those developments, when brought to market, offer features that give the new products certain advantages in price-performance or functional capability. Those advantages, in turn, attract customers (or should, anyway, if the developers have been keeping an eye on what customers want that existing products don't offer). Competing firms, in order not to lose customers, must offer equivalent advantages in their products. In fact, since matching the new product's advantages will take time, there will be an inevitable delay before competitors can offer equivalent advantages, during which time they are at risk of seeing customer loyalty dissipate. Though some competitors are willing to live with that risk, the key to the dynamics of the computer industry is that many competitors are not willing to do so. They prefer to follow a strategy of responding to new products by developing even better products if they can, thus establishing the expectation in the marketplace that loyal customers will be rewarded for waiting. This leapfrogging phenomenon explains the successive waves of innovation that have swept over the industry, producing the dramatic improvements in price-performance alluded to above.

In the case of software, the development activities involved in leapfrogging consist largely of programmers' intellectual efforts, whether expended by teams of people working for large organizations or by individuals or small groups investing their "sweat equity" to produce programs for which they hope there will be demand. No significant capital investment is required. Indeed, it has been estimated that in America farming is a more heavily capital-intensive business than programming, and it is certainly true that producing software for distribution is not like producing a processor or any other complex tangible product. Producing software does not require a factory, which means that leapfrogging can go on at an even more rapid pace.

The competitive response to innovation in software has historically come in two forms (in addition to the temporizing expedient of price-cutting on older products). Some competitors have responded by offering products based on independent design that either offer equivalent improvements or leapfrog to even greater improvements. Other competitors have responded by copying some or all aspects of the innovative product. (The ability simply to copy another competitor's product is of course constrained by law. The principal constraint, in the case of software, is imposed by the copyright law, which permits the copying of the ideas but not the expression in computer programs.) Both forms of competitive reaction have been important stimuli to technological advance in the industry, but innovation is obviously and by definition a more important factor than imitation, since without innovation there can be no advance. Given that competitive reaction of one or both kinds can be expected, however, there is a vital interest in preserving the factor that stimulates the innovator to innovate in the first place, rather than the factors that stimulate the innovator not to bother. What is that stimulus?

It is the profit motive, pure and simple. Although there are many innovators in the great centers of learning and in government research

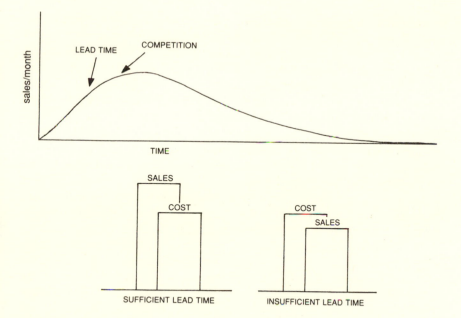

facilities, for innovation to benefit society it must be commercialized. That will happen if the innovator calculates, either explicitly or implicitly, that—despite the expectation of competitive reaction—investment in commercial development of the product in question will earn an attractive return. The desired calculus will result only if it appears both that the new product will provide added value to potential customers and that enough copies of the product can be sold to justify the risk of investment. Precisely because imitation of the new product is clearly foreseeable even when it is on the drawing boards, and because, in the case of software, imitation can be technologically effortless, the innovator will find the economic calculus attractive only if some mechanism can be found to insure the new product sufficient lead time before competitive products begin to displace it in the marketplace. For software, that mechanism is the copyright law.

3

Apple v. Franklin

The scene has occurred since times primeval: Two disputants, violently opposed in interests and views, sit mute on the sidelines and watch as their champions prepare for battle. Dominating the fray, and controlling its ebb and flow, a berobed figure presides from an elevated platform, under a graven image symbolizing tribal authority.

The time is 1982. The place, a federal courthouse in Philadelphia. The disputants are Apple Computer, Inc. and Franklin Computer Corporation. Their champions: for Apple, the firm of Seidel, Gonda, Goldhammer and Panitch, and for Franklin, the firm of Schnader, Harrison, Segal and Lewis. These two Philadelphia law firms are about to clash in an engagement that will send shock waves through the computer industry. Two years later, they will do so again in a case involving the seemingly prosaic subject matter of dental laboratory accounting programs. The instant case, however, involves operating systems, the programs that intermediate between the primitive and unwieldy language understood by computer hardware and the richer, more convenient languages in which most programmers like to write their programs. Operating systems manage the hardware resources of the computer for the customer, so that that customer who is writing other programs for that hardware need not be concerned, for example, with writing all the instructions necessary to extract information from a disk drive and insert that information into the computer's memory. Operating systems also organize the memory of the computer while it is operating, so that programmers need not worry about where to store their programs and data. The operating systems at issue in Philadelphia on the day in ques-

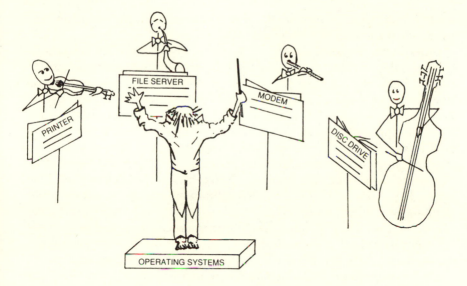

tion were those provided with the legendary home computer, the Apple II, and the classic clone computer, the Franklin Ace.

Apple had moved the court for a preliminary injunction restraining Franklin from using, copying, selling, or infringing in any other way Apple's copyrights in the Apple II's operating system. The preliminary injunction would have barred Franklin from selling the Ace until the end of the trial in the case, at which time the judge would decide whether to issue a permanent injunction. In a sense, the judge was being asked to decide in advance which party was most likely to win at trial, and to order the other party to behave until trial as though it had already lost. The requirements for issuing preliminary injunctions vary, but those that applied in the case of *Apple Computer, Inc. v. Franklin Computer Corp.* were four in number, and each requirement was a challenge for Apple. Apple's lawyers had to show (1) that Apple had a reasonable probability of succeeding at trial; (2) that the injury it was suffering by Franklin's continuing to market the Franklin Ace could not be compensated by money damages, and exceeded any injury Franklin would suffer if it had to suspend marketing of the Ace pending trial; (3) that harm to other interested persons if the injunction were granted was not likely; and (4) that a public interest would be furthered by granting the injunction. Given that in 1982 software copyright cases were still novelties in the law, that operating systems are the most functional of computer programs, and that the programs in question were largely delivered to customers in computer chips mounted on the "mother boards" or main circuit boards of the respective computers, and did not physically resemble traditional literary works, the outcome of Apple's motion was by no means a foregone conclusion.

Indeed, the lawsuit itself was something of a gamble for Apple. At the time, the Apple II was selling at a rate an order of magnitude greater than a brisk clip. Almost four hundred thousand of the funky little machines had been sold since Steve Wozniak and Steve Jobs began building Apples in Jobs's parents' living room six years earlier. Now Apple Computer, Inc., employed roughly three thousand people and had earned $335 million in the preceding fiscal year. The clones were nipping at its heels, but were not yet causing substantial damage. If Apple lost its suit against Franklin, however, the floodgates would be opened. If it were lawful to do what Franklin had done, many other firms—some much larger than Franklin—could easily start producing clones of the Apple II, and Apple's momentum and success would quickly dissipate. For what Franklin had done, by its own admission, was to copy, virtually line for line, the Apple II's operating system.

On the other hand, if Apple had taken no action against Franklin, the clone phenomenon would also have grown, albeit more slowly. Apple IIs were sold into a very price-conscious market. The hardware under the covers was not unique, and the software was easy to copy. If consumers knew that they could get fundamentally the same machine for half the price, they would do so. Apple was on the horns of a dilemma, and it chose the path of action. The principal proponent of that decision was Al Eisenstat, then Apple's general counsel. It was a bet-your-job recommendation, and Eisenstat was soon to have second thoughts about its wisdom.

Judge Clarence Newcomer listened carefully to the arguments and evidence presented at the three-day hearing. In an order and opinion issued on July 30, 1982, he denied Apple's motion, and made it clear that when the case came to trial, Apple was not likely to win. Three days after Judge Newcomer announced his decision, the Court of Appeals for the Third Federal Circuit, the court to which appeals from Judge Newcomer's court would be taken, decided the case of *Williams Electronics, Inc. v. Arctic International, Inc.*, in which the argument that computer programs could not be protected by copyright was firmly rejected. Apple immediately applied to Judge Newcomer for reconsideration of its motion in light of the *Williams* case. Its application was denied.

His company's strategy for protecting its key asset now exposed, and his own position along with it, Eisenstat called in the man from Phoenix, the Wyatt Earp of high-tech litigation, Jack E. Brown. *Apple v. Franklin* was promptly appealed to the Third Circuit Court of Appeals.

Why was Judge Newcomer so adamantly opposed to Apple's motion? There were two reasons. First, the judge had concluded that, as between

Apple and Franklin, the latter being a firm of some 75 employees which had sold fewer than a thousand computers, the injury that would result to Apple from not granting the injunction would have been far easier to bear than the injury resulting to Franklin from granting the injunction. Second, and more importantly, he had concluded that computer programs in forms not perceptible to humans were not protectable by copyright. His reasons were as follows:

If the concept of "language" means anything, it means an ability to create human interaction. It is the fixed expression of this that the copyright law protects, and only this. To go beyond the bounds of this protection would be ultimately to provide copyright protection to the programs created by a computer to run other computers. With that, we step into the world of Gulliver where horses are "human" because they speak a language that sounds remarkably like the one humans use. It is an intriguing analogy but false.

What bothered Judge Newcomer was object code. Object code is a program expressed as binary numbers comprehensible to the computer, a pattern of ones and zeros that cause the computer to execute a coherent set of operations leading to a useful result. Most programs are written in some other language more comprehensible to humans, and then are translated into object code, in which form they are delivered on a medium of storage, such as magnetic tape or diskette, to the customer. There were fourteen separate programs comprising Apple's operating system, each of which had been copied by Franklin. Among those programs were the Autostart ROM, which stored initial values in the computer's registers when the machine was turned on; DOS 3.3, which controlled the operations of reading from and writing to the Apple II's floppy disks; and Applesoft, a program that interpreted the user's programs written in the BASIC computer language and translated them into object code. All fourteen programs were delivered in object code form,

```
10101001
00110000
00011000
01101001
00100010                    X = A + B
10001101
00000010
01100000
```

Object Code   Programming Language

either in read-only memory (ROM) chips under the covers of the Apple II or on floppy disk. What bothered Judge Newcomer was the fact that, as delivered, the Apple programs—at least those in ROM—seemed to be physical devices, and copyright does not protect physical devices (except for ornamental aspects of three-dimensional pictorial, graphic, or sculptural works). The programs were also clearly utilitarian, the judge found, and they were therefore suited, if anything, for patent protection rather than copyright protection. Furthermore, the programs were not readable by humans, at least not the humans with which Judge Newcomer was familiar. Therefore, the judge concluded, although Apple had plausible arguments in its favor, the likelihood that it would be able to prove at trial that its programs were protected by copyright was low.

It was not obligatory that Apple appeal Judge Newcomer's ruling. The denial of a preliminary injunction is not a final determination of either the facts or the way the law applies to those facts. Apple could have accepted the outcome and gone forward to trial, armed now with detailed knowledge of what it would have to prove to overcome the judge's predispositions. If the decision at trial was adverse as well, an appeal could have followed, and at least then the appeal would have been based on a complete trial record in which Apple could have introduced substantially more evidence in its favor than was introduced at the three-day hearing before Judge Newcomer. In choosing to appeal the denial of the motion, Al Eisenstat had once again made a gutsy decision.

The oral argument before a three-judge panel of the Court of Appeals for the Third Circuit took place on March 17, 1983. Both Apple and Franklin knew that all the chips were bet on the outcome of the appeal: For all practical purposes, the case would be over when the appellate court ruled. Others in the industry realized that the principles at stake went far beyond the individual interests of Apple and Franklin. The Association of Data Processing Service Organizations (ADAPSO), the leading American trade association for software houses, submitted an *amicus curiae* brief in support of Apple's position. So did Microsoft and Digital Research, then the prinicipal suppliers of operating systems for microcomputers. (An amicus curiae, or friend of the court, is a person not a party to the lawsuit in question who has sufficient interest in the subject matter of the litigation to be moved to file a brief describing for the court some of the larger ramifications of the issue before it. Amici curiae make their submissions in writing only; they do not participate in the oral argument.) A company called Pro-log submitted an amicus brief in support of Franklin's position.

Franklin's arguments to the appellate panel were variations on a single theme: Operating systems, as opposed to other kinds of programs that depend on operating systems to intermediate between themselves and the hardware, are not a proper subject for copyright protection regardless of the language or medium in which they are delivered to customers. This was a broader argument than the one advanced by Judge Newcomer, who had ruled only that the object code representations of Apple's programs were probably unprotectable. There were several prongs to Franklin's argument, each of which thrust at the heart of Apple's business. The first and most dangerous prong related to the well established principle that copyright protects expression but not ideas. That principle is codified in Section 102(b) of the Copyright Act as follows:

In no case does copyright protection for an original work of authorship extend to any idea, procedure, process, system, method of operation, concept, principle, or discovery, regardless of the form in which it is described, explained, illustrated, or embodied in such work.

Franklin argued that operating systems were either "processes," "systems," or "methods of operation," and were therefore uncopyrightable. (Note how the term "operating system" works with the language of the statute to support Franklin's position.) Similarly, Franklin urged that operating systems were purely utilitarian works, and that Apple was seeking to block the implementation by others of the "useful art" described in its programs. Finally, Franklin asserted that whatever expression was contained in the Apple programs was merged with the ideas contained in those programs, and since the copyright law does not protect ideas, it could not protect the merged expression either. What Franklin was saying was that there was only one way, or at most a limited number of ways, of writing an operating system so that it would run the vast body of software written to run on the Apple II.

Apple's arguments were simple. First, it was the owner of copyrights duly registered by the copyright office. Second, Congress clearly intended that the Copyright Act protect computer programs. Third, Franklin had copied the fourteen Apple programs virtually line for line, only deleting such things as Apple's name or its copyright notice. Fourth, this was precisely the kind of activity the law was designed to prevent, and nothing in the law says that operating systems should be treated differently as far as preventing that activity is concerned.

Decisions of the U.S. Courts of Appeal are not rendered on the spot. The parties had to wait almost six months for an answer, six months, no doubt, of intense anticipation. On August 30, 1983, the opinion was issued and the fate of operating systems was determined, both in America and elsewhere, as courts in other countries came to adopt the reasoning of Judge Dolores K. Sloviter, the author of the opinion.

The Court of Appeals opinion began by recognizing that Judge Newcomer's ruling was not only fundamental to future proceedings in *Apple v. Franklin*, but also of considerable significance to the industry in general. It then set the parameters of the debate. First, the court noted the broad success of Apple, and the fact that one by-product of that success had been the development by third parties of large numbers of computer programs designed to run on the Apple II. It then described the Franklin Ace 100 as having been designed to be "Apple compatible," so that the software designed to run on the Apple II would run on the Ace 100. Franklin's copying of the Apple operating system in order to achieve that compatibility, the court said, is what precipitated the lawsuit.

(That the Apple programs had been copied was not really in dispute. An Apple programmer had imbedded his own name in one of the Apple programs. It also appeared in the corresponding Franklin program. The word "Applesoft" was contained in Apple's DOS 3.3; it was also contained in the corresponding Franklin program. All fourteen Franklin programs were virtually identical to the fourteen Apple programs. Franklin's witnesses at the three-day hearing had essentially admitted copying the Apple programs. Their explanation was that after studying the problem, they concluded that there was no other way to write a compatible operating system. Franklin's vice president of engineering had testified that the Apple programs provided too many "entry points" at which the third-party programs could connect with the operating system to permit independent development by Franklin.)

Thus, in a few sentences at the outset of the opinion, Judge Sloviter sketched out the archetypal conflict of the high-technology world, an archetype that will reappear in different incarnations in all the courtroom cases we encounter in our odyssey. Of course, the Court of Appeals did not view itself as having the responsibility to decide the outcome of an archetypal conflict. Its task was more down-to-earth: A decision had been rendered by a district court judge, and that decision had been challenged by the losing party. Unless that decision was clearly erroneous, it must be upheld. The question, therefore, was whether in any material respect Judge Newcomer's reasoning was wrong. Incidental to deciding this narrow legal issue, however, the archetypal conflict would inevitably be resolved.

Parsing Judge Newcomer's opinion, the Court of Appeals found four questions to have been decided by the lower court: first, that copyright cannot protect computer programs expressed in machine language as opposed to human language; second, that copyright cannot protect computer programs stored in the computer's read-only memory; third, that copyright cannot protect operating systems; and last, that a specific balancing of the injury to the parties was necessary to the decision whether to issue a preliminary injunction in a copyright case. If Judge Newcomer was right on any one of the first, third, or fourth items, then

Apple had properly lost in the court below. If Judge Newcomer was right as to the second point, then Apple had properly lost as to those of its fourteen programs that were delivered in ROM.

The Court of Appeals began its review of Judge Newcomer's decisions by measuring his ruling on object code against the statutory framework of the Copyright Act. That act, the court said, protects "original works of authorship" that are "fixed in a tangible medium of expression." A year earlier, you'll recall, in the case of *Williams Electronics, Inc. v. Arctic International, Inc.*, the same court had held that although this statutory language did not explicitly list computer programs as works of authorship, it included them by clear implication. That being so, the nub of the question before it now was whether it was proper to say that copyright was limited to works that could be read by people as opposed to machines. Writing for the Court of Appeals, Judge Sloviter found the answer in the statute itself. The Copyright Act defines computer programs as "sets of statements or instructions to be used directly or indirectly in a computer in order to bring about a certain result." Recognizing that a computer can only follow instructions written in object code form, the court reasoned that it could only have been programs in object code form to which Congress was referring as "used directly . . . in a computer." For that reason, the court disagreed with Judge Newcomer. When the Court of Appeals disagrees with the reasoning of a District Court judge, the latter is said to have "committed error." The first round, then, was Apple's.

The second round also went to Apple. The Court of Appeals read its *Williams* decision as having already held that software embodied in ROM was "fixed in a tangible medium of expression" and therefore suitable for copyright protection. Franklin's argument that software in ROM was essentially hardware fell on deaf ears.

With the underbrush cleared away, Judge Sloviter moved on to the heart of the matter. Were operating systems, by their very nature, not appropriate for copyright protection? Apple argued that that issue, too, had been foreclosed by the *Williams* decision. The Court of Appeals disagreed. Siding with Franklin, Judge Sloviter wrote that the issue was neither raised by the parties in *Williams* nor considered by the court. It was, in other words, open to debate, and the debate was three-headed:

—Were operating systems nothing more than "processes" or "methods of operation"?
—Are "purely utilitarian works" protectable by copyright?
—Was there only one way of writing an Apple-compatible operating system?

Notice that although these points are mixed questions of fact and law raised by the particular appeal in the particular case, they comprise,

collectively, an examination of several of the basic social-policy considerations in the innovator-follower debate as it is manifested in the software industry.

Taking Apple at its word, the court set as a baseline the postulate that
Apple was not seeking to protect the processes or methods in its programs, but only the program instructions themselves. It also set as a
baseline the principle that, generally speaking, computer programs are
protected by copyright, and set about to determine if there was something about operating systems that militated against application of that
general rule. On analysis, it seemed to the court that all computer programs, operating systems or otherwise, were inherently alike in one
important respect: They all instructed the computer to do something.
One type of program might, for example, instruct the computer to take
steps that would result in preparation of a tax return; another might
instruct the computer to take steps resulting in the translation of another
program from human-readable form into machine-readable form. If instead of computer programs the medium of expression under consideration were instruction manuals, it would not be the case that the
subject matter of the manual would determine whether the manual were
protected by copyright. A tax preparation manual would be protectable;
so would a manual on translating computer programs. In the case of
software, the court asked itself, what was the reason why the subject
of the software should determine its eligibility for protection? The reason
put forward by Franklin was that operating systems were fundamentally
part of the hardware, and hardware—except for its aesthetic elements—
is not suitable for copyright protection. That argument did not find a
receptive audience. Distancing herself from the teachings of Marshall
McLuhan, Judge Sloviter wrote that " . . . the medium is not the message.
. . . The mere fact that the operating system programs may be etched on
a ROM does not make the program either a machine, part of a machine
or its equivalent." After all, operating systems need not be stored permanently in ROM. Instead, they may be stored on a tape or diskette.
The medium in which they were "fixed," the court concluded, cannot
determine their protectability.

The question of whether operating systems were part of the hardware
raised the issue of utilitarianism. The court agreed with Franklin that
the Apple operating systems reeked of utilitarianism. That granted, the
question was whether Franklin—or anyone else, for that matter—was
entitled to copy them outright. The answer, the Court of Appeals said,
was "No." Looking to the Copyright Act as the touchstone in this area
of inquiry, Judge Sloviter found that there was nothing in that act even
hinting at a different result for utilitarian works than for other (e.g.,
aesthetic) works. (Indeed, the reader will recall, although the court did
not mention it, that the Constitution speaks in terms of granting exclu-

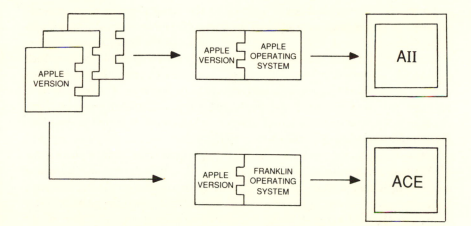

sive rights for authors in order to promote progress in the "useful arts."
It says nothing about the "aesthetic arts," and the first American copyright statute explicitly protected two utilitarian items, maps and charts.)
That Apple's operating systems produced useful results in the computer,
then, did not inform the question of infringement one way or the other.

In this fashion, the court stripped the controversy in *Apple v. Franklin*
down to the Big Issue, the one point of debate that had the software
industry holding its figurative breath. Was it unlawful for Franklin to
distribute a compatible operating system? That was what lay at the heart
of this case. Could Franklin copy the Apple operating system in order
to facilitate offering a microcomputer that would run the vast body of
application software available for the Apple II, or couldn't it?

Judge Sloviter found it necessary to sneak up on the Big Issue. It was,
she said, a matter of determining the line between idea—unprotected
by copyright—and expression. "The line must be a pragmatic one," she
said, which also keeps in mind "the balance between competition and
protection reflected in the patent and copyright laws." That balance was
struck, in the case of copyright, by allowing competitors to use with
impunity any and all ideas contained in Apple's programs, so long as
they didn't copy the protected expression. Franklin's argument, of
course, was that there was no way to copy the ideas without also copying
the expression. In terms of legal theory, the court agreed that Franklin
was right: if the ideas could not be copied without also copying the
expression, then the balance struck by the copyright law pushes the
copyright holder into oblivion. The copyright is worthless. In legal terms,
the idea and the expression merge, and copyright protection for the
expression is lost.

Therefore, the court focused on whether the ideas in the Apple operating system were susceptible of multiple forms of expression. In doing

so, the court recognized that "[m]any of the courts which have sought to draw the line between idea and expression have found difficulty in articulating where it falls." (That was a studied bit of understatement. The idea/expression dichotomy is the recurring bugbear in all kinds of copyright cases, not just software cases.) Among the courts having such difficulty, apparently, was the lower court in *Apple v. Franklin*, which had sent the case to the Court of Appeals without coming to any conclusion at all as to whether the Apple programs represented the only means of expressing the idea underlying them.

Unfortunately for posterity, also among those courts was the Court of Appeals for the Third Circuit. The task at hand—to define the ideas in the Apple operating systems, then to define the expression in those programs, and ultimately to assess whether the ideas could be expressed in ways other than those reflected in Apple's expression—proved too much for the jurists. By ducking behind the excuse that the record of the case was not sufficiently clear to allow the issue to be decided at the appellate level, they avoided making the ultimate assessment, and thereby almost managed to keep *Apple v. Franklin* out of the legal history books. Almost, but not quite. Even absent a clear record on appeal, the court was able to render an opinion as to how lower courts should distinguish the idea of an operating system from its expression, an opinion designed to help Judge Newcomer when the case was sent back to him for further proceedings. In addition to helping Judge Newcomer, of course, the opinion would serve as a guidepost for the industry at large.

Franklin had claimed that there were at best a limited number of ways to "arrange operating systems to enable a computer to run the vast body of Apple-compatible software." If Franklin were correct, and if the idea of the Apple operating system was to run Apple-compatible software, then Franklin was holding the winning Ace. To the court, however, Franklin's syllogism leaked in the middle. It made no sense to the court to describe the idea of the Apple operating system in terms of what it would take to write a compatible operating system. If it were proper to describe the idea of a program in those terms, then the commercial objectives of a competitor who came along later could suddenly convert what was theretofore protected expression into unprotected idea. A program protectable by copyright against copying by noncompatible competitors would not be protectable against compatible competitors.

The court rejected the faulty syllogism, and held instead that the idea of an operating system is simply the subject of its expression. One of the Apple programs, for example, translated human-intelligible programs into machine-intelligible programs. The idea of that program is how to translate human-intelligible programs into machine-intelligible programs. As long as other ways of expressing that idea exist, Judge

Sloviter wrote, copyright will protect the program. Franklin's wish to achieve total compatibility was simply irrelevant to that determination.

This was a very significant holding. What were its implications for the industry? Did it mean that writing compatible operating systems is illegal? That is not what the court said, nor, I think, what it meant. Compatible operating systems written without copying, if such a thing is possible, do not infringe. Remember, Franklin's objective was total compatibility, and its method was outright, line-for-line copying. One can imagine a different case, one in which the method involved avoids copying except where necessary to achieve compatibility. The Court of Appeals was not presented with that question and therefore did not address it. Subsequent cases have tested the boundaries of the answer, but never faced it squarely. In point of fact, the question is riddled with ambiguities, and can probably only be answered on a case-by-case basis, as the terms "compatibility," "copying," and "except where . . . necessary" are put into a realistic context. The factors to be considered in such case-by-case analyses, though, should be evident by the time the reader has reached the closing pages of this book.

Apple v. Franklin ends on a grace note—actually, a coup de grace note. In the lower court, Judge Newcomer had decided that, irrespective of its likelihood of success on the merits of its case, Apple had failed to make the showing of irreparable harm required to trigger the issuance of an injunction. Basically, he concluded that Apple was better able to survive the effects of denying the injunction than Franklin was able to survive the granting of the injunction. This was undoubtedly true. It was, however, not the proper test. In copyright cases, the general rule is that once the plaintiff has shown that it is likely to prove infringement on the part of the defendant, irreparable injury is presumed. There was no need, the Court of Appeals held, to go through the balancing-of-harm exercise in which Judge Newcomer had engaged, nor was it proper to do so. Apple was presumed to be suffering injury that would support an injunction.

Franklin made an attempt at appealing to the Supreme Court, but before High Court decided whether or not to hear the case the parties quickly and quietly settled. Apple had won a clean sweep, and Judge Sloviter had written an opinion that set the tone for much of what followed in the field of software copyright law. Its effects on the industry have by now become clear, at least in the United States. Although "cloning" of popular operating systems has become a commonplace commercial activity, no clone supplier who hoped to achieve substantial economic status has since relied on massive line-for-line copying in order to achieve its compatibility objectives.

Part II

Castles in the Air, and on Diskette

4

The Art of Programming

The programmer, like the poet, works only slightly removed from
pure thought-stuff. He builds his castles in the air, from air, creating
by exertion of the imagination. Few media of creation are so flexible,
so easy to polish and rework, so readily capable of realizing grand
conceptual structures.

F. P. Brooks, *The Mythical Man-Month* (1975)

Was the *Apple v. Franklin* court right? As a matter of legal reasoning and
statutory construction, unquestionably so; but from a normative perspective, ought operating systems be entitled to protection against copying, and if so, what should the scope of that protection be? For that
matter, what should the scope of protection against copying be for programs of any kind?

In order to answer these questions, it is necessary to come to some
understanding of what it is, if anything, that is expressive about computer programs. Lest the liberal mind now shut itself down in anticipation of a turgid technical exposition, I hasten to assure the reader that
developing such an understanding is neither difficult nor painful. The
way programmers express themselves in software, and the processes
they go through in setting down that expression, lend themselves easily
to analysis by traditional and sometimes even enjoyable methods of
decomposition. It is to this analysis that we now turn.

What is software? There are, fundamentally, two ways of answering
that question. One way is to state the perspective of the typical customer
for a software product. From the customer's perspective, software is
something that causes a computer to act in a particular way. The cus-

tomer's perspective is roughly similar to a concertgoer's perspective on a symphony being performed. To concertgoers, the symphony is the set of sounds that they hear. It is an aesthetic experience. Although concertgoers know that the symphony, as it was created by the composer, is in fact a sequence of instructions that must be processed by an instrumentality—the orchestra—in order to produce that aesthetic experience, the composer's score itself is of little interest to them. It is the result of the processing that counts. So it is with customers who buy computer programs.

The other way of thinking about computer programs (or symphonies, for that matter) is to consider them as compositions. Programs, like other literary works, consist of lines of text composed of symbolic characters. That, of course, is the programmer's perspective, because that is the way programmers write, or read, programs. In our concert analogy, the programmer's perspective would be akin to that of the composer. Like the composer, the programmer has in mind an end result to be delivered to the audience. That result may be a stack of printouts on a table or a series of related audiovisual images on a display screen. Whatever the result, the programmer must compose a set of instructions that will direct the instrumentality of choice to produce it.

In the case of the symphony, both the score and the resulting performance are protectable by copyright because both disclose the composer's original expression. In the case of computer programs, in reaching our conclusions as to the proper scope of protection for software we must consider the nature of programming expression both in the program itself and in the resulting output—the "user interfaces". The reader is therefore invited to experience, in this part of the book, the programmer's view of the craft. We will first examine the constraints imposed on that craft by virtue of the fact that the "instrumentality" of a program is a computer. Then we will take a short course in the elements of programming style, after which we will consider what the experts have said about the range of programming expression. Finally, we will survey the process by which programs are written, to see what that process suggests about the nature of programming expression.

5

Writing for Computers

When I consider the field of computing, two phenomena astonish me: that programmers aren't the best of writers, and that computer science has had to discover what the whole human race has known about the relative merits of chaos and order since God created the world in six days. I should have thought the discipline of programming would have made computer professionals the most polished group of writers in the country. But not only does the precision of programming fail to rub off on them, they have actually had to invent "structured programming" and discover the top-down approach, secrets quite obvious to writers—at least since Homer. I can't imagine how programmers went about their business before they, like Molière's Bourgeois Gentilhomme, suddenly discovered that they spoke prose.

Ben Ross Schneider, "Programs as Essays,"
Datamation, May 15, 1986, p. 162

It is sometimes said that computer programs differ from other literary works because they are not intended to be read by people. Indeed, as we've just seen, that assertion was given great moment by Judge Newcomer in *Apple v. Franklin*. What are we to make of that proposition, and of what consequence is it to our inquiry?

Strictly speaking, the proposition is false. All programs written for commercial distribution, and most others as well, are written with the idea that they will be read by other people. We are not talking here about bedtime reading, of course (except perhaps in the case of very hard-core byteniks). What we are talking about is the fact that in the real world there is a broad range of activities that require reading a program that someone else has written. For example, commercial programs are often enhanced by their suppliers or customers. Suppliers commonly do this by introducing a new version of the program which contains new functions and features. The original authors may or may not be involved in writing these enhancements. If they are not, the new authors must be able to read the original program in order to determine how to merge the enhancements into it. Similarly, programs are sometimes adapted by their suppliers or by customers to run on computers other than those for which they were initially designed. That adaptation cannot be done unless the new design team can read the original program. Finally, even if the program is never enhanced or adapted, there is every reason to believe that it will from time to time require service. Programs don't normally break down in the way that washing machines do, but they do frequently encounter working environments that were not anticipated by their authors, and may give unpredictable results as a consequence. Also, programmers do on occasion make errors that are memorialized as *bugs* in the resulting program. The people who correct the bugs or accommodate the program to unanticipated working environments are typically not the program authors, and those people, too, work more efficiently when the programs they service are more readable. Thus, for whatever it is worth, we can all take comfort in the fact that when program authors write programs, they have in mind a human readership.

What is at the core of concerns such as Judge Newcomer's is not the mistaken notion that programs have no human readership. It is, rather, the quite accurate notion that the primary audience for computer programs is a silicon readership. Leaving aside the screen displays and other elements of a program's user interface, the copyrighted work itself is a set of instructions intended to be carried out by a computer. Something about that fact gives many people pause; it leads them to feel that the nature of the protection afforded software should be different from that afforded literature, art, or music.

Thus, Paul Goldstein, Professor of Law at Stanford University asserts that courts should apply a

constrained infringement standard to that special form of functional work known as computer programs and hold defendant liable if he has literally copied the surface details of plaintiff's work, but should excuse the defendant who dips beneath the surface into functional elements of plaintiff's work.

Similarly, Dennis Karjala of Arizona State University states, "Infringement should be limited to verbatim or near-verbatim copying of the literal language of the program, i.e., the literal codes." And finally that most energetic crusader against traditional copyright protection for software, Pamela Samuelson of Emory Law School, proposes that the law should protect only "very low-level abstractions, e.g., instruction-by-instruction sequence of source code, as well as exact sequence of bits."

Why do these feelings arise? In part, it is because—as the quote from C. P. Snow in Chapter 1 suggests—many of us really are natural Luddites at heart. The Luddites, the reader may recall, were bands of English weavers who went around smashing textile machinery in the early years of the Industrial Revolution. The term is now frequently applied to those who dislike, distrust, or refuse to understand the workings of machines. While it can be argued that dislike, distrust, and refusal to understand are sufficient bases for discriminatory laws, that argument is neither powerful nor attractive. It would be better analytically, and more civilized as well, to seek a basis for differential protection in the substantive differences, if any, between the writings known as computer programs and other writings that arise because the primary audience for the former are machines. In that connection, the difference most often propounded is that the range of expression available to an author writing instructions for a computer is far narrower than that available to a novelist, a poet, a historian, or even a scientist. The range of expression is so narrow for the programmer, it is said, that given a particular task to be accomplished, a specific computer, and a specific programming language, there is not much opportunity for real differences of expression. This is said to be particularly true, as we have seen, in the case of operating systems.

There is no question that for a program to be machine-readable, its author must adhere to special kinds of syntactic, semantic, and constructional conventions. Whether those conventions affect the range of expression, or only its form, is a different matter, however. The range of programming expression is not substantially constrained by the special conventions of programming languages, for the reasons that follow.

Computers, as we know them today, are machines fabricated of silicon, steel, copper, plastics, and other physical materials. Conceptually, the "brains" of these machines are nothing more than arrays of elements, each capable of being in an "on" or "off" state, like a lightbulb. The state of each element is changed by the requisite switching mechanism either automatically in response to a change in another element or at the direction of an intelligent operator. Interestingly, despite the computer's mechanistic nature (or maybe precisely because of it), many scientists active in the field of artificial intelligence believe that computers can—and perhaps do—"understand" the data they are processing. Others disagree. The debate arises because we have no way of determining whether someone—or something—understands (i.e., appreciates the significance of) what we have said except by assessing whether that someone—or something—performs an appropriate act based on our words. The machine reacts appropriately, if it is properly programmed, but its reactions are strictly in accordance with the principles of physics. Although it is the assumption of most religions, and the conceit of most humans that *understanding* entails more than just reacting in accordance with the laws of physics, the existence of a serious philosophical debate as to whether computers have the capacity to understand further reduces the weight that can be given to the argument that software should be less protected than books because it is written to be read by machines.

The changes in the patterns of "ons" and "offs" that a program causes in its hardware "reader" have significance only to those among the species Homo sapiens who have designed the code expressible as sequences of ons and offs, a code in which the machine's known electronic reactions will take place in meaningful order dictated by the instructions it receives. In order for the computer to do anything useful, then, somebody has got to work the on-off switches. That could in principle be done by hand, switch by switch, like the Wizard of Oz working furiously behind the curtain. Indeed, in the earliest days of electronic computing, it was done that way. Then the lesson of the Jacquard Loom was recalled. As we've already seen, Jacquard's great invention was, in effect, to set the pattern "switches" of a loom in advance by virtue of instructions memorialized in prepunched cards. In the same fashion, it was seen that patterns of electronic ons and offs placed in a computer's memory by a program could instruct the computer's circuitry as to which switches to employ and in what sequence in order to produce a result at electronic speeds.

Use of the "stored program" technique is the underpinning of the art of programming and the basis for all modern computer systems. The power of the technique is so great that there is today not a single general-purpose computer that is composed of hardware alone. All such computers consist of (1) hardware that stores and manipulates ons and offs representing instructions or data, (2) hardware that controls the silicon switches of the computer in specified ways in response to a set of predefined patterns of ons and offs called the "instruction set" of the computer, and (3) elaborate sets of instructions—the programs—that cause the computer to perform operations that human beings can translate into intelligible and useful results.

These three basic constituents of a computer system are commonly classified according to the following slightly longer taxonomy:

Processing. The hardware device that *reads* the program is called a processor. The job of the processor is to act on data in accordance with the program's instructions. Conceptually, a processor is a very simple device. Its important elements, for our purposes, can be described as: (1) circuitry to interpret instructions one at a time; (2) storage locations, or *registers*, to hold the data to be acted on, and the instructions; (3)

circuitry to perform the arithmetic or logical operation on the data that is called for by the instructions; and (4) a pointer to the address of the next instruction to be processed.

An endemic risk for authors on computer topics is that the march of technology (actually, its headlong rush) tends to obsolete descriptions such as the foregoing even before they are published. Already, for example, "parallel processors," including the vector processors that make supercomputers "super," are experiencing commercial success, and "neural nets" that in a sense mimic the organization of the brain are not far behind. These processors or networks of processors don't conform in the strictest sense to the first element of our description. Parallel processors and neural nets today represent a modest exception, however, to the rule that today's processor hardware can process only one instruction—such as to add two numbers or compare two numbers—at a time. (The new dimension that parallel processors and neural nets add to the task of writing programs is the ability to process many elemental instructions in parallel.) What makes the processor a valuable commodity is that it can process each instruction in a very, very small fraction of a second. Because of that speed, the serial processing nature of the processor is not a significant factor in determining the nature of programming expression. Much more significant is the fact that the processor cannot process all the instructions of which the human mind can conceive. Far from it. The processor can perform only those elemental operations that are built into its circuitry. These usually number on the order of several dozen, or fewer for so-called "reduced instruction-set computers." For any given computer, the set of such operations corresponds to the series of electronic signals that we referred to above as the processor's instruction set. One rule of expression for programmers, then, is that *instructions must be expressed to the processor in terms of the elemental operations that the circuitry is capable of performing.*

Another rule of expression for programmers, obviously, is that *the processor can read only ons and offs.* That limitation forced programmers in the early days of the industry to use numerical notation systems to express their programs. In these systems, all characters are represented as, or could easily be translated by the processor into, combinations of the symbols 0 and 1. Binary numbers work very much like Arabic numbers, but they are much less compact and, as the reader can appreciate, much harder for most people to read. Take, for example, the binary number 100110. If one is not familiar with binary notation, that string of symbols is meaningless except for its decimal meaning, one-hundred-thousand one-hundred-ten. One who has been taught how the binary notation system works, on the other hand, could figure out what the number means by parsing it as follows, starting from the right: no ones, a two, a four, no eights, no sixteens, a thirty-two. An afficionado of machine-language programming, though, would know without any mental gymnastics that 100110 is the binary equivalent of the decimal number 38.

Since processors can only read zeros and ones, and since much of the information that people want from computers is not numerical at all but alphabetic, it is also common to reserve certain strings of zeros and ones to represent letters. In many computers, binary information is separated into blocks of a given length, each of which represents a single character in another language, such as a letter of an alphabet or the symbol for an Arabic number. A blocking technique used by many computers employs blocks of eight "bits" (*binary digits*, i.e., zeros and ones) to represent characters. With eight bits ranging from 00000000 to 11111111, we can represent 256 different characters, which can include the English alphabet in both upper and lower cases, the numerals 0 to 9, numerous non-English letters, and many other symbols as well. The eight-bit block is called a *byte* of information, and is a well-accepted way of organizing binary information in computers.

By happy coincidence or intelligent design, the only language that processors can digest is useful not just in arithmetic, but in formal logic as well. The two-state format, 1 or 0, is analogous to the true-or-false format of formal logic:

P	Q	P·Q		A	B	A·B
T	T	T		1	1	1
T	F	F		1	0	0
F	T	F		0	1	0
F	F	F		0	0	0

As a result, the binary notation system lends itself not just to the computation of arithmetic solutions but also to the solution of logical problems. For example, a computer may be instructed to do the following search of its data base: If (it is *true* that) a case mentions the word copyright, and (*true* that) it also mentions either computer programs or software, and (*true* that) it was decided after 1982, then the name of that case should be printed. The ability to perform logical operations as well as arithmetic operations greatly increases the range of problems that computers can handle.

As I've already suggested, there are electronic circuit elements that function in exactly the same way as binary arithmetic; indeed, they are binary arithmetic incarnate. In other words, they are capable of being in only one of two conditions, either on or off. The simplicity of such a circuit element at once conceals and represents its great power. Alone, of course, an electronic on-off switch can't accomplish much, but there is strength in numbers. For example, one type of circuit that can be constructed from such elements is called an *And* circuit. A simple And circuit has two input lines and one output line. In this circuit, current will flow (i.e., a binary 1 will issue) if and only if current has flowed on both input lines (i.e., the switches on both input lines are turned on).

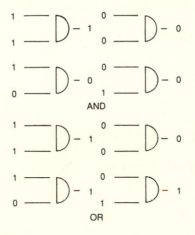

AND

OR

Another type of circuit that can be built from such elements is called an *Or* circuit. In a simple Or circuit, current will flow on the output line (i.e., a binary 1 will issue) if current is flowing on either input line (i.e., if either one input switch or the other is turned on). By combining And and Or circuits, a device known as an "adder" may be constructed that will respond to inputs in ways that we can begin to find useful. In the garden-variety adder (Biblical allusion unintended), the inputs 1 and 0 produce the output 01, the inputs 1 and 1 result in the output 10, and the inputs 0 and 0 result in the output 00.

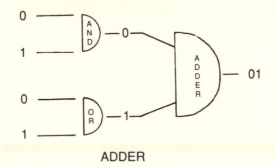

ADDER

From the elementary on-off switches, elementary circuits that perform basic logic operations—such as And, Or, and Not—can be fabricated. From those elementary circuits, elementary devices that perform basic arithmetic operations, such as adders, can be fabricated, and from those elementary devices, interconnected in large numbers, powerful processors capable of performing millions of instructions per second can be fabricated. By calling on various combinations of the devices and circuits in the processor according to patterns specified in software, the processor is directed to solve problems, and because of the ability to change the software just as the cards in the Jacquard Loom could be changed, the range of problems that processors can be directed to solve is infinite even though the number of instructions in their instruction sets is distinctly not.

Storage. Just as there are electronic circuits that can perform logic operations, there are also electronic circuits whose function is to store a bit or a byte of information—a 1 or a 0, or eight ones and zeros—to report on what is stored when queried and to change the contents of storage on command. Because the storage of information, like the storage of screws or shirts or books, lends itself to the use of orderly arrays of receptacles that are basically the same, large numbers of storage circuits can be fabricated on a single semiconducter chip. At the beginning of the 1980s, the storage chips in widest manufacture could hold sixteen thousand bits of information. Today, million-bit ("megabit") chips and four-megabit chips are widely available, and the sixteen-megabit chip is just entering the scene. Although experts in the field all accept the notion that such miniaturization cannot continue indefinitely, they also agree that the end is not yet in sight.

For our purposes, it is sufficient to think of storage circuits in a computer as a collection of cells or mailboxes, each of which can hold a bit or a byte of information. The information may be data, such as customer names, chemical formulas, or the characters comprising the text of a letter. It may also be the instructions of a program. Each cell has an associated address, and the processor sends information to, or receives information from, a cell by referencing its address.

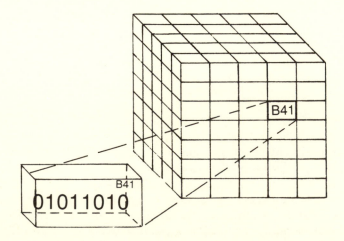

Electronic storage is temporary storage for data or instructions immediately needed by the processor. That data or those instructions may change constantly as processing proceeds. Like all generalities, this last generality has its exceptions. As we saw in the case of *Apple v. Franklin*, computers can contain permanent electronic storage known as read-only memory, in which are stored the program instructions that the hardware will require no matter what the customer wants it to do. Nonetheless, long-term permanent storage for customer programs and data is usually provided by disk drives, tape drives, or other devices that store the information magnetically, or even optically as points formed on the surface of a disk by bursts of light from a laser. These latter devices offer much larger storage capacity than electronic storage, but retrieve data much more slowly because they are in part mechanical. One job of the program author (generally the author working on the operating system) is to solve operational problems that arise because of the differences in speed between the various components of a computer system.

Input and Output. The information processed by a computer must originate outside the computer itself or be derived from information originating outside the computer, and, to be useful, results of that processing must sooner or later be delivered outside the computer itself. (There are, no doubt, deep philosophical implications in that assertion, akin to the Zen question about whether a tree falling unheard in a forest makes a sound, but I leave them to the reader to ponder.)

The information provided to the computer may be categorized in one or more of several different types. Five common types are:

1. Data, that is, numerical or alphabetic records to be sorted, added, integrated, or otherwise manipulated formulaically;

2. Text, such as what you are now reading;

3. Graphics, for example, bar charts, cartoons, or hand-drawn pictures;

4. Images, or digitized photographs and video signals; and

5. Voice and other sounds.

The components of a computer system that receive the input may also take any number of forms. Common input devices are punched card readers; tape drives, disk or diskette drives; keyboards on video display terminals; optical character readers; magnetic character readers; speech recognition devices; sensors of temperature, motion, or chemical composition; and video cameras. In addition, computers are increasingly coming to serve as input devices for one another. A personal computer connected through a network to a large mainframe computer, for instance, can receive data from the mainframe, process it, and dump it back into the mainframe for storage. Indeed, many think that a personal computer cannot serve as an effective general-purpose office workstation unless it is capable of communication with mainframe resources, especially data bases.

Output may also take several forms. It may be printed on a printer, displayed on a screen, spoken by a voice response unit, stored on magnetic disk or tape, graphed on a plotter, punched as holes in cards, or translated into action by a robot. Each type of input or output device has a particular way of conversing with the processor: its own language or communication conventions. The ability for the processor to communicate with a variety of devices is generally provided by means of software. Using software for this purpose gives suppliers the flexibility to add conventions for new devices easily and, from the customer's point of view, cheaply. Thus, one of the tasks typically performed by the authors of operating system software is to facilitate the input and output of information between the processor and the profusion of input and output devices that may attach themselves to the processor, each with its peculiar linguistic tics.

Control. Computer systems are assemblages composed of a number of interacting devices. The interactions between these devices must be controlled in order that electronic gridlock does not occur or electronic chaos does not reign within the system. For the most part, controlling the devices that make up a computer system is the task of the software writers. Their programs tell the hardware what to do, how to do it, and where to find the information to be acted on. The creative efforts of those writers transform the hardware world of electronic pulses, of elemental logico-mathematical operations on streams of ones and zeros, into a coordinated, whirring, blinking ensemble that can store and retrieve vast libraries of information, transmit messages among thousands of workstations, and allow users at those thousands of workstations to share the resources of a mainframe processor as though it were their own. "Control", in the sense I am using the term, then, denotes the imaginative elaboration of imperative sentences; sentences that take as a given the processor's instruction set—a sort of Basic English with adjectives, adverbs, and most nouns, verbs, and prepositions filtered out—and build on that limited base a complex, richly articulated environment that, because of the speed of processor circuitry, responds in almost miraculous ways to the prompting of human users.

Communication. The same telephone system that allows us to talk to one another over great distances also allows computer systems—and even parts of the same computer system—to communicate with one another. (Actually, computer scientists would prefer to have a higher-fidelity and more reliable telephone system than the one that humans use, but they are making do for now.) The personal computer behind a lawyer's desk can access caselaw data bases stored in a mainframe

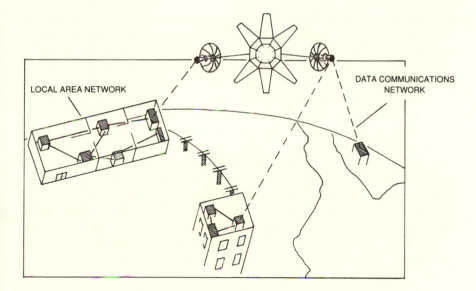

LOCAL AREA NETWORK

DATA COMMUNICATIONS
NETWORK

system hundreds of miles away. An international enterprise's computers around the globe can transfer information to one another via satellite. The teller terminals in a bank's branch offices can communicate with a processor at headquarters over telephone lines. When they do so they are said to form a "data communications network." The workstations at the bank's headquarters can communicate with each other through wires buried in the walls of the building. If they do, they are said to form a "local area network." What makes such networks work is software. Networking programs instruct computers to behave like a combination post office and central telephone exchange.

Processing, storage, input, output, control, and communications: In deciding what capabilities to implement in achieving these six functions, and how to implement them, program authors must make large numbers of decisions, choosing sometimes from options presented to them by the hardware environment, by international standards, or by other external factors; and sometimes from options that bubble up out of their own imaginations. For personal computers, the number of such decisions is typically tens of thousands or hundreds of thousands. For large computers, the number ranges from hundreds of thousands to millions, to tens of millions. Each decision made by the program authors translates into one or more lines of programming text, called *code* because it resembles coded text.

Obviously, the fact that programs are written with one eye to the need for them to be executed by computer hardware imposes certain requirements on program authors that authors of other kinds of literary works do not have to accommodate. On the other hand, program authors are freed from many of the constraints that plague other kinds of authors. Computer programs do not need to have happy endings, for example. They don't have to rhyme, or hold a meter. In programs, it is not necessary that Good be seen to triumph over Evil, or that characters be believable. Escaping those shackles only to be bound to a machine world of zeros and ones might not seem a felicitous trade from the standpoint of free expression, but the binary arithmetic requirement provides a view of programming at its most primitive level, a level like that of an Ur-language that is no longer employed in actual discourse. Instead, programmers have created languages more akin to human languages, which the computer itself can translate into the patterns of zeros and ones that it can assimilate. In the next chapter, we will consider the different types of programming language in common use today, and also relive a courtroom drama that involved programming languages, thereby advancing our sense of the available range of programming expression.

6

Programming Languages: The *SAS* Case

I speak Spanish to God, Italian to women, French to men and Ger-
man to my horse.

Charles V, Emperor of the Holy Roman Empire

The computer for which the company known as SAS Institute, Inc., had
written its statistical analysis program was the IBM System/370, actually
a family of large and mid-sized computers all members of which con-
formed to the same instruction set. The SAS program was one of the
most popular programs of its type. A number of customers who used
computers other than IBM System/370s began to think to themselves (in
words or substance), "My, wouldn't it be nice if I could run SAS on my
non-System/370 computer." In data processing terms, this is the equivalent of the Parisian filmgoer wishing for a version of *Who Killed Roger
Rabbit* dubbed in French, or the Japanese businessman eagerly awaiting
a Japanese version of Clyde Prestowitz's book on East–West economic
rivalry, *Trading Places*.

SAS Institute discovered in the course of its market research activities
that customers particularly wanted a version of SAS that ran on computers manufactured by the Digital Equipment Corporation (DEC). Accordingly, the company set in motion a development project to adapt
SAS to the language of the DEC instruction set. In the computer industry,
however, there are opportunists behind every disk drive. One of the
most pronounced characteristics of the industry, in fact, is that every
conceivable customer requirement is seen as a raging demand that must

be supplied. Competitive opportunities tend to be seized as fast as they arise. Sometimes faster. In short, SAS Institute was not the only actor in the industry to notice the customer demand for a DEC version of SAS. The S&H Computer Systems company also saw an opportunity to satisfy the wishes of DEC's customers. S&H undertook to rewrite SAS so that it worked with the DEC instruction set. The process was essentially one of translation, and resulted in a kind of paraphrasing of the SAS program in another programming language.

SAS Institute was offended by what it viewed as the misappropriation of its intellectual property and, more importantly no doubt, its potential customers. To appreciate the issues at play in this case, we need first to explore the nature of programming languages. That exploration will also serve as a platform from which to obtain a better perspective on the task of program writing generally. After we've had our look at the various types of programming languages, we'll review the outcome of the case styled *SAS Institute v. S&H Computer Systems*.

One of the first programmable electronic computers ever built was the ENIAC. Designed and constructed at the University of Pennsylvania in 1946, the ENIAC weighed thirty tons, contained seventeen thousand vacuum tubes and occupied eighteen hundred square feet of floor space. To realize that today's hand-held calculators are more powerful information processors than was this behemoth is to feel the frenetic rhythm of the computer industry. The driven people in the world aren't going to medical school any more. They're becoming computer entrepreneurs and leading the industry on a merry chase for ever greater price-per-formance.

ENIAC was a war baby. It was born out of the wartime need for a better means of calculating trajectory tables for artillery shells. During the war, such tables had been calculated by teams of people sitting at calculating machines. It was an inefficient and frustrating process, and the military knew there had to be a better way. A contract was let to the University of Pennsylvania engineering department to pursue a then-staggering idea: creating a machine that would perform those calculations in its "head." The Penn researchers rose to the challenge and created the machine, and although ENIAC did not actually see wartime service, it did launch a revolution of its own.

Though its mission was to perform trajectory calculations, it was capable of being adapted to the solution of other kinds of problems as well. In order to adapt the ENIAC, its operators had to reset some six thousand switches on the machine and replug hundreds of cables, much like telephone operators at old-fashioned switchboards. Or like the Wizard of Oz. In effect, they were rewiring the connections among the ENIAC's circuits in order to change its processing logic. The technicians who did this work no doubt used written instructions from the machine's designers; instructions that indicated in human-readable diagrams and language how switches should be set and cables plugged in order to cause the machine to produce the desired result.

Replugging the computer and resetting its switches every time a new kind of computation needed to be made was obviously a cumbersome, error-prone process, and if it hadn't been mechanized there would likely be no commercial computer industry today. I cannot report to you who invented the solution to that problem without treading into a swirl of historical controversy, but it is generally accepted that the great mathematician John von Neumann was instrumental in popularizing the invention. Von Neumann and others recognized that the instructions for resetting and replugging the ENIAC were in themselves a kind of data. This was a brilliant insight (even though, in a way, Jacquard had had the same insight almost two centuries earlier). It meant that the instructions could be stored in the computer just like the data on which the computer was meant to operate. Von Neumann proposed differentiating the stored instructions from stored data by preceding the former with a 1 and the latter with a 0, so that the processor could distinguish between them. By running the instructions—which we now call a program—through the computer along with the data, and thereby indicating to the processor at each step through which of its circuits the data should flow and in what sequence, the task of resetting and replugging could be eliminated and the computer would become a general-purpose problem-solving tool.

That concept, the concept of the stored program, is the key to the computer industry and the key to understanding the computer. By storing a variety of programs in a form readily accessible to the processor, such as on magnetic disk or tape, we give the processor the capability to change its character by calling each program into its memory on command. In that way, the same processor can be made to process a payroll, look up a customer's payment history, book an airline reservation, send an item of electronic mail, play chess, simulate a hurricane, or keep track of inventory.

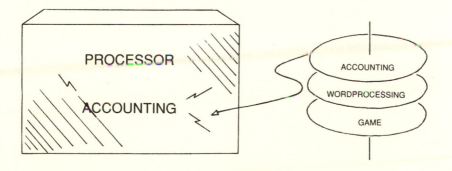

The instructions that comprise a program must be written in a language that the processor reads. Strictly speaking, each processor can read only the machine language for processors of its type. The IBM 3090 cannot read the machine language of the UNISYS 1100. The word "read," in this context, really means only "can execute." Lest we risk anthropomorphizing the machine, I should make clear that a processor's machine language is nothing more than the set of instructions—also called, not surprisingly, the instruction set—that the machine is designed to execute when they are presented in proper form to its circuitry. The instruction set of a computer, then, is a specific set of strings of binary numbers, each of which has the following "meaning" to the processor. When each such string is presented as input to the processor, it causes the processor's circuitry to perform one of the actions that the processor is capable of taking.

Machine language. Programs in machine language are expressed as strings of numbers. Each machine-language program consists of sequences of instructions. Speaking broadly, one can describe machine-language programs as taking the following form: a command to the processor to perform some elementary operation, such as Move an item of data or Compare two items of data, together with the identification of the parameter(s) on which the operation is to be performed and the location(s) in processor storage where the action is to take place. One such instruction, translated into English from its binary form, might be: "Move parameter A to memory location 110."

Machine-language programs typically contain long sequences of such instructions, all written as sequences of numbers. In the very early days of computing, almost everyone who wrote computer programs did so in machine language because it was the only way to instruct the machine. Typically, these early programs were written in decimal (0–9), hexadecimal (0–15), or octal (0–7) versions of machine language, which the computer itself translated into ones and zeros. Nonetheless, even for the binary bards of the 1950s, machine language was a long, tedious, and error-prone way of expressing one's thoughts. Because writing programs as series of numeric sequences directly referencing storage addresses and other machine elements was such an unsatisfying task, some clever people came up with the idea of writing programs that would make it easier to write other programs, by serving as translators between symbols that humans can more readily understand and the binary strings that machines understand. These translation programs are something like the translators at the United Nations. Programmers write their texts in languages other than machine language, and the translation programs convert the texts into machine language. Some translator programs are simultaneous translators. As each instruction presents itself for processing, it is translated. Simultaneous translator programs are called

```
10101001                    ADDROUT L  2, DATA 1  ┐
00110000                             A  2, DATA 2  ├ instructions
00011000                             ST 2, SCORE  ┘
01101001                                 ⋮
00100010                                 ⋮
10001101                    DATA 1   DS  F         ┐
00000010                    DATA 2   DS  F         ├ data definitions
01100000                    SCORE    DS  F         ┘
```

Machine Language   Assembler Language

"interpreters." Other translation programs prepare complete translations before their output is presented to the processor for processing.
Those programs are called "assemblers" or "compilers".

What interests us, from the point of view of programming expression,
is what languages these translation programs can accommodate, since
the vast majority of programs are no longer written directly in machine
language. The languages in which they are written may be classified
and described as follows:

Assembler language. This is simply machine language written in symbols
more readily comprehensible to humans than binary notation. The commands are the same as those in machine language, so that every statement is an elementary command to the processor in which the verb is
one of those in the processor's instruction set, but instead of 1's and
O's, we find the verbs expressed as alphabetic characters. Parameters
are represented as Arabic decimal numbers or as hexadecimal numbers.
Hexadecimal is a base–16 numbering system in which the first six letters
of the alphabet are combined with the ten digits so that, for example,
the decimal number 10 can be expressed in one symbol, A. Most significantly, memory locations are referred to by name as well rather than
by their actual binary addresses, thus freeing the programmer from the
need to keep track of the specific location of the data on which the
program is operating.

Assembler language is far more accessible than machine language,
but is still a difficult language to read. "Cryptic" would be an understated
description of an assembler-language program. There is a capability,
however, that becomes available with machine-language programs and
remains available in most higher-level languages, and that vastly im-
proves the readability of programs. The capability is called "commenting." Comments are little aides-memoire that programmers may write
in the margin alongside any line of a program. They usually translate
the instruction into human language for later reference by the author
or another reader. The computer ignores them when it is processing the
program.

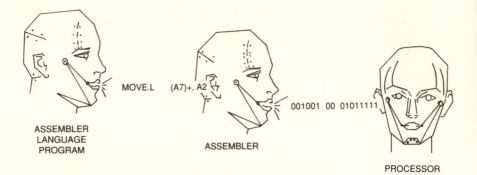

ASSEMBLER
LANGUAGE
PROGRAM

MOVE.L   (A7)+, A2

ASSEMBLER

001001 00 01011111

PROCESSOR

Actually, the computer would also ignore the rest of an assembler-language program, which it can't read directly either, were it not for the existence of programs called assemblers. An assembler actually causes the computer to translate assembler-language programs into their binary, machine-language form, which the computer can then process.

Like machine language, assembler language reflects the way computers are designed rather than the way people think. Assembler-language programs must specify each elementary action that a computer will take to accomplish a particular result. Given the limited and inflexible set of instructions that a processor can follow, specifying those actions is a tedious job indeed. Although assembler language was and still is a means of writing software that is finely tuned to the hardware it is designed to control, it was not the breakthrough that would create a generation of computer programmers.

That breakthrough came in the mid–1950s, about a decade after the ENIAC, as people began to recognize that programs could be written that would convert a single high-level instruction into appropriate strings of assembler-language or machine-language instructions. Recognition of that possibility led to the development of high-level programming languages.

High-level languages. These are based on the notion that the job of translating a program written the way people think (high-level) into a program written the way computers are designed to work (low-level) could be automated, so long as the high-level statements were sufficiently formalized. The first formalized high-level language available commercially was FORTRAN (short for FORmula TRANslator), created at IBM in the late 1950s. Since then, many others have been created. FORTRAN was designed to facilitate the writing of programs that would solve scientific problems:

	ADDROUT L 2, DATA 1	
10101001	A 2, DATA2	
00110000	ST 2, SCORE	
00011000		
01101001		
00100010		
10001101 =		= X = A+B
00000010		
01100000	DATA 1 DS F	
	DATA 2 DS F	
	SCORE DS F	

Machine Language   Assembler Language   FORTRAN

COBOL was designed for business applications. BASIC was developed at Dartmouth with a view to providing a language easy for students to use. LISP is used in writing "artificial intelligence" programs, which cause computers to simulate—in a rough way—some aspects of human reasoning.

Just as assembler-language programs are translated into machine language by assemblers, high-level languages are translated into machine language (or, often, into assembler language) by programs called compilers. Compilers expand a single high-level instruction into many low-level instructions. By doing so, they remove from the programmer the burden of knowing precisely how a specific processor works or, in other words, knowing the processor's particular machine language. As a result, the programmer can express the program in a language that is at once easier to use, more economical of the programmer's time and more comprehensible to another human reader.

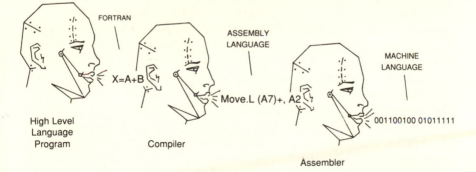

An additional benefit of high-level-language compilers is that they make it possible to run the same programs on processors with very different instruction sets. The reason this works is that if the program author writes a program in, say, standard COBOL, then any processor

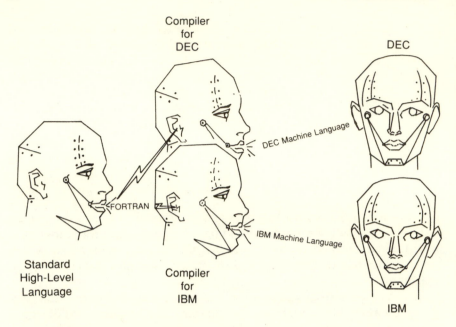

for which a COBOL compiler is available will have a means of translating that COBOL program into that processor's machine language.

There are two points to be taken from the foregoing reading. First, we have seen that computers can be programmed in languages that are increasingly natural for people to use. Indeed, research continues into the possibility of programming computers in "natural English" or other human tongues. From that observation, we are led to conclude that any argument that computer programs should be treated differently under the copyright law from other literary works because programming languages are different from natural languages proceeds from a fundamentally erroneous premise. Second, we are led to conclude that there is no linguistic basis for distinguishing between the legal protection to be afforded to programs expressed in high-level languages and the legal protection to be afforded to programs expressed in assembler or machine languages. That is so because an assembler- or machine-language version of a high-level-language program is nothing but a translation (and in most cases, a mechanical translation) of the same expression from one language into another.

We are now ready to return to the *SAS* case. Let us take up at the point at which S&H concluded that there was a market for a statistical analysis program that ran on DEC computers.

The company's first effort was to design a program of its own. They even chose a name for it: PASQUEL. When S&H determined that it would be much easier to market a package modeled after SAS, however, the PASQUEL project was quickly abandoned. Instead, S&H obtained a license to SAS from the SAS Institute and embarked on a project to convert SAS from the IBM environment to the DEC environment. Internal notes pointedly describe the project's goal as being "conversion—fully compatible." At the time, S&H officials apparently thought—without having checked with the institute—that once their conversion was complete, the institute would gladly embrace the S&H product and market it for S&H. Although S&H did not disclose to the institute the purpose for which it was licensing SAS, the company did disclose its intentions to DEC personnel, who questioned the legality of the project.

Undaunted, S&H proceeded with its conversion activities. And now, questions of credibility began to creep into the picture. S&H witnesses testified that the only purpose for which they had licensed the SAS program was to run it against test data in order to compare the results it produced with those produced by the S&H program. The undisputed evidence, however, was that having received the SAS program under a standard customer license, S&H immediately loaded it onto a DEC computer. SAS could not run on the DEC computer, of course, because the DEC computer could not read SAS's IBM-oriented instructions. (The reason was that there was no DEC compiler that would translate SAS from its IBM-oriented high-level language into DEC machine language.) Therefore, the program could only be stored as a text file on the DEC machine. It could not be executed against test data, or any other data for that matter. As a result of the disclosure of that evidence, the trial judge, Thomas A. Wiseman, Jr., refused to believe what the S&H witnesses had said about their purpose in licensing SAS. As much as anything else, that loss of credibility predetermined the outcome of the case.

The court also found that S&H personnel printed out listings of the SAS code, and—worse—that they sat at their terminals and, using text-editing programs, rearranged, changed, or moved lines of SAS code or blocks of code to create the S&H program. In large measure, that finding was based on circumstantial evidence, in particular, the following:

1. The existence of forty-four examples of S&H code segments so similar to the SAS code that they must have been copied;

2. The fact that S&H destroyed the original source code for its product shortly after it allowed SAS's president to look at it and before SAS's expert witnesses could review it;

3. The fact that the S&H code had been altered in nonfunctional ways before being provided to the court-appointed expert (for example, originally, the S&H program printed the words "Statistical Analysis System" at the beginning of its output, which caption was later changed);

4. The fact that in early versions of the S&H code the acronym "SAS" appeared in at least 145 different statements, which appearances were later removed by what the court concluded was a text-editing process;

5. The coding standards document distributed to programmers on the S&H project, which indicated that the modular structure of its program was intended to duplicate SAS, that the names of the "driver routines" (internal names, not visible to users of the program) written by S&H programmers were to be "as close as possible" to those in SAS, and that in only one instance were the S&H programmers instructed not to use a particular SAS routine;

6. The lack of design documentation for the S&H program, when compared even to the documentation available for the aborted and incomplete PASQUEL program;

7. The fact that the same people whose testimony about licensing the court had found to be incredible were responsible for breaking the SAS conversion project into parts and providing necessary information to the programmers working on the individual parts; and

8. The fact that S&H admitted "carefully and precisely" reproducing portions of the SAS user commands and instructions not documented by SAS in its manuals and therefore not visible elsewhere than in the SAS source code.

As to the last point, S&H argued that those user commands had to be duplicated in order that the S&H program would be "compatible" with the SAS program. S&H's expert witness testified that the creation of compatible programs was a common practice in the computer industry. While accepting that possibility, the court noted that there was no evidence that industry practice included the misuse of proprietary and copyrighted materials.

Obviously, the court's findings of fact were all adverse to S&H. Having thus badly lost the factual battle, S&H argued that under the law applicable to the facts, there was no infringement, following the pragmatic rule that, in court, you play the hand that you are dealt as best you can. One of the basic principles of copyright law, as we have seen, is that expression is protected and ideas are not. All that S&H had taken from SAS was its ideas, S&H claimed, not its expression. As the reader will appreciate, that defense is a common one in software copyright cases, as it is in any copyright case where the copy is not identical to the original. It throws the court into a gray area and gives the defendant's lawyer room to maneuver, in particular, to offer expert testimony and put forward arguments not really directed to the idea-expression dichotomy at all, but to other reasons why the defendant should be let off the hook. In the case at hand, however, there were no other reasons. The judge had concluded that S&H witnesses were liars. He had no sympathy for their position. Accordingly, he gave S&H's defense fairly short shrift. While S&H was perfectly free to make the DEC machine do the same statistical analyses that the IBM machine did when running SAS, the judge said, it should have done so by its own creative effort. Just as the copyright in a play may be infringed without using its dialogue, the copyright in a computer program may be infringed without producing a literally identical program. (Indeed, translating a program from one machine environment to another would be expected to result in a product that was not literally identical to the eye; yet copyright unquestionably protects against unauthorized translation.) S&H had produced a program so similar that it must be said to have copied SAS's expression.

S&H also claimed that the actual examples of copying presented by SAS Institute were so few and far between as to be trivial under the law; that is, insufficient to establish the "substantial similarity" required to prove copyright infringement. The judge made several points in the course of rejecting that defense. First, he said, the test of substantial similarity is qualitative, not quantitative. The taking of even a quantitatively small fragment of a protected work might be qualitatively substantial because of the disproportionately large value of that fragment. Second, forty-four examples of copying could not be said to be an insubstantial number. Third, if S&H had not destroyed or masked the evidence of copying, there would have been many more examples. And finally, the evidence of copying presented at trial implicated not merely the particular lines of code that were similar, but the organization and structure of the SAS program which, the evidence showed, must have been copied pervasively by S&H. Although the S&H program might indeed contain substantial original work, it was, the judge concluded, substantially and pervasively "based on" the SAS program.

S&H's final defense was that it had excised—or could excise—the examples of copying, and in any case should be allowed to market the portions of its program that the SAS Institute had not challenged. The court rejected that defense in its entirety. It did not accept the proposition that the copying was limited to the examples presented by the institute, nor did it accept the idea that the unchallenged portions of S&H's program were free of copying.

The upshot, for S&H, was that it was enjoined from marketing its product, or any products derived from that product, or any products derived from SAS. The upshot for the industry was that programmers learned that translation of a program from one machine environment to another is the exclusive prerogative of the copyright owner.

Given the facts of the *SAS* case, the result was not surprising. One might ask, as we did in the context of *Apple v. Franklin*, whether the principle articulated in *SAS* is salutary or not; that is, whether people in fact ought to be prohibited from translating one another's computer programs and offering the translations as their own. Such, of course, is the rule imposed by the copyright law. However, there are voices in a sometimes strident chorus, in the United States, in Europe, and particularly in Japan, crying out for repeal of the copyright law as applied to software. The aim of their crusade is precisely to allow suppliers to translate successful programs of other suppliers for profit just as S&H Computer Systems did. What is the reason for this crusade? These voices say it is because software is not like other literary works, and treating it as a literary work creates economic mischief. We will explore their arguments next, beginning with the question of whether there is similarity between computer programs and works that all agree are protectable against translation.

7

Programming Structures: The *Synercom* Case

I believe I told Renée that certain frank remarks she had made were as suitable to her as a silk hat to a monkey.... As a sequel to this incident, I still have the brief note she sent me, very imposing in its form:

You gravely offended me last night, Colette, and I am not one who forgives. Adieu. Renée.

However, the other Renée, the good and charming Renée, saw to it that I had a second note two hours after the first one. It read:

Forgive me, dear little Colette, God only knows what I wrote to you. Eat these lovely peaches as a toast to my health and come to see me. Come dine with me as soon as you can, and bring along our friends.

Colette, *The Pure and the Impure* (1932)

There is good programming style and bad programming style. There is elegance in program authorship, and inelegance. There are individual quirks, habits, modes of expression, and flights of creativity that mark the expression in a programmer's source code. There is a book called *Elements of Programming Style*. There are books on the psychology of computer programming.

Nonetheless, many commentators within and outside the legal community continue to resist the notion that programs are literary works. Most of those commentators know little about computer programming. They are arguing on the basis of faith rather than knowledge. In the next four chapters, we examine the elements of programming style with a view to illuminating a subject now often being debated in the dark. As we gather knowledge as to what programming is all about, we will also push open the doors of various courtrooms wherein our knowledge will illuminate the issues being argued.

I signalled my viewpoint at the outset of this work. In my opinion, programs are literary works, not just in a copyright sense, but as a matter of social taxonomy. That is not to say that programs are literature. Rather, they are particular kinds of literary works, in the way that a musical score or a "shooting script" for a movie are literary works: One doesn't read them through like a novel, but they have the attributes common to all literary works. Those attributes are structure, flow, logic, design, naming conventions, commentary, and resultant style. We are going to examine those attributes one by one. This chapter is devoted to the first of them: program structure.

Take a book from your shelf: any book, fiction or nonfiction. Open it and consider its contents without regard for their meaning but only in terms of the parts of it that are separately recognizable. Even if you've selected *Finnegan's Wake*, you'll find that the book can be decomposed into structural elements. At a "coarse" level of analysis, the book is structured into chapters, and sometimes the chapters are grouped within larger structures called "sections" or "parts." Within chapters there may be recognizable subchapters or, in a novel, scenes. A closer look reveals that within these coarse structural elements there are finer, or "detailed," structural elements: paragraphs, sentences, parts of speech.

Programs, too, have structure, both coarse and fine. The coarse structure of a program is often called "modularity." Large programs are usually organized into sections called "modules." Typically, each module will be devoted to one of the major capabilities of the program. It seems to be a commonly accepted tenet of good programming style that the individual modules of a program be reasonably self-contained in terms of purpose, and that they refer to one another in a minimum number of ways. However, a program may be split into modules in a number of different fashions. The division may be based on the functions provided by the program, on the sequence of the program's intended execution, on the anticipated relationships among the parts of the program, or on some combination of the foregoing.

Modules are roughly equivalent to chapters in a book. In a very large program, modules may be collected in groups into larger elements called "components." In the other direction, a module may be broken down into recognizable submodules, just as a chapter may have subchapters or scenes.

The fine or "detailed" structure of a program includes, in addition to its individual sentences (called "statements") and the parts of speech of which they are made, two distinct types of structural elements: blocks

of code and data areas. Blocks of code are simply collections of statements. They may be linear or reusable. A linear block of code is simply
a series of contiguous statements. A reusable block of code is a series
of contiguous statements that is susceptible of being incorporated by
reference where desired and as many times as desired in the writing of
a program. Reusing the same set of statements at different places within
the flow of a program, normally with somewhat different content each
time, is a fundamental technique of program authorship. Roughly similar
techniques are found in poetry:

> Fear no more the heat o' the sun,
>   Nor the furious winter's rages;
> Thou thy worldly task has done,
>   Home art gone, and ta'en thy wages.
> Golden lads and girls all must,
>   As chimney-sweepers, come to dust.
>
> Fear no more the frown o' the great;
>   Thou art past the tyrant's stroke;
> Care no more to clothe and eat;
>   To thee the reed is as the oak.
> The sceptre, learning, physic, must
>   All follow this, and come to dust.
>
> Fear no more the lightning-flash,
>   Nor the all-dreaded thunder-stone;
> Fear not slander, censure rash;
>   Though hast finished joy and moan.
> All lovers young, all lovers must
> Consign to thee, and come to dust.
>   William Shakespeare, "Fear No More"

In the case of programs, various approaches have evolved for marking
segments of code for reuse, for pointing a program statement to the
location of the desired reusable segment, and for returning the program
to the next proper statement once the reusable block of code has served
its purpose. These distinguishing features differentiate the different
types of reusable blocks of code. Some of the principal types of reusable
units of code are "macros," "routines," "subroutines" and "entry
points."

The term "macro" is a contraction of "macro-instruction," a facility
commonly provided by assembler programs. The term refers to a reusable block of code that can be incorporated by reference using a convenient procedure provided in the assembler program. The procedure
allows a desired block of code, located in or available to the assembler,
to be assigned a symbolic name. When another program refers to the

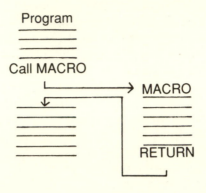

macro by its symbolic name, the assembler can find the macro's code automatically. In other words, a programmer writing a program to be used with that assembler need only specify the macro name in order to arrange for insertion of the macro code in the program. Thereafter, code from the macro having that name will be included in the program as if it had been written out in sequence at that place in the program's flow.

Generally, macros are written in such a way as to allow the using programmer to customize the code to be inserted by specifying certain values, or "parameters." In a sense, such a macro is like a form letter that can be customized by filling in the blanks. The "blanks" that await filling in a macro are the "formal parameters" of the macro, and the values inserted by the using program are the "actual parameters." For a program such as an assembler that provides macro capabilities, deciding what macros to offer and defining the formal parameters that a macro will support are important parts of the design process and reflect the creativity and style of the particular programmer or group of programmers who write a given program.

Macros have many uses in computer programming. First and foremost, they enable program authors to avoid writing detailed series of instructions over and over. They can also be used to simplify communication between two programs. Communication between programs must be effected more carefully than communication between two people. For example, if I ask you for your address and phone number, and you reply by giving your phone number first and then your address, I will nonetheless be able to understand you. Try this with a computer, though, and you will get an angry beep, an error message, or a garbled data base record. Computer programs, for the most part, don't have the same flexibility as do people in the realm of communications. One of the purposes for writing macros, then, is to save program authors from having to remember cumbersome and detailed rules for program-to-program communications. (A distant telephonic analogy to calling a

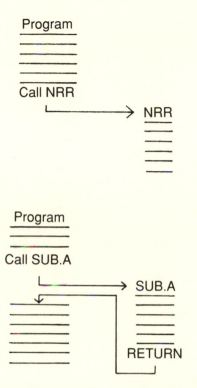

macro for this purpose would be pushing the speed-dial button on a programmable phone.)

Definition of a macro is one of several ways of marking a reusable block of code. For present purposes, though, the procedure just outlined is adequately descriptive of alternative methods for "blocking" sets of instructions for reference or reuse. Briefly, these alternative methods are:

Nonreturning routines. These are sets of instructions that have a self-contained purpose and are callable by reference to a symbolic label or name, but have no provision within themselves for returning control to the part of the program that "called" them in.

Subroutines. These are routines that return control to the next instruction following the instruction that "called" them (or to another specified part of the program). From the programmer's standpoint, calling a subroutine entails no more than writing the subroutine's symbolic label and any necessary variable parameters; the assembler does the rest.

Entry points. These are labels to which a program can *branch* if the author wishes it to perform some, but not all, the functions of a routine.

So much for reusable blocks of code. We now turn to the other major feature of detailed structure that distinguishes one program from an-

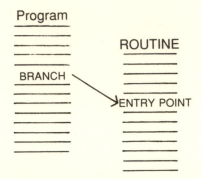

other: the way the program organizes and refers to the data that it uses. The facilities for accomplishing that organization are known as the program's "data areas" or "data structures." Almost all programs provide some way to refer to an item of data by assigning the item a name or identifier. Some of the data so named may be constants whose value never changes. For example, pi might be assigned the value 3.14159 for all purposes. Other data will be variables that can be assigned new values by statements in the program, so that their values cannot be known until the program is run. The variables CIRCUMFERENCE and DIAMETER, for instance, might take on new values each time a calculation is performed.

A data structure, then, is an organized collection of data. There are numerous kinds of data structures; some commonly occurring ones are as follows:

Arrays   indexed groupings of data;

Sets   groupings of data in which the order within the set has no significance;

Lists   sequentially organized and accessible groupings of data;

Stacks   lists in which entries are created or deleted on a last-in, first-out basis; and

Queues   lists in which entries are created or deleted on a first-in, first-out basis.

Like macros, data structures are used for a number of purposes. For economy of exposition, I will treat here only one of those purposes, the organization of data to help in the control of processing of the program by the processor. Data structures used for this purpose are sometimes called "control blocks."

A control block is an area of the computer's main memory reserved in accordance with instructions from a program, and used as a "filecard" or "notepad" to store information that the program will need from

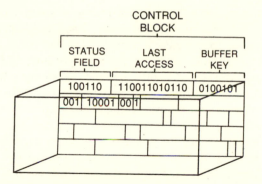

time to time to carry out its tasks. Control blocks are somewhat similar to sets of reference tables that one finds at the front or back of lengthy novels to help the reader keep track of the identities and relationships of characters. A control block consists of a series of "fields" in which discrete items of information are to be filed. The fields of a control block, and sometimes even the individual bits within a field, are assigned symbolic names. Each named element is a variable of some separate significance to the program. The control block, then, is defined by the variable it contains, the order in which such variables are stored in memory, and the size (i.e., number of bits) of each variable. Other data structures are defined similarly.

The definition of individual data structures, the selection of the information to be stored in those data structures, and the reservation of fields of particular sizes to hold presently needed information or information that may be needed in the future are matters within the discretion of the program author. The choices made by a program author in establishing data structures can substantially affect the quality and efficiency of the resulting program. Indeed, those choices often affect the design of the rest of the program. More importantly, those choices are generally made from a wide range of alternatives based on the programmer's training, experience, and writing style. Let's now consider a case in which the nature of data structures was not appreciated.

Popular programs inevitably become targets for competition. Innovators are like prospectors staking out claims in a new territory and striking it rich. Other prospectors inevitably gather around. Such was the experience of Synercom Technology, Inc., a Texas corporation formed in 1969 to develop and market software that automated the task of performing structural analyses, the complex set of calculations that engineers do to calculate the stresses on the structures they have designed.

Synercom's program, called STRAN, and the manual that accompanied it, were derived from existing public domain works. A public domain work is one that has intentionally been published without reserving a copyright. In the case at hand, IBM had for some time been offering an uncopyrighted structural analysis program called FRAN and an associated uncopyrighted user's manual. Customers had not found the IBM offerings to be terribly attractive even though they were free of charge, and the Synercom people thought they knew why. FRAN was a complicated program, and difficult to use. In particular, users required a great deal of training in order to learn how to prepare the information to be input to FRAN, and training cost money. If the process of preparing input could be simplified, demand for the program would, the Synercom people thought, be markedly increased. They set to work modifying FRAN, and transformed it into STRAN, a program that they first offered in a form that ran on CDC computers rather than IBM computers. (Later, exercising the copyright owner's exclusive right to translate, Synercom adapted STRAN to run on IBM computers and UNIVAC computers as well.) Parts of STRAN were still public domain software, in that they were unmodified portions of FRAN; however, the parts of STRAN that comprised modifications made by Synercom were original work and protected by copyright. Along with STRAN, Synercom developed a new user's manual, for which it was also true that parts were unmodified public domain material and parts were original.

What was particularly original about STRAN was the way users prepared data for input to the program. This task was accomplished by filling out one or more of thirteen forms called "input formats," which were designed to give the image of an 80-column punched card, with notes indicating what data was to be entered on the card and where. Once the input formats were filled in, they could be given to card punch operators to prepare the cards that would actually be input into the computer for processing by STRAN. (The punched card is obsolescent now, of course. The *Synercom* case arose during the Dark Ages of computing. Nonetheless, the use of formatted input is still a requisite for introducing data into computers, just as the use of a restricted vocabulary is a requisite for authors of children's books.)

The reader will properly have concluded that the STRAN input formats are a kind of data structure. Each input format was separately registered with the Copyright Office and bore a notice of copyright. Synercom quickly discovered that once customers were trained in the use of the new input formats, they became STRAN enthusiasts.

Enter EDI. Formed in 1973, when STRAN had been in the market for four years and Synercom had invested approximately five hundred thousand dollars in training customers, EDI was an engineering firm familiar with Synercom's program. For reasons veiled in the mists of computer-law history, this particular engineering firm decided to go into the busi-

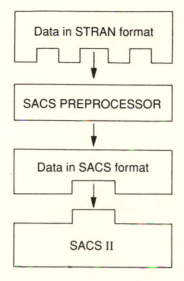

ness of marketing a structural analysis program that would compete with STRAN.

EDI did not copy the code of STRAN. Instead, a public domain program that had been written by Boeing was used as a base for developing EDI's program. EDI called its program SACS II. SACS II came with a "preprocessor" program that accepted as input data formatted using the STRAN input formats and converted that data into a form comprehensible to SACS II. From the user's perspective, therefore, SACS II was completely compatible with STRAN. The manuals written by EDI to accompany SACS II contained substantial amounts of material copied verbatim from Synercom's STRAN manuals. EDI's marketing strategy was to offer a wholly compatible alternative to STRAN at a price considerably lower than Synercom's. To add insult to injury, EDI entered into a marketing arrangement with UCC (later UCCEL and still later swallowed by Sterling Software), an organization that had been marketing STRAN for Synercom. UCC produced its own manual for SACS II, which also was copied verbatim from Synercom's user manual.

Sorely aggrieved, Synercom sued EDI and UCC for copyright infringement in the Federal District Court in Dallas, drawing the Honorable Patrick Higginbotham as trial judge. (Judge Higginbotham was later elevated to the Court of Appeals for the Fifth Circuit, a seemingly irrelevant fact the significance of which will become evident in a later chapter.) Judge Higginbotham is a thoughtful individual who does not take kindly to abuse of the judicial process. In light of that attitude, EDI's litigation strategy was a substantial mistake. Its lawyers initiated a substantial amount of what Judge Higginbotham found to be "needless discovery": thousands of interrogatories addressed to Synercom, which under the Federal Rules of Civil Procedure Synercom was obligated to answer or object to in writing, and nearly thirty depositions under oath. EDI also filed numerous motions that had no merit and in the judge's view were filed solely to delay the trial and increase Synercom's cost of litigation. Further, throughout the pretrial period, EDI denied copying Synercom's manuals at all, asserting instead either that there were no similarities or that any similarities were coincidental. Those assertions were never made at trial, however, and Judge Higginbotham's view was that EDI knew them to be untrue when made. Finally, EDI had counterclaimed against Synercom for unfair competition, fraud, and antitrust violations, but abandoned its counterclaim before trial, for the reason— in the judge's view—that substantial portions of it were completely groundless.

There are courtrooms where attorneys can get away with such tactics because the judges are lax in supervising the process or are distracted by the press of other work. Judge Higginbotham's courtroom was not one of them. He found that EDI and UCC had infringed Synercom's copyrights in its manuals. The relief he ordered indicates the vigor of his rejection of the defendants' arguments. EDI and UCC were ordered to stop printing the SACS II manuals, to give Synercom a list of all customers who had received copies of the SACS II manuals, to recall all copies of the SACS II manuals, and to deliver all recalled copies to Synercom within sixty days. They were also ordered to pay Synercom's court costs and attorneys' fees. As you can see, the fate of the copyright infringer in the marketplace can be a very unhappy one.

That's not what is most interesting about the *Synercom* case, though. What is most interesting about the *Synercom* case is its treatment of the claims of infringement as to the STRAN input formats. Synercom's complaint also charged that EDI had copied those formats. EDI and UCC did not do so directly, however, in the sense of reproducing the input format documents under their own names. Rather, the SACS II user manuals made it clear that users were to use 80-column paper as an aid to input creation, and were to place data on that paper in sequences that were the same as the sequences on Synercom's STRAN input formats. If they did so, EDI's preprocessor could convert the data from STRAN format to SACS II format. The real question, therefore, was whether EDI's preprocessor program, which accepted data in those sequences, infringed the copyrights in Synercom's input formats.

That was a difficult question, particularly in 1978 when Judge Higginbotham had to decide it, as there were precious few cases on software copyright to rely on as precedent. In order to prove infringement of its formats, Synercom had to demonstrate that it held a valid copyright in the formats and that they had been copied. The Copyright Office registration for the formats was prima facie proof that Synercom held a valid copyright, but the defendants contested validity. Passing the validity question, in order to prove copying Synercom could either bring forward direct evidence (e.g., a confession from an EDI employee) or it could prove that EDI had had access to the STRAN formats and that the work created by EDI was substantially similar to the STRAN formats. Access was not an issue. Whether the expression in EDI's preprocessor program was substantially similar in nontrivial ways to the expression in the STRAN printed formats was a very formidable issue, however. That sort of cross-medium proof can succeed, and (as we'll see later) has succeeded, but it is no mean feat to compare a computer program to a diagram, illustration, or manual. Even if they cover the same subject matter, the structures of the two works being compared are quite unlikely to be similar to the untutored eye and their contents will invariably seem on the surface to be substantially different. Of course, where the program produces output that is comparable to the expression in a diagram, illustration, or manual, the case is easier; but that was not the case in *Synercom*. Whatever similarity to the STRAN formats there was in EDI's preprocessor was not on the output side but on the input side, in the EDI code that accepted data prepared in accordance with those formats.

Judge Higginbotham did not go very far down the torturous path of examining EDI's preprocessor to see if it was similar to Synercom's format sheets. Instead, the judge asked himself a preliminary question, and in answering that question he disposed of this part of the case without having to assess similarities in detail. The question the judge asked himself was whether the STRAN formats—even though Synercom had registered copyrights on them—were in fact protectable by copyright. In other words, were Synercom's format copyrights valid? The Copyright Office, after all, is not infallible, but rather far from it. Copyright registration is largely a perfunctory act. The Copyright Office performs little or no research to determine if the work sought to be registered is original or not, or whether the material in the work meets the definition of copyrightable subject matter. In 1978, protectability of program input formats was a perfectly legitimate question.

Even though he was sympathetic to Synercom's claims—as the disposition of the manual-infringement issues demonstrates—the judge had difficulty concluding that the formats were protectable by copyright. In copyright cases, as in other areas of law, the paradigm chosen by the court as the underpinning of its analysis usually determines the outcome of the issue. The paradigm selected by Judge Higginbotham was "blank forms." He started his analysis from the principle that blank forms are not protectable by copyright. The classic case in this area is *Baker v. Selden*, an 1879 case involving accounting worksheets, which is often misapplied in software copyright cases. In *Baker v. Selden*, it was held that a copyrighted exposition of a new method of accounting could not prevent others from reproducing the formats of the worksheets displayed in the copyrighted work. Later cases have put a spin on *Baker v. Selden* by holding that forms that convey information are protectable to the extent of the expression of that information. Thus, for example, answer sheets for multiple-choice tests can, at least sometimes, be protected by copyright. More significant for purposes of the present inquiry, computer screen displays generated by programs are protectable to the extent of their expressive elements, as is made clear by cases that we will examine as we come to the heart of the "look and feel" issue.

Did Synercom's input formats convey information? The judge concluded that they must have done so. Since EDI's instruction manual incorporated the ideas from the Synercom formats, those formats must have imparted the information necessary for EDI to achieve that incorporation. The information conveyed was a particular way of sequencing data for simplified input to a structural analysis program.

That conclusion led Judge Higginbotham to his second paradigm: copyright law protects expression, but not the ideas contained in that expression. Because of that principle:

EDI was free to "read" Synercom's formats and employ their teaching; it was not free to "copy" the formats, and contends that it did not. Thus the issue is whether EDI copied expressed ideas or expression. EDI put forward an alternate argument that because use of the idea required substantial duplication of Synercom's arrangement and sequencing, copyright protection should not be allowed.

That "alternate argument" was what is known as the "merger" doctrine, under which it is asserted, as we saw in *Apple v. Franklin*, that if there is only one way of expressing an idea, the expression is not protected.

There was no question that EDI's preprocessor program duplicated the sequence of the STRAN input formats. There were, the judge found, 3,628,800 different possible sequences (10 factorial, suggesting that there were ten different variables) for the input data called for by the STRAN input formats, and EDI's preprocessor used exactly the same sequences as did STRAN. No accident, that; but, the judge concluded, sequence was all that EDI had duplicated. (That conclusion, by the way, was surely not correct. Synercom's choices as to what types of data should be used as input to STRAN and the precise meaning that Synercom assigned to each of those data types were other design choices reflected in the input formats and duplicated in SACS II. It may have been the case that those choices were dictated by the mathematics of structural analysis or by industry practice—in which case copyright protection would not attach to them because they were not "original"—but the judge made no such finding.) If all that EDI had copied was the sequence of STRAN's input formats, then according to the court, there could be no infringement, because the way data is sequenced constitutes idea, not expression.

In a thoughtful footnote, Judge Higginbotham likened what EDI had done to the action of translating the Synercom manual into a computer program. Although he accepted the principle that translating the STRAN user manual from one human language to another would be infringement, and that translating the STRAN program from one computer language to another would be infringement, he rejected the notion that translating the manual from a human language to a computer language could constitute infringement, because the manual did no more than "prescribe a problem involving a set of ordered inputs in a particular arrangement," and the conversion of that problem statement into a computer program

requires substantial imagination, creativity, independent thought, and exercise of discretion . . . the program and the statement are so different, both in physical characteristics and intended purpose, that they are really two different expressions of the same idea, rather than two different versions of the same expression.

Because the foregoing footnote was dropped (lawyers talk about "dropping footnotes" the way others talk about "dropping hints") at a point in his opinion where Judge Higginbotham was discussing his view that the H-pattern on a gearshift lever was idea and not expression, some commentators have sought to generalize the footnote's conclusion that EDI's program could not be a copy of Synercom's manual into a general rule that copying elements of a manual into a computer program can never be infringement. That generalization is unjustified. A manual that is more than just a statement of the problem that the computer program solves, and which can be converted into a computer program without any substantial exercise of "imagination, creativity, independent thought, and exercise of discretion," can indeed be infringed by translation from human language into programming language. Some years after *Synercom* was decided, in fact, a lawsuit presenting just that issue was brought in Massachusetts. In that case, *Williams v. Arndt*, the plaintiff had written a book describing in step-by-step detail a particularly unambiguous approach to trading in the futures market. The defendant rewrote that description into a computer program, and was held thereby to have infringed the copyright in the plaintiff's manual. That holding, while idiosyncratic, reflects a proper reading of Judge Higginbotham's footnote which, in a passage universally disregarded by those who favor narrow copyright protection for computer programs, observes that

it would probably be a violation to take a detailed description of a particular problem solution, such as a flowchart or step-by-step set of prose instructions, written in human language, and program such a description in computer language.

Alternative to finding that EDI did not infringe Synercom's copyrights in the STRAN formats because it had simply copied ideas, the court held that if the only expression in the formats was their sequencing and ordering of data, then the formats were not copyrightable in the first place. The fate of Synercom's format copyrights was thus doubly sealed. The reader will have gathered, however, that the court's ruminations on copyright protection for input formats came as cold comfort to EDI, which had been ordered to recall its customer manuals from the marketplace, an embarrassment of the first order and, potentially, a very serious blow for the SACS II program. For the rest of us, however, the *Synercom* case set the terms of the debate concerning whether copyright protection could be used as a barrier to compatibility. Following Judge Higginbotham's reasoning, if all that was copied in order to achieve compatibility was the structure inherent in the sequence and order of ten different variables in data to be input to a program, compatibility could be achieved without infringement. If, on the other hand, what was done was to translate a detailed description of the problem solution implemented by the target program into a compatible computer program, there probably would be infringement. Where Judge Higginbotham's reasoning breaks down is in the conclusion that the only information copied by EDI was sequencing. What was copied was content, sequence, and meaning. Thinking back to *Apple v. Franklin*, we can now see that the court there was faced with an extreme case of an asserted need to copy content, sequence, and meaning in the name of compatibility, and we can see that the Third Circuit was not sympathetic to that assertion.

Synercom is not the last or best word on copyright protection for data structures, as we shall see, but it did serve as an excellent introduction to the issues and has therefore been cited frequently, sometimes favorably and sometimes unfavorably, in cases that have been decided since.

8

Programming Flow

This first Book proposes first in brief the whole Subject, Man's disobedience, and the loss thereupon of Paradise wherein he was plac't: Then touches the prime cause of his fall, the Serpent, or rather Satan in the Serpent; who revolting from God, and drawing to his side many Legions of Angels, was by the command of God driven out of Heaven with all his Crew into the great Deep. Which action past over, the Poem hastes into the midst of things, presenting Satan with his Angels now fallen into Hell, describ'd here, not in the Center (for Heaven and Earth may be suppos'd as not yet made, certainly not yet accurst) but in a place of utter darkness, fitliest call'd Chaos: Here Satan with his Angels lying on the burning Lake, thunderstruck and astonisht, after a certain space recovers, as from confusion, calls up him who next in Order and Dignity lay by him; they confer of their miserable fall. Satan awakens all his Legions, who lay till then in the same manner confounded; They rise, their Numbers, array of Battle, their chief Leaders nam'd, according to the Idols known afterwards in Canaan and the Countries adjoining. To these Satan directs his Speech, comforts them with hope yet of regaining Heaven, but tells them lastly of a new World and new kind of Creature to be created, according to the ancient Prophecy or report in Heaven; for that Angels were before this visible Creation, was the opinion of many ancient Fathers. To find out the truth of this Prophecy, and what to determine thereon he refers to a full Council. What his Associates thence attempt. Pandemonium the Palace of Satan rises, suddenly built out of the Deep: The infernal Peers there sit in Council.

John Milton, *Paradise Lost* (published 1671)

The next characteristic of computer programs that we will put under our intellectual microscope is "flow." All programs have it. The flow of a program is roughly akin to the flow of plot in a fictional work. The flow of Book I of *Paradise Lost* is summarized in Milton's Argument for Book I just quoted. Flow answers the question, "What happens next?" There are two types of flow in computer programs: flow of control and flow of data.

In the case of flow of control, the question, "What happens next?" can be put put in the following terms: "What instruction is presented to the processor next?" Control of the processor rests with the program that is being processed, and is passed from instruction to instruction in that program in various fashions. The simplest fashion in which control is passed among instructions is *seriatim*. Unless the author decides differently, the instructions in her program will be presented to the processor in the order in which they appear in the text of the program.

For good reason or for convenience, however, the program author can decide that control of the computer should be passed from one part of the program to a remote part rather than to a contiguous part. This can be done by calling a macro, for example, or by branching to a subroutine. Programs can also loop through the same sequence of instructions a number of times before moving on. (The purpose of looping is not to cause the computer to repeat the same operations on the same data, like a phonograph needle stuck in a groove on a scratched record, although a badly written program might get "hung-up" in such a loop now and again. Rather, the purpose of looping is to cause the computer to repeat the same operation on data that differs with each pass through the loop. For example, the calculation of compound interest may be achieved by repeating a simple-interest computation for as many times as the interest is to be compounded, each time using as principal the result of the previous computation.)

The flow of control in a program is dependent on two factors: the extent to which the program employs reusable blocks of code and the extent to which separate modules in the program interact to accomplish a single purpose.

Many types of literary works have a flow of control that is other than seriatim. An example: "If you already have an understanding of contract law, skip to chapter 3," or, "For the recipe for Bernaise Sauce, see page 42." There are even novels that are not intended to be read straight through from page 1. The premiere modern example of literature of this sort is the *Dictionary of the Khazars* by Milorad Pavic. According to the *New York Times Book Review* for December 4, 1988, this imaginative work "should be read just about any way except cover to cover," and allows readers, "to make [their] own story, or hundreds of them." On a less literate level, there are interactive children's novels such as Edward

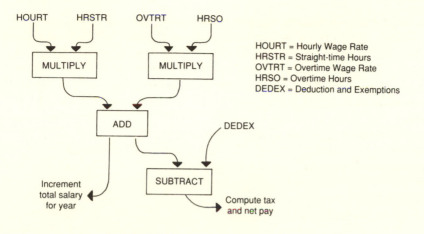

Partial Data Flow Diagram for a Hypothetical Payroll Program

Packard's *Sugarcane Island,* wherein choices made by the reader at the end of each chapter determine which part of the book should be read next and which should be skipped altogether. Of course, in the realm of computer-based interactive fiction, such as ICOM Simulations' intensely engrossing quest game Shadowgate or Chris Crawford's masterful Cold War simulation Balance of Power, non-seriatim flow of control is essential to the enjoyment of the work. The nonlinear flow of control in such works does not diminish the copyright protection accorded to their authors' creations, and the protection accorded computer programs should not be diminished on the grounds that their flow of control is nonlinear, either.

The other aspect of flow that is recognizable in computer programs is called "flow of data." In the case of data flow, the question "What happens next?" is rephrased as "Where is which data sent next?" One computer scientist has suggested that analyzing a program's data flow is similar to observing the way gossip is propagated. A different kind of analogy, but one that also serves, is to view items of data in a computer program as characters in a novel. They each have names (usually called "labels"), and they each have a recognizable role to play in achieving the program's purpose. As I've already described, some of them are constant and unchanging, while others are transformed by events occurring under the control of the program.

The items of a program's data are stored in data structures set up by the program within the computer's memory. These structures are often called "data areas," as they are simply sections of the processor's main memory or permanent storage that are organized according to structures imagined by the program author and expressed in the program. The control blocks discussed in Chapter 7 are data areas. An item of data flows (or, more accurately, is copied) out of the data area when its name is called, and then is either compared to some other data, modified and replaced, or otherwise acted on. One of the distinguishing features of any program is the pattern described by the movement of data into and out of data areas. This pattern consists of several elements: When each item of data is called, from what part(s) of the program each is called, where else in the program each item is then passed (if anywhere), and the ultimate disposition of each item of data. A tracing of the flow of data in a program produces a roadmap to all the "characters" in the literary work that the program represents.

9

Program Logic and Other Elements of Expression

Computers are to computing as instruments are to music. Software is the score, whose interpretation amplifies our reach and lifts our spirit. Leonardo da Vinci called music "the shaping of the invisible," and his phrase is even more apt as a description of software.

Alan Kay, "Computer Software," *Scientific American*, September 1984

A third distinguishing characteristic of any computer program is its particular logical development. In fact, structure, flow, and logic are the attributes that are the essence of the expression in a computer program, as in literary works generally. The fact that software contains logical progressions, however, is often held out by critics as proof that this particular class of literary work should be treated differently, and less well, under the copyright laws. The critics are playing a semantic trick. The term "logic" has many possible meanings, including some (such as "principles of reasoning") that describe levels of abstraction not protected by copyright. As will be clear from what follows, however, the logic of a computer program includes much more detailed elements, which must be protected if copyright coverage of software is to be at all meaningful. The late Professor Melville Nimmer, during his lifetime America's foremost expert on copyright law, warned against the very tyranny of labels that seem to have swayed a number of commentators critical of copyright protection for software:

The crucial question is whether a particular word describes only an idea or whether it refers to the concrete expression of an idea in a program. Where such words as "logic," "flow," or "structure" refer to expression . . . they refer to copyrightable subject matter.

Logic is a characteristic that all literary works exhibit. Instruction manuals are conceded by all to be of value only to the extent that they are logical. Works of persuasion, such as philosophical tracts or sociopolitical theses are also generally recognized as proceeding in logical fashion, using various kinds of rigorous reasoning to impel the reader to follow—and accept—the author's arguments. Less universally recognized is the fact that fictional works require logical development as well, to maintain tension, keep the reader engaged, and sustain believability. The logical relationship among words, sentences, paragraphs, and chapters in a novel is an important element of the novel's expression. John Gardner, in his 1983 book *The Art of Fiction*, put it this way:

Perhaps the logical first step in the fictional process is the writer's conscious or intuitive recognition of the nature of narrative, and his acceptance of the shackles imposed by his decision to tell a story. . . . By definition—and of aesthetic necessity—a story contains *profluence*, a requirement best satisfied by a sequence of causally related events, a sequence that can end in only one of two ways: resolution, when no further event can take place . . . or in logical exhaustion, our recognition that we've reached the stage of infinite repetition. . . .

As for fiction . . . it seems fair to say that, since no narrative beyond a certain length can hold interest without some such profluence as a causal relation of events (by either real-world logic, comic mock-logic or poetic logic), no narrative except a very short one can escape real-world relevance. . . . Fiction seeks out truth.

Computer programs seek out truth, too, the truth that is inherent in the programs' logic.

As in the case of program structure, so too logic can be defined on a coarse level of abstraction or a fine (or detailed) level of abstraction. The coarsest, or highest, level of program logic is simply the statement of the program's major capabilities and the relationships among those capabilities. Thus, for example, the high-level logic of a payroll program might be described as follows:

This program instructs the computer to read time-card information and update the Employee Time Record for all employees. That updated record is then used to compute compensation for each employee for the pay period just ended. Straight-time and overtime are computed separately and then summed. The summation is used to compute taxes and Social Security deductions. Those deductions as well as any other deductions for the pay period are summed. The deduction sum is offset from the compensation sum for each employee, and checks and paystubs are then printed.

The detailed logic of a program comprises the sequence of individual steps that make up the program. These sequences describe in detail the specific way in which, through a series of elementary statements conforming to the grammatical rules of a programming language, a program author has instructed a computer to provide each of the capabilities specified in the program. There are literally hundreds of programming languages, and the characteristics of many of them are radically different. As in the case of different human languages, not all elements of expression exist in all programming languages, but certain elements recur frequently enough to warrant our attention here.

One common element of logic expression is the form IF-THEN-ELSE. This form instructs the computer that IF a certain condition exists, THEN it should next execute a specified instruction, or ELSE (if the condition does not exist) it should next execute an alternative, also specified, instruction. The IF-THEN-ELSE logic sequence is one way for the computer to test the status of a data item and take an action depending on the outcome of the test.

Programmers also use IF and THEN statements without ELSE statements in order to accomplish a conditional result without specifying an alternative action. ("If your shoes are muddy, then take them off before you come in.") IF will usually test a variable to see if it is equal to, less than, or greater than a specified value, as in "IF counter = 0." THEN may be followed by an instruction, or it may be followed by one or more IF statements. (E.g., "IF Johnson's birthday is March 29, THEN IF today's date is March 27 or before, and IF today's date is after March 15, THEN send a birthday card.")

The actions that can follow a THEN are the same kinds of actions that may be taken without IF-THEN statements preceding them. They are, in fact, the other forms of logic expression. Typical examples are:

—Set Variable A equal to some value, either constant or variable. E.g., VARA = 3.14159. Or, VARA = R15 (where R15 refers to the contents of Register 15 in the computer).

—CALL a macro or Subroutine.

—GO TO another part of the program. In other words, transfer control to another part of the program.

—DO a series of steps. The steps referenced by the DO command may be presented repeatedly if desired, using DO WHILE or DO UNTIL, where WHILE and UNTIL insert tests of the conditions under which the steps are to be done. E.g., DO UNTIL WEIGHT > 50.

Taken individually, of course, no one of the above described logic elements can be said to be intrinsically highly expressive. That observation, while true, however, would seem to be entirely beside the point.

In a computer program, the combinations and sequences of these logic elements, and the many others that are used to write software, can be representative of exceedingly creative expression. Out of such elementary logic elements, programs of great elegance and complexity have been written. The choice of logic elements, and their pattern, sequence, and significance, are as fundamental to programmers' expression as the choice of words and their pattern, sequence, and significance are to poets' expression. To make the sweeping statement, as some do, that "program logic" is not protected by copyright, is to display a profound ignorance of the nature not just of programming languages but of language in general. One could as well conclude that musical themes cannot be protected by copyright. Taken individually, for example, neither a three-quarter-note middle C nor a whole-note rest nor an A-minor chord nor for that matter even an A-minor 6th/9th aug/11th—try that one on your guitar!—is intrinsically very expressive. Taken in combination and in context, however, so that their pattern, sequence, and significance can be appreciated, aggregations of music notational elements express a vast body of highly creative effort.

Logic, flow, and structure: Taken together, these attributes define the "design" of a computer program. A program's design may be considered from 50,000 feet or, put more formally, at a high level of abstraction. From such a perspective, we might find in a particular case that the program under observation is divided into twenty modules and makes heavy use of macros. The same program can also be examined under a microscope or at a low level of abstraction. From that close-up perspective, we might find that at a particular juncture the program tests to see if the number of years of an employee's service exceeds ten, and if it does, the program branches to a subroutine that calculates the pension amount and stores the result in the field called "Retmnt" of the data area called "PersBen." This low level of abstraction, which represents the program's "detailed design," is a complex web of structure, sequence, pattern, and organization. The resulting combination is a tapestry of decisions and actions that is the essence of the author's expression.

We are now ready to take on the *Whelan* case, the case that until the "look and feel" lawsuits were filed was considered by those commentators most closely identified with the Luddite philosophy to be the most scandalous copyright suit since the founding of the republic because of the case's solicitude for the structure, logic, and flow of programs. Before we turn to *Whelan*, though, I should for completeness' sake describe four other attributes of programming expression that serve to give each computer program its individuality. These are naming conventions, comments, user interfaces, and style.

Naming Conventions. Unless programmers are writing in machine language, they must invent names for numerous elements of their programs. Reusable blocks of code, data items, and variables are generally referred to by name. The names chosen by the program author are as discretionary as the names of characters are to a novelist, since names of program elements are converted into memory addresses when the program is translated into machine language by the assembler. The processor itself therefore sees only the references to specific memory addresses; it does not in fact see the names when it is processing the program. Thus, subject only to very modest constraints (word length or prohibitions on using names already used in the particular computer system, for example), the author's range of choice for naming conventions is very broad indeed. As one would therefore expect, the selection of names tends to reflect the personality and experience of the author. Since most programs are intended to be read by persons other than the author, it is preferable to use names that convey some sense of the purpose of the thing being named, but the reference may be explicit or cryptic, abbreviated or full, related to the name of another program element or unrelated, or completely arbitrary, at the whim of the author.

Comments. It is a standard practice for programmers to insert running commentary in their programs to assist themselves and others in understanding those programs. The comments are prose descriptions of the program's statements. Three different kinds of comments can be identified. *Directory comments* appear at the beginning of a lengthy program, and provide, in effect, a table of contents. *Prologue comments* appear at the beginning of each significant structural segment of the program, and explain the purpose for that segment. Milton's Argument for Book I of *Paradise Lost* is in the nature of a prologue comment. *Explanatory comments* appear beside individual lines of code and explain what those lines of code, and perhaps the next few lines, are intended to accomplish. Like the names chosen by the programmer, the comments are not processed by the computer when the program is executed. The computer simply ignores them, and therefore—again with only modest constraints—program authors may write whatever comments they wish. Comments may be numerous or sparse, expansive or concise, abbreviated or full text. The context of the comments and the aspects of the program on which the author chooses to comment are also among the arbitrary choices made by the author.

User Interfaces. The user interfaces to a program fall into two principal categories: screen interfaces, namely, the format and content of the visual displays by which the program author communicates to the users through the program the ways and means to utilize the program, the effects of that utilization, and such other information about the program (or about anything else) that the author wishes to communicate visually; and programming interfaces, which are the specified things that a user must write into his or her program if it is to communicate with the author's program. In an original program, the user interfaces are both highly creative and highly valuable. Alan Kay calls them the " 'user illusion' . . . the simplified myth everyone builds to explain (and make guesses about) the system's actions and what should be done next." Whether they are written on the basis of the author's personal image of the program as it should appear to the user, or on the basis of years of market research into ease-of-use factors, a program's user interfaces determine the degree of the program's user friendliness, a highly qualitative characteristic that has a substantial impact on marketplace success.

Programming Style. Not surprisingly, each programmer develops a personal style of expression. To some extent, that style reflects the program author's education or training, imagination—or lack thereof—and intellectual horsepower. To some extent, it may result from conventions adopted within the program author's department. To some extent, a program's style may reflect the environment in which it is written. For instance, the composition of a programming team can engender distinct differences in structure for programs having the same function. A team composed of four trainees and one experienced programmer might be expected to produce a program consisting of one "main program" component and several relatively small subroutines, whereas a team of three experienced programmers might be expected to produce a program consisting of three modules.

Style is reflected in the logic elements that a programmer tends to favor and in the way those elements are employed. It is reflected in the modularity of the program and the extent to which modules are self-contained or interdependent. It is reflected in the user interfaces and data structures chosen by the author and in the numerous other discretionary decisions the author makes. Some programs are elegant; others are clumsy. Some are written to execute very rapidly in a processor; others are written to take up little memory. Some are written using techniques that reduce the programmer's writing time, irrespective of the resulting execution time or memory space utilization. Some are written to be easily readable, using naming conventions and comments that convey clearly the author's meaning; others leave it to the reader to decipher the meaning from the programming language statements. All these choices, and others, combine to give programs the same individuality that makes one novelist's work different from another's.

There is even a Strunk and White for programmers, or more precisely a Kernighan and Plauger. Brian Kernighan and P. J. Plauger are the authors of *Elements of Programming Style*, a style handbook for people writing in programming languages.

Before certain critical readers begin frothing at the mouth, I should quickly add that it is a settled principle of copyright law that style in and of itself is not protected by copyright. I mention this because a common, if intellectually bankrupt, tactic of those opposed to copyright protection for software (and also those accused of copyright infringement) has been to focus on individual attributes of programs and assert that, individually, such attributes are not protected by copyright. Thus, we might hear it asserted that "GO TO" is unprotectable because it is "logic," that style is unprotectable because it is not "expression," or that the notion of using a macro for a particular purpose is not protectable because it is idea, not expression. As tiresome and disingenuous as these arguments are, they turn up in one law review article after another, and in brief after brief. As best I can discern, they never succeed, for the reasons suggested in our music analogy above.

That is perhaps a long-winded way of saying that although overall style itself may not be protected by copyright, evidence of similarities in style is, under the law, evidence of copying. Similarity of stylistic features may certainly be cumulated with other, more detailed evidence of similarity in structure, logic, flow, or other program elements to prove copyright infringement.

Now, let's examine *Whelan*.

10

Whelan v. Jaslow

This story has it all: trust and betrayal, greed, deteriorating relationships, the eternal battle of the sexes. To think of the *Whelan* case as simply a software copyright case is to miss the point completely. Indeed, at the core, most copyright cases have the same point: the vindication of Good, the vanquishing of Evil. The good author or composer triumphs over the evil purloiner of his creation, or the evil author fails in his efforts to prevent the good readers benefiting from the ideas they have read. What makes one party good and the other party evil in copyright litigation, and indeed in litigation of any kind, is not usually the law itself. It is usually the motivations of the parties to the suit, as discerned by the trier of fact, be it judge or jury. The scent of skulduggery, rapaciousness, overreaching, or insensitivity to the rights of others will usually attach itself to one side or the other as the trial progresses. We saw earlier how this happened in the *SAS* case. It also happened in *Whelan*. Indeed, even the critics of the *Whelan* decision will usually concede that the judiciary reached the correct result, and that the only problem is in the reasoning the courts used to reach that result. Let's see for ourselves.

Once upon a time in Pennsylvania, a fictional person was created and given the name Whelan Associates, Inc. This fiction was sanctioned by the state's corporation laws, and in 1979 Whelan Associates, Inc., entered the world as that type of legal fiction known as a Pennsylvania Corporation. Less than a decade later, Whelan Associates, Inc. would be defunct, the victim (though victor) of a costly and protracted court battle; but in 1979, all was hope and promise.

The real person behind the corporate fiction was Elaine Whelan, a woman with substantial experience as a computer programmer and systems designer. Elaine Whelan was president and controlling stockholder of Whelan Associates, Inc. Prior to forming her company, Ms. Whelan was a principal in and half-owner of a small custom software house called Strohl Systems Group, Inc. It was in 1978 that the strands of fate began to wind Elaine Whelan into the cascade of events leading to the formation, temporary success, and ultimate demise of Whelan Associates, Inc.

At that time, Rand Jaslow was a young man working in his father's business. Edward Jaslow was president of Jaslow Dental Laboratory, Inc., a successful service business to the dental profession that was of a size sufficient to warrant, and to need, data processing capability. Rand Jaslow decided to make a contribution to the family business that his father would see as a major accomplishment: he decided personally to automate the company's ordering, inventory control, cost control, and customer list maintenance operations. In this decision, we see a kind of self-confidence born of ignorance, for Rand Jaslow had had no formal training or experience in computer programming. That shortcoming did not deflect him from his goal, however. He went to a Radio Shack store and purchased a TRS–80. Even by the standards of 1978, the TRS–80 that the younger Jaslow bought could be seen as little more than a novelty. It had no printer capability and only limited storage capacity. By today's standards, it is simply horrifying to think that an intelligent adult would propose to automate a sizable business operation on such a machine. However, the younger Jaslow did not know enough to be horrified.

Not surprisingly, Rand Jaslow did not succeed, despite his best efforts. In the end, he swallowed his pride and contacted Strohl Systems. In August and September of 1978, Strohl Systems submitted a proposal to Jaslow Dental Laboratory to design and implement a computer system for the business. The proposal provided that Elaine Whelan would lead the design and implementation team, that the software would be implemented on an IBM Series/1 computer (a minicomputer, not a personal computer) and that the programs developed by Whelan would be owned by Strohl Systems, not by Jaslow Laboratories. Strohl Systems would market the programs to other dental laboratories, and Jaslow Laboratories would receive a 10 percent royalty for every system sold. This seemed a satisfactory arrangement to the Jaslows. They accepted the proposal.

In the indelicate vernacular of the trade, good systems designers really "get into bed" with their customers. They come to understand their clients' business as well as the clients themselves do, or maybe better. They examine its dynamics and its procedures in detail, the better to design software that will successfully replace the preexisting methodologies.

Though clearly no love was lost between Elaine Whelan and Rand

Jaslow, Whelan consulted Jaslow extensively for advice as to how the laboratory operated, and learned in depth the way in which the Jaslows conducted their business (except, of course, for the manufacturing processes, which were not being automated). She conferred with him about features, capabilities, and functions that might be desirable for the system to provide. From these discussions and her own independent study of the dental laboratory business, Elaine Whelan constructed the software that would automate Jaslow Dental Laboratory, Inc.

The software was written in Event Driven Language (EDL) a programming language understood by the IBM Series/1, and became operational at Jaslow Dental Laboratory around March 1979. Over the next six months, Elaine Whelan's team made a number of changes to the system at the request of Jaslow personnel, and billed the laboratory for each one.

During 1979, Strohl Systems began marketing the system under the name Dentalab. Also during 1979, Elaine Whelan came to a parting of the ways with Myles Strohl, the other half of Strohl Systems. Ms. Whelan took Dentalab with her in exchange for giving up her half interest in Strohl Systems, and she set up Whelan Associates, Inc., to market that software. In recognition of the fact that her expertise lay in programming and design, and that Jaslow Laboratory had superior knowledge of and contacts within the dental laboratory business, Whelan Associates entered into an agreement under which the laboratory would act as sales representative of Whelan Associates for one year starting July 1980, and thereafter subject to termination on thirty days' notice. Compensation to Jaslow Laboratory would be a commission of 35 percent of the gross price of each system sold.

A smooth curve fit to the foregoing data points would allow one to predict a bright future for Dentalab, Whelan, and Jaslow. Cooperatively, they could have gone forward to conquer the world of dental laboratory automation. Alas, curve fitting is not a terribly reliable way of predicting the future of human relations. For two years, the business relationship worked successfully. Then things began to turn sour between Whelan and Jaslow. The laboratory began to feel that it should receive a higher commission, as well as extra compensation for after-sales support. There may have been other problems between the parties as well, although the judicial opinions don't disclose them. The real curve-breaker, however, was a completely extraneous event: the announcement in late 1980, and the subsequent success, of the IBM Personal Computer (PC). The IBM PC provided substantial capability for automating small- to medium-sized firms. Among the many thousands of firms installing the new hardware were a number of dental laboratories. Programs written in EDL could not run on the desktop machine, however, and those laboratories that had bought IBM Personal Computers were therefore not interested in Dentalab.

By mid–1982, Rand Jaslow was at it again. This time, he was trying his hand at writing a dental laboratory package in the BASIC programming language for the IBM PC. In May 1983, the lawyer for Jaslow Dental Laboratory wrote a remarkable letter to Whelan Associates. Besides purporting to terminate the sales agency, the letter asserted that after the termination the laboratory would be the exclusive marketer of Dentalab. He warned Whelan that Dentalab contained Jaslow trade secrets that Whelan could not lawfully disclose. Even more surprisingly, he demanded return of "all materials related to the Dentalab package including source and object codes and other pertinent documents," and claimed that the laboratory was the exclusive owner of Dentalab.

Matters went rapidly downhill from there. In June 1983, Jaslow Laboratories sued Whelan Associates for allegedly misappropriating the laboratory's trade secrets. In the same month, Joseph Cerra, Whelan's marketing vice president, resigned, after assuring Elaine Whelan that he was not going to associate himself with Rand Jaslow. In August 1983, Cerra, together with Rand Jaslow, Jaslow père, and one other individual formed Dentcom, Inc., for the purpose of marketing software, including Dentalab, to dental laboratories. By that time, Rand Jaslow had failed once again as a programmer, and he and the laboratory had employed an expert programmer to write the dental package for the IBM PC. That programmer utilized the work that Rand Jaslow had done.

There were two kinds of problems with Rand Jaslow's work. First, it contained numerous errors and was amateurish in its design. Those sorts of problems the expert could and did fix. The second kind of problem was one that the expert could not fix, however: In writing his defective program, Rand Jaslow had had access to and used a copy of the source code of Elaine Whelan's program. Since access to an original copyrighted work in the course of preparing another work, together with substantial similarity between the new work and the original work, are sufficient to make out a prima facie case of copyright infringement, Rand Jaslow—by using the Whelan source code—had put the laboratory, Dentcom, his father, Whelan's former vice president, and himself at a technical disadvantage in the ensuing litigation.

What really counts in the courtroom, though, is which party ends up representing Good and which one Evil, and by this measure Rand Jaslow had taken a substantial misstep, since he was never authorized to have in his possession a copy of the Dentalab source code, and had obtained his copy surreptitiously and without the consent of either Strohl Systems or Whelan Associates. Then, further tangling himself and others in a web of his own unfortunate design, he set about to duplicate the data structures, flows, screen formats, language and acronyms, collating methods, and all the functions of Dentalab. As if that were not enough, when the expert had completed the PC package based on Rand Jaslow's work, Dentcom put it on the market under the names "Dentalab" and "Dentlab," thus seeking to capitalize on the existing notoriety of Elaine Whelan's product. This is the moral equivalent, in programming terms, of setting out to create a book about the Watergate affair that duplicates the structure and flow of events of *All the President's Men* and then marketing that "creation" under the very same title.

Whelan Associates' copyright infringement suit was filed in September 1983, in the same courthouse in which, a year and a half earlier, Apple Computer Company had sued Franklin Computer, Inc. Whelan Associates was represented by the Philadelphia law firm of Seidel, Gonda, Goldhammer and Abbott, the firm that, under a slightly different partnership name, had represented Apple at the trial level in its suit against Franklin. The defendants were represented by Schnader, Harrison, Segal and Lewis, the firm that had represented Franklin in the earlier suit. Plus ça change, plus c'est la même chose.

The Jaslows and their companies denied all liability. In their answering papers, they put forward several different arguments. They claimed that Whelan Associates' copyright in Dentalab was invalid, both because Rand Jaslow was a coauthor of the program but had not been listed as such on the copyright registration form, and because Rand Jaslow had hired Whelan Associates to create Dentalab for him and therefore was in fact the owner of the program. Further, they claimed that Dentcom's program was created independently by Rand Jaslow, and the copyright law does not protect a copyright owner against someone else independently producing a similar work. Finally, defendants claimed that Whelan Associates was engaging in unfair competition.

The defendants' earlier trade-secret suit was combined with the plaintiff's copyright-infringement suit, and the defendants quickly went on the offensive. In particular, they sought a preliminary injunction to prevent Whelan Associates from using the laboratory's trade secrets. After a three-day hearing, their motion was denied, however, and a theme was sounded by the court that the defendants did not find to their liking: in addition to ruling that the defendants had not met the legal standards of proof for obtaining a preliminary injunction, the presiding judge held that the defendants had come to court with "unclean hands" by virtue of using the name of Whelan's program in marketing the Dentcom program. The term unclean hands is a quaint legal phrase that is shorthand for, "You come in here seeking that I order the other side to stop misbehaving, but it appears to me that you're the one who has been misbehaving, so you'll get no help from me."

In due course—about nine months after the copyright suit was filed, which is reasonably speedy for federal court—the case came to trial before Judge Donald Van Artsdalen. By that time, the Jaslows and associates had wisely abandoned their trade secret claim. The trial was a short one—only three days, no longer than the Jaslows' preliminary injunction hearing—but it was short because the evidence already taken at the preliminary hearing was made part of the trial record. The principal witnesses at trial, fittingly, were Elaine Whelan and Rand Jaslow. Their testimony was supplemented by that of two technical experts, one hired by each party.

To demonstrate that he was coauthor of Dentalab, Rand Jaslow testified that the original conception of automating the paperwork of a dental laboratory was his, and that he had disclosed to Elaine Whelan in detail the operations and business methods of Jaslow Laboratories. He said that he had explained to Ms. Whelan the functions to be performed by the program, and helped design the language and format of some of the program's visual displays. He claimed that the extensive knowledge he had gained in computers allowed him to give valuable assistance to Elaine Whelan.

As a first order of business in the written opinion in the case, the judge swept aside each of those contentions. He found that Elaine Whelan alone was the author of Dentalab; that it was her expertise and creativity by which the data structures, work flows, screens, and interrelationships among parts of the program were designed. Rand Jaslow's intellectual contribution was no more than that made to an architect by the owner of a building to be constructed, except, of course, that Jaslow did not obtain ownership of the finished product. Strohl Systems, and later Whelan Associates, did.

No surprise here: The only question that may occur to the reader at this stage is why the Jaslows let this case go to trial, rather than settling out of court. On that score, it must be accepted that hindsight is a great source of objectivity. For the players in this drama, before the trial, during the trial, and during the appeal, there was little or no objectivity. This was a clash of wills, an emotional tempest based on strongly held convictions. That it was also a complete waste of their time and money was beside the point.

For the rest of us, of course, the case was not a waste. Whelan and Jaslow spent their time and money to provide us, through the opinions of the courts, with a new articulation of the copyright law as it relates to software. The real issue in *Whelan* was not who owned the copyright in Dentalab but, as Judge Van Artsdalen put it, "whether the IBM-PC program developed by Rand Jaslow on behalf of all the defendants constitutes copyright infringement." This was not a case, he noted, of direct translation from one computer language, EDL, to another, BASIC. In fact, a literal translation from EDL to BASIC would be very difficult, if not impossible, and in all events would be a most inefficient way of translating the program from one language to the other. Instead, the judge seems to have concluded, Rand Jaslow copied the way Dentalab instructed the computer to receive, assemble, calculate, hold, and retrieve and communicate data, and also copied the way data flowed sequentially from one Dentalab function to another. He found the Dentcom program's screen displays to be almost identical to Dentalab's in format, terminology, and use of abbreviations. He noted that prospective customers at trade shows had said there was no substantial difference between Dentalab and the Dentcom program. Finally, as between the two expert witnesses, Judge Van Artsdalen found Whelan's expert to be more credible.

In his formal judgment, the judge awarded Whelan Associates $101,000 in damages and, more importantly, enjoined the defendants from marketing the Dentcom program, from marketing the Dentalab program, from using the Dentalab name, and from using the source code for either the Dentalab program or the Dentcom program (except that the Jaslows could continue to use the Dentalab program in connection with the operation of their own laboratory). Defendants were also ordered to pay Whelan Associates' legal fees. They promptly appealed.

Almost immediately, commentators who favored narrow copyright protection for software waded in to criticize Judge Van Artsdalen's opinion. To understand why, consider the way the Court of Appeals that reviewed Judge Van Artsdalen's decision framed the issue in the case when its opinion was published in 1986:

This appeal involves a computer program for the operation of a dental laboratory, and calls upon us to apply the principles underlying our venerable copyright laws to the relatively new field of computer technology to determine the scope of copyright protection of a computer program. More particularly, in this case of first impression in the courts of appeals, we must determine whether the structure (or sequence and organization) of a computer program is protectible by copyright, or whether the copyright law extends only as far as the literal computer code. [Footnote omitted.]

Until Rand Jaslow and his fellow defendants appealed the ruling in favor of Whelan Associates, no Federal Court of Appeals had spoken on the question of what elements of a program were protected by copyright. The only question that had therefore reached the appellate level was whether programs—in particular operating systems—were protected by copyright at all. Thus, what had begun as a private mudslinging brawl between Whelan and Jaslow now suddenly spread itself across a much broader canvas. Japanese bureaucrats and industry representatives, who were wrestling with the very question articulated by the Court of Appeals in the context of modifying their own copyright statutes as they related to computer programs, were now most interested in how that Court would deal with the *Whelan* case. Would it really do, they wondered, to provide for narrow protection for software in Japan if in the end Japanese program authors would want to export to America programs based on software originally authored in America? If the *Whelan* Court of Appeals ruled that software was entitled to full copyright protection, so that its detailed design including structure, logic, and flow were protected in the same way that the plot of a novel is protected, then a program derived from someone else's program might not be infringing under a narrow-protection rule in Japan, but might well be infringing if marketed in the United States. Similarly, the Commission of the European Community, which had undertaken a study of copyright laws in light of new technology, including software, was also trying to assess whether it was in the interest of the member states of the Common Market to protect computer programs in the same way as other literary works were protected, or more narrowly. Would narrow protection be an advantage to European software suppliers in local markets, or a disadvantage? Would it result in a stronger or a weaker industry than would full protection?

In addition to these foreign governmental interests, suppliers of compatible or "clone" software and suppliers of completely original software in the United States were of course watching the *Whelan* debate very closely.

Parties with opposing perspectives on the issues in *Whelan* rushed to print with articles and commentary, hoping to influence the Court of Appeals. As heated as that debate was before the Court of Appeals' decision, though, it became even more heated after the decision, for reasons that will make themselves clear as we step through the court's analysis.

At the outset, the way programs are developed seemed important to the court. The opinion describes the process as being composed of "several steps, moving from the general to the specific." The first step is to define the problem. In the *Whelan* case, the problem was to automate recordkeeping for a dental laboratory, a problem that the court believed to be unique in at least some respects. The next step is to outline the solution. "The outline can take the form of a flowchart, which will break down the solution into a series of smaller units called 'subroutines' or 'modules.' " The arrangement of these units, the court found, is an important factor in determining the efficiency of the resulting program. (As we've already seen, "efficiency" can be measured in many different ways, and indeed can mean many different things, including speed of execution, utilization of memory, and ease of use. There is no single definition of the "most efficient" program.) A third step in developing a program is structuring the data. "The programmer must make decisions about what data is needed, where along the program's operation the data should be introduced, how the data should be inputted, and how it should be combined with other data." The court found that there were interrelationships between data structures and logic structures, that there were many different ways to organize data, and that each solution "may have particular characteristics—efficiencies or inefficiencies, conveniences or quirks—that differentiate it from other solutions and make the overall program more or less desirable." Elaine Whelan's detailed outline of the Dentalab logic structures and data structures was over two hundred pages long.

Once the detailed design of these structures is complete, the coding step can begin. After coding, the program is "debugged," that is, purged of errors. Documentation is written. After the program is on the market, the supplier must provide maintenance services. Considering all the steps in the software development process, the court concluded that coding constitutes "a comparatively small part of programming," and that "by far the larger portion of the expense and difficulty in creating computer programs is attributable to the development of the structure and logic of the program, and to debugging, documentation and maintenance."

These factual determinations made, the Court of Appeals turned to the legal issues. On appeal, the defendants had made two arguments. On the one hand, they urged that since Judge Van Artsdalen did not find any literal similarity between the Dentcom program and Dentalab, his ruling must be incorrect because copyright covers only the literal elements of programs. On the other hand, they asserted that even if copyright covers the structure, sequence, and organization of programs, the plaintiff had not shown sufficient evidence of substantial similarity between the two programs to prove infringement.

Dealing with the two arguments in order, the court, in the person of Judge Edward R. Becker, first observed that generally speaking a copyright in a literary work can be infringed even though there is no substantial similarity between the literal elements of the original work and those of the accused work. "One can violate the copyright of a play or book by copying its plot or plot devices." In the words of the late Melville Nimmer, if the accused work displays "comprehensive nonliteral similarity" with the original work, infringement may exist. Thus, on first blush, it would appear that Judge Van Artsdalen was right.

Defendants claimed, however, that computer programs are not like other literary works because the structure of a program is its idea, and therefore is unprotectable under a law that does not protect ideas. Judge Becker turned for guidance to *Baker v. Selden*, the accounting forms case we discussed earlier, and in particular to the following quote from that old Supreme Court case:

[W]here the art [i.e., the method of accounting] it teaches cannot be used without employing the methods and diagrams used to illustrate the book, or such as are similar to them, such methods and diagrams are to be considered as necessary incidents to the art, and given to the public.

Judge Becker concluded that just as *Baker v. Selden* focused on the end to be achieved by Selden's book, so too in the programming context the line between idea and expression could be drawn with reference to the end sought to be achieved by the program. It is here that the Court of Appeals is said by some to have gone astray. I do not agree, for reasons that will be explained later, but I wish to focus the reader's attention particularly on the following language from Judge Becker's opinion: "the purpose or function of a utilitarian work [including a computer program] would be the work's idea, and everything that is not necessary to that purpose or function would be part of the expression of the idea." Thus, a program's structure, logic, and flow (which the court called "structure, sequence and organization") is protected by copyright except to the extent that elements of structure, logic, and flow are necessary for accomplishing the purposes of the program.

The Court of Appeals stated its belief that such a rule would advance the basic purpose of the idea-expression distinction in the copyright law, which is to preserve the balance between competition and protection. Anyone is free to copy whatever is necessary to achieve the same purpose as an original program, but if one goes beyond that and copies structural, logic, and flow elements of a program, which the court had found to be among the more significant costs of developing the program, one risks being held an infringer. The court's confidence in its rule was unshaken by arguments that the rule was too vague to be useful, or that one who copied only structure, logic, and flow would still have to undertake substantial work in order to produce a finished product. As to the latter point, Judge Becker observed that such copying, even though nonliteral, was of substantial value in relation to competitors who do not copy the structure, logic, and flow of others' programs. As to the former, he agreed that a rule limiting software protection to literal copying would be simpler, but said that producing a simplistic rule was not a goal that overrode the other considerations in the case.

The court also took note of another argument against full copyright protection for software: the argument that progress in the area of computer technology is a "stepping-stone" process that necessarily entails some degree of plagiarism of works that have come before. Judge Becker

responded that copyright law had always recognized, and accommo-
dated, the fact that all intellectual pioneers build on the work of their
predecessors. The trick was to balance the conflicting objectives of protection and dissemination, and there did not appear in this regard to be
any difference between progress in computer technology and progress
in other areas of science or the arts.

Turning to the Dentcom program, the court noted that there were
other dental laboratory programs on the market that performed the same
functions as Dentalab but had different "structures and designs." It held
that the purpose of Dentalab was to aid in the business operation of a
dental laboratory, and as that could clearly be done without copying the
detailed structure of Dentalab, the detailed structure was part of the
expression, not the idea, of the program.

Judge Becker was mindful that the Court's rule might put it in conflict
with *Synercom*. Though *Synercom* might be distinguishable on the basis
that the input formats were structurally simple and programs were structurally complex, it had to be admitted that the input formats were a kind
of data structure. In *Synercom*, Judge Higginbotham had asked what
Judge Becker now considered a "powerful rhetorical question": If sequencing and ordering are expression, what separable idea is being
expressed? Judge Becker had an answer for that question in *Whelan*: The
separable idea is the idea of efficiently organizing a dental laboratory.
To the extent that *Synercom* held that there was no idea separate from
sequence and ordering in a computer program, and therefore, that there
was a difference between the protection of structure, logic, and flow in
the computer context and the protection of those elements in any other
context, *Synercom* was wrong. (Please note for later reference that Judge
Becker's court, the Court of Appeals for the Third Circuit, did not hear
appeals from Judge Higginbotham's court. Appeals from Judge Higginbotham's court went to the Court of Appeals for the Fifth Circuit, which
would have its own occasion before long to compare *Whelan* and *Synercom*.)

To Judge Becker, the data structures in Elaine Whelan's program were
so comprehensive, detailed, and complex that they were, in themselves,
protectable by copyright. He saw no conflict here with cases holding
that "blank forms" are not protectable, because the forms at issue in
those cases did not rise to the same level of expressiveness as did the
data structures in Dentalab. (As already noted, it may be that differences
in the expressiveness of the data structures at issue may have been
another reason for the differing rulings in *Whelan* and *Synercom*.)

The court also mentioned the fact that the screen displays in the
Dentcom program were highly similar to those in Dentalab. While these
similarities were not directly relevant because Whelan Associates did
not claim infringement of the screen displays, they were nonetheless

probative of copying because of the likelihood that there was some relationship between the screens and the underlying program. (One member of the three-judge appellate panel, Judge Rosen, disagreed on this point. His view was that proof of display similarity was not at all probative that the underlying program was copied, since identical screens can be produced by programs that are written very differently. I'll return to that issue in a later chapter, in connection with a 1989 case dealing with the visual displays of a cost-estimating program.)

Finally, the court addressed the argument that the quantity of copying was not large enough to constitute infringement. Whelan's evidence of logic copying was based on similarities in only five subroutines. Quantitatively, that did not comprise a great deal of the Dentalab program. Nonetheless, the court found that Whelan's evidence was sufficient to prove substantial similarity, both because the subroutines chosen for comparison by Whelan's expert were the most important ones, and because the comparison of the subroutines showed that they were highly similar. Its ruling in that respect highlighted the fact that there is no quantitative threshold below which copying is excused. In *Harper & Row v. The Nation*, for instance, the Supreme Court held the defendant magazine to have infringed the copyright in President Gerald Ford's memoirs by copying only four hundred words. Why? Because they were the most important four hundred words in the book—the words that dealt with the pardon of former President Nixon.

For a number of reasons, therefore, the Court of Appeals concluded that the Dentcom program was properly held to have infringed the copyright in the program written by Elaine Whelan.

The defendants petitioned the Supreme Court in an effort to overturn the Court of Appeals' decision, but could not interest the minimum four justices necessary to obtain a hearing. Judge Becker had had the last word.

The howls of protest and the cheers of approbation from different sectors of the computer industry and the legal community that greeted the *Whelan* opinion are best left, I think, to be analyzed after we've studied a few more cases. For the moment, I'd simply like to present the reader with two items of evidence of similarity between the Dentcom program and Dentalab. You may assume there is substantial additional evidence to the same effect. Knowing what you now know about Rand Jaslow's behavior, about the elements of expression in computer programs, and about the copyright law, I'd like you to consider how you would have ruled in *Whelan v. Jaslow*.

The first item of evidence is a chart comparing the structure, flow, logic, and naming conventions in the "order entry" modules of the two programs.

ORDER ENTRY PROGRAMS

Dentalab System	*Dentcom PC Systems*
Primary Menu, choose [1]	Primary Menu, choose [1]
Production SCHEDULING	Production MENU
Production Menu, choose [1]	Production menu choose [1]
ORDER ENTRY	ORDER ENTRY
DL1000 program (Order entry)	ORDER ENTRY program
"ENTER ACCOUNT OR NAMEKEY	"ENTER ACCOUNT NAME KEY:
"Check CUSTMAST for valid cus-	_____
tomer. Read CUSTMAST file on	Check CUSTMAST for valid
this customer.	customer. If valid, read
	CUSTMAST file for this
	customer.
Increment sequential order no.	If yes, increment order # in
in ORDERS. Display customer	ORDERS
name, address.	
Display entry screen (6.6).	Display entry screen, patient
patient shade, remake, call	shade, mould, remake, call Dr.?
	Dr.?
Pan #. Dr's. request date.	case/pan #. Drs. request date,
	final case status T. F. B. R.
	IS THIS SCREEN CORRECT?
Ask for first department number.	If yes ask for first department
Display dept. order screen (6.8	number. Display dept. order
-6.11)(list of items in this	screen (P10)(list of item in
dept. from ITEMMAST)	this dept from ITEMMAST
User entry choices	User entry choices

Dentalab System	*Dentcom PC Systems*
System adds days in dept. [DAYVAL] to present date to find due out date. System computes workload for dept/day out by product of load factor x quantity.	System adds days in dept. from COMPANY to present date to find due out date. Time is of AM, "Noon" or PM. System accumulates case load by product of item load factor x quantity
ITEMMAST	ITEMMAST
Adds this to load already in DAYVAL for date out.	Adds this to load already in DEPTLOAD for date out.

The second bit of evidence consists of a portion of the testimony of Whelan Associates' expert, Dr. Thomas Moore, in connection with two subroutines found in both programs: the invoicing subroutine and the month-end subroutine. Like live testimony in most cases, it is confused in places, but its thrust is clear.

In the Dentalab system, the same kind of thing again, same information is up there, description, unit price, extension, items and program reads all those things in from te [*sic*] number of files actually, and displays them and then gives the operator a number of options to change the order as it appears on the screen to skip this one, to cancel it, or to accept it.

The same choices are given in Dentalab [*sic*] systems, change, skip, cancel.

Assuming that the order is accepted, both systems then calculate the money, calculate the amount of money that will be billed, and at this point they use the price code to find which of the four prices are to be charged for this particular customer. Both systems do that. They pick that one of four prices and calculate the total amount, write then the record of this invoice that has been formed to show the invoice's file, sets the flag in the order's file to show that this order has now been invoiced so that it doesn't get reinvoiced.

Q. What is a flag?

A. Well, a flag would be, in this case, a certain location is marked I for invoices, just an indicator that invoicing has been done on this record.

Q. Both used it?

A. Both used a flag. I don't remember whether Dentcom uses a letter I or some other symbol, but there is a flag there that it's a field number 12, in which it's indicated that this file has been invoiced or this order has been invoiced.

. . . .

Q. Do you have any comment about the invoicing?

A. Well, I think it should be clear, it was clear to me from going through these programs that there is a very marke[d] similarity between the two, that they, item by item, are doing pretty much the same thing with the same fields in the same files, and accomplishing roughly the same results.

So there was quite a match, line by line, between these two, flow in these two.

Q. What do you conclude from that?

A. Well, back together with the file's structure, sort of set up with the—how the programs have to proceed. I would think that the person who designed or constructed Dentalab system must have been thoroughly familiar with the Dentcom system. [*Sic.*] The person who constructed the Dentcom system must have been familiar with the Series/1 system, because the same file structure and the same program steps are followed, same overall flow takes place in both systems.

....

Q. What did you find in month-end?

A. Okay. Month-end, the calling program in Dentcom, this obviously is done at the end of each month.

In the Dentcom system there is a program called MOEND, which chains all these other programs, that is, MOEND calls MOPRDL, and after that program runs, goes back to MEEND [*sic*], calls the print sale and so on.

In the Dentalab system, there is a supervisory program also called MOEND, and that system calls or runs a series of programs doing various functions.

Now if we look at the functions done by the programs in order, we find that they are the same except for a flipping of the order in the first two things.

The Dentcom system, it first prints product group reports, and then prints the monthly customer sales analysis.

In Dentalab, just reverses, prints sales analysis first, product group report second.

After that, both systems do the same thing in the same order.

They now do accounts receivable aging, since a month has gone by they have to update all the 30 days, 60 days, et cetera, calculate service charges. Then they print the monthly AR reports that had to do with service charges, only those that involve service charges, they both do that. Then they both print the age file balance, balance report, and following that they print the month and [*sic*] accounts receivable report. That's the total accounts receivable rport [*sic*].

Then they both go through and look for accounts that are not active that month, and print a list of these accounts, accounts not serviced, an account that doesn't have any access.

The final thing that the Dentcom system does is to calculate the new AR total for the entire lab, which I mentioned is contained in the company file.

Dentalab does not keep that total, so that's the last item, that is not as far as I can tell, done by Dentalab. I may have said—did I say Dentcom keeps that total? Dentalab does not. That's the only difference.

Readers unfamiliar with data processing may be wondering whether Dr. Moore's description isn't possibly a mere reflection of the way all dental laboratory programs have to work. I remind those readers that there was substantial evidence that other dental laboratory programs accomplished the same purpose as Dentalab without having the same design. I'd also remind the reader that Judge Van Artsdalen found the design of Dentalab to have been Elaine Whelan's sole creation, and not simply the natural consequence of implementing Rand Jaslow's generalized requests.

I'd like you now to be the judge. Ask yourself two questions. Was justice done in *Whelan v. Jaslow*? Did the Court of Appeals explain the line between idea and expression in a way that overprotects software?

We started the first chapter of this book in a steaming hall in Philadelphia in the summer of 1788. We have been back to Philadelphia twice since. The courthouse where *Apple v. Franklin* and *Whelan v. Jaslow* were tried is just down the street from Independence Hall. The decisions in those two cases, while not in the same league as the decisions made by the Framers of the Constitution, have served to protect the rights of software authors as fully as the Copyright Act passed under the authority of the Constitution protects other kinds of literary works. In Part III hereof, we deal with the policy implications of that protection. Does it make sense as an element of an (intentional or accidental) industrial policy, on a domestic scale and on an international scale? Does it properly balance the interests of innovators and followers? Does it engender software "monopolies" that are inimical to consumer welfare? We will explore these and other policy questions in the succeeding pages.

Part III

The Shaping of the Invisible

11

The Range of Programming Expression

We wanted to uncover the magic and the mystery that surround the development of an operating system or an application program: Where did the idea for the program come from? How difficult was it to bring to fruition? What did it feel like to develop a major program? Is programming an art or a science, a craft or a skill? What does it take to be a successful programmer?

This common set of questions supplies a framework—a way to highlight the similarities and differences in approaches to programming and to allow the nuances and the philosophies of each programmer to shine through. Even so, certain themes recur: simplicity, balance, conciseness, elegance. These seem qualities befitting poetry, not programs for power users.

Susan Lammers, "Programmers at Work,"
PC World, September 1986, p. 187

Over the long history of copyright law, one of the basic rules that has evolved in the caselaw is that not all works of authorship are entitled to the same level of copyright protection. Specifically, literary works in which only a narrow range of expression is possible receive only limited protection. Typically, the literal expression in the work may not be copied, but the structure, logic, and flow of the work may be copied. Those who favor limited copyright protection for software like to analogize software to those literary works for which limited protection has traditionally been accorded. In this chapter, I'll try to explain why such a generalization is not just wrong, but wrong-headed.

Consider first the kinds of literary works for which it is commonly said that only literal copying constitutes infringement: maps, for example. A map is a visual representation of the physical structure, logic, and flow of part of the earth's geography. One cannot copyright the earth's geography. The relative location of roads, towns, mountains, rivers, and other geographical features are facts the existence of which and the physical relationships among which can only be accurately depicted in one way: as they exist in the real world. Coloring, shading, typeface, and emphasis techniques may vary from mapmaker to mapmaker, but New York City is always going to be shown as south of Albany and on the east bank of the Hudson River. Since copyright law only protects original expression, not the underlying facts being expressed, the mapmaker's copyright protects only the originality displayed in the way he or she has chosen to express the geographic features in question. In part this rule results from the pragmatic recognition that it would be next to impossible in most cases to prove that a second mapmaker copied the structure, logic, and flow of the earth from the first mapmaker's map as opposed to deriving it in other ways. In part, the rule is a reflection of the fundamental principle that the copyright law protects only expression, not ideas. Facts, it is thought, belong to the realm of ideas, at least in the sense that everyone ought to be free to describe them, and in the sense that descriptions of the same facts will often of necessity be highly similar.

Note that these rationales do not apply to maps that are nonfactual. The map of Middle Earth, drawn to illustrate the geography described in J. R. R. Tolkien's *The Hobbit* and showing the relative locations of the Lonely Mountain, the Iron Hills, the Desolation of Smaug, the Grey Mountains, and the Withered Heath whence came the Great Worms is entitled to as much protection for its structure, logic, and flow as is Tolkien's textual description of that imaginary territory. Similarly, for Saul Steinberg's satiric map of America from a New Yorker's perspective, in which the distance from Fifth Avenue to the Hudson River appears to exceed the distance from the Hudson to the Pacific Ocean, the protection is broader than merely for the literal words and lines on the page. And what if Rand MacNally were to put a few fictitious towns, creeks, and roads on its map of Indiana? (Map copiers beware! Cartographers have been known to engage in this practice specifically for the purpose of helping them catch infringers.) Clearly the structure (i.e., relative locations) of those fanciful elements, and not just their names, would be part of the original expression of the map.

Phone directories are another type of writing protected under the copyright law as literary works, but accorded very narrow or "thin" protection. Certainly, in the case of a directory that lists all telephone numbers in a specific area alphabetically by owner, no one could argue that the structure, logic, and flow of the directory is fanciful or original. However, that rule does not apply to all directories. If the author has exercised selectivity in choosing the entries to the directory (e.g., all Oriental restaurants in England and Wales), and has arranged those entries in a fashion that is in some way unique, creative, or arbitrary (e.g., sorted by region of cuisine, then by price, then city, then ambience), protection is very likely to extend beyond the literal words of the directory to its structure, logic, and flow. Indeed, to the extent the literal words are nothing more than name, address, phone number, and region of cuisine, they might not be protected at all, while the directory's structure, logic, and flow would be.

Dictionaries. It is said that these are only thinly protected as well, for, after all, how many different ways are there to define "tiresome"? Again, the natural limitations on the number of different ways that definitions of words can be expressed do not apply to fanciful dictionaries. I have already referred to *The Dictionary of the Khazars*. In addition to offering the opportunity for non-seriatim reading, *Khazars* is a collection of definitions that—where they are not wholly imaginary—are highly imaginative. There are numerous other examples in the world of fiction. Dig out your copy of Richard Adams' *Watership Down*, and check the "Lapine Glossary" at the back. Or sample Edward Lear's "Nonsense Botanies." Such dictionaries are traditionally accorded broad copyright protection.

Computer programs are also frequently likened to recipe books by copyright defendants and "narrow protectionists." Recipe books generally receive "thin" copyright protection because there is little difference between the ideas they convey and the expression necessary to convey those ideas. Put differently, copyright law does not protect the recipe, and since there is only a limited range of expression available to any writer of the same recipe, there is a merger of idea and expression, or something very close to a merger. From what we've already seen about the nature of computer programs, I hope that readers will conclude for themselves that the comparison to recipe books is simply not apt, since for computer programs the ingredients chosen, what those ingredients are called, the quantities in which they are used, the order in which they are added to the mix, and many other variables can be altered markedly without affecting the end result.

In sum, it has not proven constructive to analogize software to factual lists, compilations, or expositions, the so-called *petite monnaie* (small change) of copyright law. There are two reasons. First, software is simply not factual. The lines of code are not statements of fact; they are directions to the computer to manipulate intellectual constructs, most of which are created by the program authors themselves for purposes of manipulation. Second, the range of constructs and manipulations from which the program author selects are constrained more by the author's imagination than by the relatively weak constraints imposed by the nature of the desired result.

In support of this dual assertion (if the evidence presented in Chapters 7 through 10 is not sufficient), I offer the testimony of individuals who should know: people with substantial experience writing software and managing software development projects. Consider first the following description of the craft of writing computer programs, written by Dr. Frederick Brooks, for many years the head of the Computer Sciences Department at the University of North Carolina at Chapel Hill, and in the mid–1960s responsible for a milestone software development project at IBM, the development of the operating system for the System/360 family of computers:

Why is programming fun? What delights may its practitioner expect as his reward?

First is the sheer joy of making things. As the child delights in his mud pie, so the adult enjoys building things, especially things of his own design. I think this delight must be an image of God's delight in making things, a delight shown in the distinctness of newness of each leaf and each snowflake.

Second is the pleasure of making things that are useful to other people. Deep within, we want others to use our work and find it helpful. . . .

Third is the fascination of fashioning complex puzzle-like objects of inter-locking moving parts and watching them work in subtle cycles, playing out the consequences of principles built in from the beginning.

Fourth is the joy of always learning, which springs from the nonrepeating nature of the task. In one way or another the problem is ever new, and its solver learns something: sometimes practical, sometimes theoretical, and sometimes both.

Finally, there is the delight in working in such a tractable medium. The programmer, like the poet, works only slightly removed from pure thought-stuff. He builds his castles in the air, from air, creating by exertion of the imagination. Few media of creation are so flexible, so easy to polish and rework, so readily capable of realizing grand conceptual structures. . . .

Programming then is fun because it gratifies creative longings built deep within us and delights sensibilities we have in common with all men.

                                        F. P. Brooks, *The Mythical Man-Month* (1975)

The petite monnaie of copyright, indeed! I once heard software thus deprecatingly described, at the outset of a major academic conference on copyright protection for software, by Professor Jerome Reichman of Vanderbilt Law School. My reaction was to read him from the audience the foregoing quotation from Brooks's *The Mythical Man-Month*, thereby provoking a dialectic that continues each time we meet.

The Mythical Man-Month deals with the problem of managing large software development projects. The book grew out of Brooks's experience in managing very large operating systems development projects. It is quite significant that even in the context of commercial projects of considerable size, employing large numbers of programmers, and in the context of operating systems—programs whose purpose is to manage the other hardware and software resources of a computer system—we find the core of the task described as "exertion of the imagination," "building castles in air" in a medium "readily capable of realizing grand conceptual structures," and bringing delight that "must be an image of God's delight in making things." In assessing what range of alternative expression is available for program authors, we should certainly give substantial weight to Brooks's characterization.

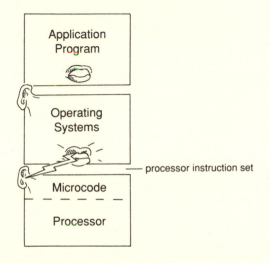

Recognizing that one swallow does not make a summer, however, it is helpful to know that Dr. Brooks's observations square with those of others active in the field. The corroborative views of Carl Alsing are quoted in Tracy Kidder's *The Soul of a New Machine*. Alsing is a microcoder. Microcode inhabits a nether world of its own. To most programmers, it looks like part of the computer's hardware. To hardware engineers, it looks like software. You'll recall that every processor has an instruction set, the set of commands that, if presented in proper form, the processor can execute. Operating systems are written to conform to instruction sets of particular processors, and the authors of those operating systems assume that everything behind the instruction set interface is hardware. That assumption is not always accurate. In fact, in many if not most cases, behind the instruction set interface is a much more primitive interface to the hardware itself, and between the instruction set interface and the more primitive interface lies microcode. Microcode is software that helps create the hardware's instruction set. It

occupies specially allocated memory in the processor. Accordingly, it is
the most utilitarian, machine-oriented software that can be conceived,
and the untutored observer might expect that it would permit of an
exceedingly narrow range of expression; that the process of writing
microcode would be tedious drudgework completely lacking in the opportunity for creative expression.

Alsing describes what it's really like to write microcode:

Writing microcode is like nothing else in my life. For days there's nothing coming
out. The empty yellow pad sits there in front of me, reminding me of my
inadequacy. Finally, it starts to come. I feel good. That feeds it, and finally I get
into a state where I'm a microcode writing machine. . . .

You have to understand the problem thoroughly and you have to have thought
of all the myriad ways in which you can put your microverbs together. You
have a hundred L-shaped blocks to build a building. You take all the pieces,
put them together, pull them apart, put them together again. After a while,
you're like a kid on a jungle gym. There are all these constructs in your mind
and you can swing from one to another with ease.

I've done this in short intervals for a short period each year. There's low
intensity before it and a letdown at the end. There's a big section where you
come down off it, and sometimes you do it awkwardly and feel a little strange,
wobbly and tired, and you want to say to your friends, "Hey, I'm back."

The comparison here to periods of writer's block and then inspiration,
muse-driven productivity, and even the exhaustion that follows periods
of intense creativity is inescapable, and again there is a reference to the
broad range of expression available to the microcode author: the "myriad
ways" of arranging the microverbs to solve the assigned problem, and
the sense of swinging "like a kid" from one imagined construct to another.

If two swallows make a summer as far as the reader is concerned, feel
free to branch to the next chapter. If not, consider next the opinion of
Gary Kildall, the author of CP/M, one of the principal early operating
systems for personal computers. Kildall was interviewed by Susan Lammers for the article from which the quote at the beginning of this chapter
was taken.

When a program is clean and neat, nicely structured and consistent, it can be
beautiful. I guess I wouldn't compare a program to the Mona Lisa, but a good
program does have a simplicity and elegance that's quite handsome. Stylistic
distinctions of different programs are intriguing, very much like the differences
art critics might see between Leonardo's work and a Van Gogh. I like the LISP
programming language because it's so pleasing. There's a concise form of LISP
called the M expressions. When you write an algorithm using M expressions,
it's so beautiful you could frame it and hang it on the wall.

What Kildall adds to our understanding of the subjective nature of program writing are the notions of "beauty," "simplicity," "elegance," and the idea that there can be stylistic variability between two programs on the same order of magnitude as the difference between fifteenth-century representational art and nineteenth-century Impressionistic art. He goes on to say that programming is both art and science, and indeed "is very much a religious experience for a lot of people."

Lammers asked Bob Frankston, coauthor of VisiCalc, the first commercial spreadsheet program, which art form programming most closely resembled. His stream-of-consciousness answer:

In music, and in various forms of art, we try to operate within rules, but you have to know when to break the rules and when to follow them, just as in programming. In art, you also ask yourself how people will perceive your work—you're trying to create a perceptual impression. When you communicate, whether in writing or in a program, what you say must be understood by the recipients. If you cannot explain a program to yourself, the chance of the computer getting it right is pretty small.

Lammers also spoke with Robert Carr, who wrote the program Framework, about whether programming is art or science:

It's really a combination of both. . . . Certainly, some very scientific, well-grounded principles are tremendously important for software development, but good software goes beyond that. Looking at the sketch of the decision-tree that led to the design of *Framework*, you'll see I spent a lot of time thinking, scribbling—a lot of subconscious activity. That's where the art is. In art, you can't explicate how the end result was achieved. The best software comes from the realm of intuition.

Small wonder, given the foregoing views, that in a book otherwise dense with the highly specialized wisdom of computer science, J. F. Leathrum's *Foundations of Software Design*, we find it asserted that the decision to write a program "is very much like the decision to write a novel or write a poem. In both software and the literary analog we are dealing with a highly creative activity."

I promised in Chapter 1 to deal with the subject of CASE, or Computer-Assisted Software Engineering. CASE is a generic industry term for a range of products and techniques that program authors can use to make themselves more productive. These range from programs that will automatically generate lines of code given high-level instructions by an author and programs that will store and organize an author's favorite subroutines for easy retrieval in the future, to disciplined methods of project management and code writing wherein a computer may or may not help to impose the discipline. I have already noted that the fact that

some in the software industry choose to refer to the job that program
authors do as "software engineering" does not mean that programming
is engineering or that programmers' work is not authorship, any more
than referring to Tom Paine or Upton Sinclair as "social engineers"
means that their work was engineering or that their writings were not
authorship. The proof is not in the terminology, it is in the nature of
the work produced. If a programmer uses computer programs to become
more productive, the literal text produced may be original and highly
innovative or it may be a series of cliche routines common in the industry. The detailed design of the program is still the essence of the
programmer's expression, however, and that design is something that
CASE tools do not create. Musician Herbie Hancock uses programs
similar to CASE programs to make himself more "productive" (I think
he would say, "To expand my range of creative possibilities"). Musician
Pierre Boulez does also. However, no one proposes that, purely on
account of their use of those tools, their music is entitled to lesser protection than that of Miles Davis, Leonard Bernstein, or others who do
not use such automated assists.

CASE practitioners may write programs that are organized in more
"in-line" fashion and utilize fewer branching techniques. They may write
programs that have certain stylistic similarities. They may write programs that, in some measure, aren't even original. There may develop,
because of CASE, a class of hack programmers, like the hack writers
who turn out sitcom scripts on schedule week after week. Such a development, if it arises, should not affect the scope of copyright protection
afforded computer programs, any more than the existence of hack writers affects the scope of copyright protection for television programs
generally. The only effect CASE should have in software copyright cases
is to reduce the ability to infer copying from the existence of similarities
that arise from the serindipitous use of common CASE techniques.

It is important to realize that none of the quotations cited in this
chapter was given for the purposes of influencing the copyright treatment of software. Each was a sincere assessment of the degree of creativity involved in program authorship. None of those quotations, or the
ideas expressed in them, is ever dealt with by the commentators who
favor thin copyright protection for software. Nonetheless, quite clearly
one of the most important determinants of the scope of copyright protection for software is whether writing programs is like writing a novel
or like writing a phone directory. As to that determinant, I have firmly
concluded that software is basically a written work of imagination. The
medium of expression is constrained, to be sure, by the intended purposes the program is to serve, but as we have seen those constraints
are much the same as the constraints imposed by the decision to write
a mystery novel, a thriller, or a juvenile novel.

If the reader has reached the same conclusion, he or she is in good company. CONTU, the presidential commission whose recommendations were the basis for the 1980 software-related amendments to the American copyright laws, concluded that in software the "availability of alternative noninfringing language is the rule rather than the exception." Judges, in the face of vigorous arguments to the contrary mounted by copyright defendants, have been even more definitive in their conclusions than CONTU. In the *SAS* case, Judge Wiseman put it this way:

[T]hroughout the preparation of a complicated computer program such as SAS, the author is faced with a virtually endless series of decisions as to how to carry out the assigned task. . . . The author must decide how to break the assigned task into smaller tasks, each of which must in turn be broken down into successively smaller and more detailed tasks. . . . At every level, the process is characterized by choice, often made arbitrarily, and only occasionally guided by necessity. Even in the case of simple statistical calculations, there is room for variation, such as the order in which arithmetic operations are performed. . . . As the sophistication of the calculation increases, so does the opportunity for variation of expression.

A year later, the Canadian Federal Court, Trial Division, had occasion to consider the same issue, in a case brought by Apple against suppliers of clones of the Apple II who readily admitted to having copied the Apple operating system from the chips inside the Apple II, but predictably claimed that there was only one way of expressing the ideas in the Apple object code. In rejecting that argument, Judge Reed said:

There is no doubt that computer programs are highly individualistic in nature and contain a form of expression personal to the programmer. No two programmers would ever write a program in exactly the same way (except perhaps in the case of the most simple program). Even the same programmer, after writing a program and leaving it for some time, would not write the program the same way on a second occasion. The sequence of instructions would most certainly be different. The possibility of two programmers creating identical programs without copying was compared by the *defendants'* expert witness to the likelihood of a monkey sitting at a typewriter producing Shakespeare. (Emphasis added.)

In *M. Kramer Mfg. Co., Inc. v. Andrews,* a case involving computer programs that caused a computer to play poker, the U.S. Court of Appeals for the Fourth Circuit also faced the argument that the plaintiff's program contained no expression separate from the ideas it embodied, and also rejected the argument, saying:

In the computer field "[t]here exists a virtually unlimited number of instruction sequences that would enable a programmer to construct a program which performs even the more basic algorithmic or mathematical procedures." . . . It follows, therefore, that normally in the computer field, courts are concerned with expression and not idea, as those terms are defined in copyright law.

The argument that limited possibilities for alternate expression exist often arises in connection with a firm's business strategy to offer programs that are, in one sense or another, "compatible replacements" for the programs of another firm. That was the case, as we saw, in *SAS*, *Apple v. Franklin*, and *Whelan*, and that scenario will ultimately be the focus of our policy analysis. At present, however, we are concerned only with what, if anything, the existence of a compatibility strategy can tell us about the range of expression available to the writer of the program being cloned. The replacer claims that its compatibility strategy dictates close conformity, if not identity, with the expression in the target program, and thus that the idea and the expression in the target program have merged. Even if it is so, however, that the clone-writer's range of expression is limited (a question we have yet to explore), that fact says nothing about the range of expression available to the author of the target program. As Judge Sloviter pointed out in *Apple v. Franklin*, the fact that one firm establishes a compatibility business plan cannot ipso facto cause a merger of idea and expression in another firm's program in which, prior to the stranger's compatibility plan, there had been no such merger. In its pithiness and pointedness, Judge Sloviter's treatment of this issue is worth reading:

Franklin claims that whether or not the programs can be rewritten, there are a limited "number of ways to arrange operating systems to enable a computer to run the vast body of Apple-compatible software." . . . This claim has no pertinence to either the idea/expression dichotomy or merger. The idea which may merge with the expression, thus making copyright unavailable, is the idea which is the subject of the expression. The idea of one of the operating system programs is, for example, how to translate source code into object code. If other methods of expressing that idea are not foreclosed as a practical matter, then there is no merger. . . .

Franklin may wish to achieve total compatibility with independently developed application programs written for the Apple II, but that is a commercial and competitive decision that does not enter into the somewhat metaphysical issue of whether particular ideas and expressions have merged.

Obviously, in the broader context that we must utimately address, the relative interests of innovators and followers must be weighed in assessing the proper application of the old wine of copyright law to the new bottle that is software; but in terms of the immediate question—the range of expression available to writers of original programs—the existence of followers is irrelevant. What is relevant is the nature of program writing itself, concerning which the views of authoritative spokespersons and respected jurists have been presented in this chapter. If, ultimately, we determine that programs should be given only thin copyright protection as a way of balancing the interests at stake, we can now see that we will be doing so in the face of the fact that programs are works of imagination; literary works of a type traditionally granted full protection for their literal text and detailed structure, logic, and flow under the copyright law.

12

NEC v. Intel

"I intended to end it as follows: when the Inquisitor finished speaking, he waited some time for the Prisoner's reply. His silence distressed him. . . . The old man would have liked him to say something, however bitter and terrible. But he suddenly approached the old man and kissed him gently on his bloodless, aged lips. . . . There was an imperceptible movement at the corners of his mouth; he went to the door, opened it and said to him: 'Go and come no more— don't come at all—never, never!' . . . The Prisoner went away." . . .

"You see, old man, I thought that when I went away I would have you at least in all the world," Ivan said suddenly with unexpected feeling. "But I can see now, my dear anchorite, that there's no place for me in your heart. I shall never repudiate the formula of 'everything is permitted,' but you will repudiate me for it, won't you?"

Alyosha got up and, without uttering a word, kissed him gently on the lips.

"Plagiarism!" cried Ivan, suddenly looking very delighted. "You've stolen it from my poem!"

Fyodor Dostoyevsky, *The Brothers Karamazov* (1880)

A sort of legal halfway house en route to assessing the policy considerations surrounding legal protection for software is the case of *NEC Corporation v. Intel Corporation*. The *Intel* case is a halfway house because, although it defines the respective rights of an innovator and a follower, it does so in the context of a licensing arrangement between the two, not in terms of the apportionment of rights that the copyright law would make in the absence of a licensing arrangement. Nonetheless, the case is instructive because it indicates the sort of balanced analysis of which the federal courts are capable in a realm that narrow protectionists argue is too complex for judicial determination.

NEC, a licensee under Intel's patents to the 8086 and 8088 microprocessor chip, sued its licensor in the District Court for the Northern District of California. The basis for the suit was that Intel was accusing NEC of infringing the copyright in the microcode residing in the Intel microprocessors, and NEC sought a judicial declaration of noninfringement. NEC was licensed not only to intel's patents, but also to copy that very microcode in connection with the NEC uPD 8086 and uPD 8088 microprocessors and "improvements thereon developed by NEC." The question was whether the new NEC V20 and V30 microprocessors were merely improvements on the uPD 8086 and uPD 8088, and if not, whether the NEC microcode for the V20 and V30 was an unlawful copy of the Intel microcode. Taking the issue to the limit, NEC also asserted that microcode was not a proper subject for copyright protection, and any similarities between its microcode and Intel's should also be excused on that ground.

Judge William Gray picked up the case after the judge originally assigned to the case, William Ingram, stepped down as a result of NEC's successful effort to disqualify him on the grounds that he owned Intel stock ($81 worth through a fifteen-person investment club). Before he disqualified himself, Judge Ingram had ruled as a preliminary matter that microcode was protectable by copyright, but he vacated that ruling when he stepped down, and left the issue for Judge Gray to decide again. The trial consumed eighteen courtroom days in 1988. There was no jury, and Judge Gray issued his opinion on February 6, 1989.

Most people think that NEC prevailed, as the company was held not to have infringed Intel's copyright. That conclusion is somewhat shortsighted, however. Intel knew early on that its copyright would not be enforced against NEC, and although it is true that NEC was found not to have infringed, Intel established what was to that company and all other computer companies an invaluable point of principle.

That principle was stated by Judge Gray at the outset of his opinion, in considering NEC's arguments that microcode was not proper subject matter for copyright. The judge concluded that for microcode to be protectable, it had to meet three requirements. First, it had to be a computer program, as opposed to hardware; second, it had to be "fixed in a tangible medium of expression" (a requirement for all copyrightable works); and third, it had to be original. As microcode is a series of instructions that tells a microprocessor what circuits to actuate in order to carry out the tasks directed by the "macrocode," or software, it falls clearly within the statutory definition of "computer program," the judge

held. In addition, NEC did not contest that the burning into ROM of
Intel's microcode constituted fixation in a tangible medium of expression.
Finally, the requirement of originality simply means that the work was
created independently and exceeds the modicum of originality one might
find in a short phrase or fragmentary work. Intel's microcode exceeded
that threshold, in the judge's view. Accordingly, Intel's microcode was
protectable subject matter.

That ruling, of course, is what Intel was after. In terms of technology,
the 8086 and 8088 chips were obsolescent by the time the case was
decided, but the principle that had been put forward by NEC (which,
you remember, was the plaintiff in this lawsuit), that microcode could
be freely copied in order to achieve compatibility, posed a substantial
threat to the viability of Intel's ongoing investment in microcode development.

Having won the war, Intel went on to lose the battle. There were two
reasons why Judge Gray gave the decision to NEC, only one of which
is particularly interesting to us. The uninteresting reason was that Intel
had failed to mark its notice of copyright on the ROM, and had failed
to cause licensees of its chips to mark notices of copyright on the chips
they manufactured. The result of this failure to give notice, the judge
ruled, constituted a forfeiture by Intel of the copyright in the 8086/8088
microcode, under the rule that "whenever a work protected under this
title is published . . . by authority of the copyright owner, a notice of
copyright . . . shall be placed on all publicly distributed copies." It was
because of the judge's foreshadowing of his feelings about this rule when
he took over the case that Intel knew early in the case that it was not
going to prevail. (The quoted rule, by the way, is an anachronism as of
March 1989. The United States has decided to adhere to the Berne Copyright Convention, the major international copyright compact, and under
Berne notice is not a requirement for protection of a published work.
The "©" symbol has thus become an item of "don't-tread-on-me" nos-
talgia rather than a legal prerequisite.)

The—to us—interesting reason for NEC's victory in the battle was that
by Judge Gray's lights even if Intel had not forfeited its copyright, NEC
had not infringed that copyright. The similarities between the two programs—and there clearly were a substantial number of them—could not
be attributed to copying. Unfortunately, just as he came to that part of
his opinion, the judge turned laconic:

In preparing this portion of this memorandum, I am assuming that it will be of
particular interest only to Intel and NEC and their respective counsel, and therefore that anyone who reads it will be familiar with the facts. Accordingly, I shall
refrain from the extremely arduous and lengthy task of describing or explaining
the background circumstances involving the specific issues.

In that assessment, Judge Gray was quite wrong. He may have been wrong procedurally in not fully discharging his obligation to state his findings of fact in such a way that they would be meaningful to the appellate court in the event of an appeal. Whether or not that is so, his judgment about the interest of third parties was certainly wrong. Many people not associated with either Intel or NEC were intensely interested in his findings of noninfringement because of the context in which they arose. NEC had written microcode that made its chips compatible with the Intel 8086 and 8088. If the similarities between the two programs were excused on the grounds that they were necessary in order to achieve compatibility, the case would serve as support for the clones, a counterpoint to *Apple v. Franklin* and *Whelan v. Jaslow*. Indeed, some lawyers who represent clones have seized on the *Intel* case as evidence that the law is in conflict or that courts are retreating from the principle of full copyright protection for software.

Such conclusions are reflective of wishful thinking rather than rigorous legal analysis, since it is impossible to construct a rigorous legal analysis around Judge Gray's shorthand explanation of the evidence of copying presented by Intel and the defenses presented by NEC. This much can be said, however: NEC put its microprogrammer on the witness stand and subjected him to cross-examination by Intel, and the judge believed the young man's testimony that he did not undertake to copy the Intel microcode. Intel's evidence of copying was all inferential, and the judge found the inferences not strong enough to discredit that testimony, in large measure because of what the court found to be legitimized constraints on NEC's range of expressive choice in writing its microcode. Some of those constraints were imposed from "below," if you will, by the interface to the Intel chips. Those constraints from below were legitimized, Judge Gray said, by the license granted to NEC under Intel's patents to copy those chips. The other principal set of constraints, imposed from "above" the microcode, were represented by the instruction set of the Intel chips. Those constraints from above were legitimized, so far as the trial was concerned, because Intel did not challenge NEC's copying of the instruction set itself.

Both NEC's expert witness and Intel's expert witness testified that if the underlying hardware were the same, the range of expression available to the NEC microprogrammer would have been limited substantially. Intel sought to reduce the impact of that evidence by asserting that NEC could have used a different chip architecture and written different microcode that would still have implemented the Intel instruction set. The judge was unimpressed:

Having granted to NEC a license to duplicate the hardware of its 8086/88 to the extent comprehended by the Intel patents, and having conceded at trial that

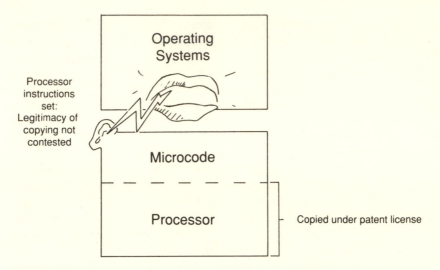

Processor
instructions
set:
Legitimacy of
copying not
contested

Operating
Systems

Microcode

Processor

Copied under patent license

NEC had a right to duplicate the hardware of the 8086/88 because it was not otherwise protected by Intel, Intel is in no position to challenge NEC's right to use the aspects of Intel's microcode that are mandated by such hardware.

He seems to be suggesting that it was not acceptable for Intel to sell the license with one hand and try to take away its economic benefit with the other hand.

Given what Judge Gray found to be the credibility of the NEC microcoder and the effect of the licensing arrangement, Intel's evidence of substantial similarity was not sufficient to raise an inference of copying. (In the end, NEC's other license to copy the Intel microcode in its uPD 8086 and uPD 8088 chips was not a factor here, because the judge found that that license did not extend to the V20 and V30 chips.) There were approximately ninety instructions in the Intel instruction set. For each instruction, there was a "microroutine" in the Intel microcode. Intel acknowledged that about forty of those microroutines were not substantially similar to NEC's microcode, and Judge Gray found that most of those nonsimilar blocks of code were longer than the blocks of code that Intel claimed to be infringing. Most of the shorter microroutines, some of which were only a few statements in length, involved what the court called "simple, straightforward operations in which close similarity is not surprising." NEC's case was further bolstered by a clever device, the use of which was made possible by the Intel license and trial concession: a "clean room" exercise. NEC submitted the Intel hardware specifications and instruction set to a microprogrammer who had never seen the Intel code, in an insulated environment, and asked that microcoder to create microcode for the NEC chips. The judge found the results of this exercise profound: "The similarities between the Clean Room microcode and [the accused NEC microcode] are at least as great as the similarities between the latter and the Intel microcode. . . . The strong likelihood follows that these similarities also resulted from the same constraints." In light of the constraints he felt to be operative, Judge Gray found that the expression in the shorter, simpler microroutines was protectable only against virtually identical copying, and concluded that "NEC properly used the underlying ideas, without virtually identically copying their limited expression."

Does the court's reasoning in this regard constitute an implicit rejection of *Apple v. Franklin*'s teaching that an accused infringer's compatibility objectives are irrelevant to the assessment of what is idea and what is expression in a computer program? Does *NEC v. Intel* constitute a rejection of *Whelan v. Jaslow*'s teaching that copyright protects against more than just line-by-line copying? Are Carl Alsing's rushes of creativity irrelevant to the protectability of microcode, or of other computer programs? Not at all. Where a case does not involve the copyright owner's legitimation of the constraints a compatible supplier imposes on itself, the *Intel* case is not an instructive precedent. We will see this in the litigation we examine in later chapters. It is also true, however, that neither the *Apple* case nor the *Whelan* case involved such legitimation, and of course the results in those cases were quite different from that in *NEC v. Intel*.

Even on its own terms, though, the *Intel* case stands as an affirmation of *Whelan* rather than a rejection of it. The best evidence of this is that, in analyzing the similarities in the two programs, Judge Gray quoted and sought to follow the admonition in the law review article out of which this book grew:

Where the accused work reflects an accumulation of similarities, the totality of the taking is to be considered: "When analyzing two works to determine whether they are substantially similar, courts should be careful not to lose sight of the forest for the trees." In programming infringement cases involving comprehensive nonliteral similarity, the "trees" are the individual lines of code, and the "forest" is the detailed design. [Citation omitted.]

By adopting the methodology recommended by my coauthors and me in that article, the judge affirmed that infringement can indeed occur in cases where there is no literal similarity, and also affirmed that the detailed design of a program, not just its literal text, is part of its protected expression. Further, he agreed with Intel that the test of infringement is "whether the work is recognized by an ordinary observer as having been taken from the copyrighted source." The "ordinary observer" test, a fundamental and long-standing technique for assessing copyright infringement, is a qualitative test that encompasses similarities of detailed structure, logic, and flow in literary works, not just similarities of individual words and sentences.

Some argue that the court's conclusion that the expression underlying the ideas of the short microroutines in Intel's microcode was protectable only against virtually identical copying indicates a more particularized definition of "idea" than *Whelan* would allow. According to this view, *Whelan* teaches that the ideas of a program are its purposes or functions and everything necessary to its purposes or functions, while *Intel* teaches that the ideas in a program include the ideas underlying each subroutine. The reasoning of that argument is too facile, however. It disregards the peculiar circumstances of the *Intel* case, in which the accused infringer was authorized or permitted by the copyright holder to copy elements of the program that constrained the expression available for the other elements asserted to be infringed. It also ignores the fact that the functions of the Intel microcode were in many cases represented in microroutines consisting of only a few statements, so that—in this particular computer program—there may have been an unusually close nexus between purpose or function and subroutine structure. Most particularly, though, it ignores the evidence that Judge Gray considered this very argument and recognized that *Whelan* was the precedent to be followed in this area:

Let us assume, for purposes of this discussion, that when Mr. Kaneko [the NEC microcoder] faced the task of writing these microsequences for Rev. O [an intermediate draft of the NEC microcode, in which the sequences to which Judge Gray referred were "very similar" to sequences in the Intel microcode] he sought to recall how Intel had handled this difficult problem, or even referred to his [*sic*] character string to make that determination. Let us also assume for purposes of this discussion that he directly copied what he learned into Rev. O. If he had stopped there and caused Rev. O to be the final microcode, a difficult question would arise as to whether what he had taken from the disassembled 8086/8088 constituted the technical "idea" for a solution or the "expression" thereof. *See* 17 U.S.C. Sec. 102(b); *Whelan Assoc. v. Jaslow Dental Laboratory*, 797 F. 2d 1222, 1234 (3d Cir. 1986).

Ultimately, Intel must be seen as consistent with both *Franklin* and *Whelan* both of which cases Judge Gray cites repeatedly.

There is one area that Judge Gray may not have analyzed correctly, however, and that is in assessing the importance of similarities between two microroutines in the Intel microcode and the corresponding microroutines in Rev. O ; similarities that did not appear in the final version of the NEC microcode. The judge held that evidence of the close similarities between the original and a draft of the accused work was irrelevant, since in the accused work itself the two microroutines had been changed so significantly as not to be substantially similar any longer. There are two weaknesses in this part of the opinion. First, the "substantial similarity" test is an inferential test of copying. The copyright owner may, and indeed should if possible, offer direct evidence of copying. Such evidence might be an admission by the alleged infringer, or it might be evidence of the process by which the alleged infringer created the accused work. The latter type of evidence is what Intel offered, in the form of excerpts from Rev. O. Though it may be true that the two subroutines were substantially changed from Rev. O to Rev. 2, the fact that they were so similar in the draft NEC code as to cause Judge Gray to concede "Of course these microroutines in Rev. O could have been copied" stands as evidence that the NEC microcode as a whole may have been produced by a process of copying. It may not have been sufficient direct evidence of copying to be conclusive in and of itself, but it certainly should not have been disregarded, particularly in a case where there were numerous other close similarities between the two programs, which similarities were sought to be excused on the basis of "constraints."

That leads to the second problem with this aspect of the *Intel* opinion. One cannot tell for certain, but it seems that Judge Gray may have been aware that the two microroutines in Rev. O were legitimate evidence of a process that entailed copying, and sought to meet that argument with a dubious parry. He cited authorities holding that "a defendant may legitimately avoid infringement by intentionally making sufficient changes in a work which would otherwise be regarded as substantially similar to "the original." What makes the parry dubious is that a development process that includes preparing a draft that is substantially similar to someone else's original is a process that contains an illegal step. The draft itself is an infringement. Some commentators have argued that such a draft should be considered to come within the "fair use" exception to infringement. The Copyright Act describes research as being a fair use of a copyrighted work, possibly permitted depending on a number of factors. Unfortunately for the supplier who prepares a draft that is substantially similar to an original program on his way to developing a final product, competitive use is almost never "fair use." Fair use is typically confined to the realms of higher learning, criticism, or parody.

Thus, Rev. O may in itself have constituted infringement and, again, in a context in which NEC was arguing that "The constraints made me do it," a development process based on producing an infringing work and then modifying it so as to disguise the similarities would seem a powerful counter to the assertions of constraint. The question of whether a programmer may lawfully write a program by marking up someone else's original work to the point where it is not substantially similar any longer is an interesting hypothetical question that lawyers and programmers can spend many happy hours debating. My advice is not to waste those hours, and not to develop programs that way.

13

Bright Lines and Gray Areas: The *Frybarger* Case

"But tell me, sir, is this book printed on your own account or have you sold the copyright to a bookseller?"

"I am printing it on my own account," replied the author, "and I expect to gain a thousand ducats at least from this first edition of two thousand copies. They will sell like hot cakes at six *reals* apiece."

"You are very good at figures," said Don Quixote, "but it is very clear that you do not know the tricks of the printing trade.... When you find yourself saddled with two thousand copies of a book you will find your back so sore that it will frighten you...."

"What then?" exclaimed the author. "Would you have me give it to a bookseller, who will pay me three farthings for the copyright and even think he's doing me a kindness by giving me that? I don't print my books to win fame in the world, for I am already known by my works. I want profit, for fame isn't worth a bean without it."

Miguel de Cervantes Saavedra, *Don Quixote* (1615)

If a person writes a play and another person copies the play without authorization and markets it as his or her own, we generally feel that the first person has been wronged. There may be some cultures in the world where no sympathy whatever is engendered by the original author's plight, but in the developed world the reaction of informed citizens will be that a property right has been violated. Conversely, if the second person sees a performance of the original play, learns from it various writing techniques and ideas about character and plot development, and uses those techniques and ideas, along with other techniques and ideas, in writing plays of his or her own, our sense of propriety and justice is not offended. As we have seen, the copyright laws embody this moral precept in terms of the idea-expression dichotomy, with the social and economic consequences that flow from it. In the statement of that precept in the first sentence of this paragraph, there is little question that if we substitute the word "program" for the word "play," the reaction of informed people would be no different. The question we are now closing in on is whether there are policy reasons why the traditional moral line between protected expression and unprotected idea should be drawn differently for software than it is for other literary works of equivalent creative content.

I've been fairly harsh on the "narrow protectionists" to this point because they have behaved irrationally, like Luddites smashing machinery. In order to achieve the outcome they desired, they have misrepresented the nature of program authorship, and have falsely analogized the writing of programs to the compilation of maps, telephone directories, and other types of works in which imagination plays little part. However, we are now past that point. We must now ask ourselves whether, despite the fact that programs are works of imagination, there are overriding policy reasons for limiting the protection that the law would normally provide for such works. In copyright lingo, what we are asking is whether the line between idea and expression should be drawn closer to the literal text of a program than it is for other kinds of literary works for which the range of potential expression is similarly broad.

We will have reference to two paradigmatic examples as we consider this question. The first example concerns translation. The second involves cloning. Both examples are based on the same assumed set of facts. Assume, as the law professors say, that Federated Computers, Inc. (FCI), writes a new program for its line of computers. Assume further that the new program is an instant success and materially advances the sales of FCI's computers. Posit a second computer company, Consolidated Computers, which offers a competing line of systems.

In our first hypothetical example, Consolidated translates the new FCI program into a language understood by Consolidated's systems and offers the translation commercially, thereby increasing the competitiveness of Consolidated's computers against FCI's. Because of differences between the language in which FCI's original program was written and the language understood by Consolidated's computers, slavish line-by-line translation is not possible, but the translation is as effective as, say, Richmond Lattimore's translation of Homer's *Iliad*, although like the latter translation it bears little immediate visual resemblance to the original. Should Consolidated be held to have infringed FCI's copyright?

In our second example, Consolidated adopts a more sophisticated product development strategy aimed at accomplishing the same end. Its programmers write a program that offers the same functions, the same user interfaces, and the same programming interfaces as the FCI program, but other than as necessary to achieve those ends, Consolidated's program is not similar. This "compatible program" is offered commercially and increases Consolidated's competitiveness vis-à-vis FCI. In this second case, should Consolidated be branded an infringer?

One policy reason advanced in favor of drawing the protectability line, for programs, at the literal text of the work—and therefore answering both of the above questions in the negative—is that any other line would be too difficult to administer. To deal with that argument, we need to retread somewhat more carefully the ground that was covered by the Court of Appeals in *Whelan*. Specifically, just as Judge Becker did, we need to consider the process by which an original program is written so that we can tell whether or not there is a reasonable frame of reference for administering the traditional idea-expression dichotomy in the case of software.

At the risk of compartmentalizing too rigidly what is usually an iterative and flexible process, we may characterize the writing of a new program as being likely to comprise in some way or other the following phases:

Product definition, in which a general idea is developed of what the program should be able to do. For a commercial program, customer requirements and competitive capabilities inform this determination.

Generalized or high-level design, in which the general statement of the program's performance objectives is translated into a plan for writing the program. Here, the overall job the program is to accomplish may be broken down into separate components to make the task of programming more manageable.

Intermediate design, in which the components defined in the high-level design are elaborated in more detail, resulting in definition of the major structures of the program. Here, individual module structures and data structures are identified, and the information that will be passed from component to component within the program is specified.

Detailed design, in which the program's design is articulated into codable units (e.g., subroutines, macros, and individual data areas). At the end of this phase, the design of the program will be so detailed that the starting point for each codable unit is defined with sufficient particularity to allow the assignment of codable units in parallel to different programmers—if the size and schedule of the project warrant it—with reasonable confidence that the pieces will work together when they are brought together after coding. The detailed design of the program may be documented in the form of "pseudocode" (a programming language–like shorthand) or flow charts that fully define in human-readable terms what the code of each unit will accomplish. Detailed design documents constitute a complete articulation of the program in English or in symbolic language.

Coding, in which the English or symbolic representation of the program contained in the detailed design documents is translated into a specific programming language. As the Court of Appeals in *Whelan* noted, this part of the process can often be routinely entrusted to a beginning programmer.

In the real world, of course, the process of writing programs is often less rigid and less linear than the above parsing would suggest. Some of the steps may be collapsed into one another; some may recur; some may at times be implicit rather than explicit. In addition we have not described the testing or documentation phases mentioned by the *Whelan* court, as they do little to inform the present inquiry. Nonetheless, our brief outline of the program-writing process is sufficient to teach us that the detailed design of a program, being the equivalent of a paragraph-by-paragraph outline of a novel, is a complete expression of the program, an expression of which the actual coded text is fundamentally a translation.

That is not to say that the earlier phases of the process do not contribute to the expression of the program; they do. However, just as copying no more than the chapter organization of a book will not normally constitute infringement, copying the high-level design, and only the high-level design, of a program should not normally constitute infringement. In the *Whelan* example, it was not the mere fact that both programs had an invoicing routine and a month-end routine that was taken as evidence of infringement, but the fact that both routines in both programs were implemented in the same way.

On the other hand, copying the detailed design of a program should clearly constitute infringement. In *Whelan*, the comparison of the detailed designs of the two order entry routines shows sufficient similarity in flow, structure, and naming conventions to permit an inference of copying of expression. (Remember, though, that had the Jaslows been able to prove those detailed design similarities to be necessary to achieving the purpose of order entry, then even the detailed design of that module would not have been protected.)

Where the line may be fuzzy is at the level of intermediate design. Here, what may be idea and what expression may be difficult to determine. Further, the instances of "necessary" expression are likely to be higher in the intermediate design of a program than in the detailed design. That the line may be fuzzy, though, doesn't mean that the test is unadministerable. Like many tests that judges deal with every day, there are boundaries that are sharply defined and gray areas in between where the facts of the particular case may make a large difference. The *Whelan* court's ruling that where a structural or organizational element is essential to the achievement of the result that the program accomplishes, then that element may be idea and not expression, was its way of cutting a path through the gray area. That rule gives us one significant guidepost; the judiciary will certainly develop others. Thus, although the gray area will always be gray, since it is and has always been in the nature of the idea-expression dichotomy to be highly dependent on the facts of a particular dispute, deciding software cases in the gray area is no less administerable than deciding gray-area cases concerning other kinds of copyrighted works. Indeed, given the semblance of discipline in the program-writing process, the gray area may be smaller and picking one's way through it may be easier than it is for other works.

Which brings to mind the case of *Tricky Trapper v. Mouser*, more formally styled *Anthony James Frybarger v. International Business Machines Corporation, Gebelli Software, Inc. and Nasir Gebelli*. In *Frybarger*, the Court of Appeals for the Ninth Circuit found itself in the dread gray area, charged with describing the difference between idea and expression in an entertainment program—a program that caused a personal computer to behave like an arcade game machine.

The name Nasir Gebelli is legendary in computer game circles. It is safe to say that almost anyone who meets both of the following qualifications: (1) has owned an Apple II, and (2) can read, knows who Nasir Gebelli is. His exotic name appeared on the logo screen of numerous early games for the Apple II, lending an air of underground collectibility to his works. In the summer of 1982, Gebelli had occasion to review the design drawings and flow charts for a game program called Tricky Trapper developed by Frybarger, then one of Gebelli's employees. He later received a copy of the program itself, with comments, but did not choose to market it. During this period, Gebelli was widening his horizons to include the IBM PC, and entered into an agreement with IBM to produce three computer games for the PC, one of which was called Mouser. Mouser was produced by Gebelli and distributed by IBM in 1983. Frybarger, having fallen out with Gebelli, and finding a certain correspondence between Mouser and Tricky Trapper, sued Gebelli, Gebelli's company, and IBM in the Federal District Court for the Eastern District of California for infringing the copyright in Tricky Trapper.

IBM promptly moved for summary judgment of noninfringement. After Judge Milton Schwartz had viewed videotapes of the two games in operation as well as videotapes of four other computer games, had examined color photographs of the visual displays of the two games, and had read the affidavits of the several experts offered by each side, he granted IBM's motion, concluding as a matter of law that no reasonable jury could find that Mouser was substantially similar to Tricky Trapper. The ruling was extended to Gebelli and his company, thereby making Frybarger's loss complete, and he appealed.

Both Tricky Trapper and Mouser are chase games. In the visual displays of each, there is a protagonist with whom the player is expected to identify, who negotiates a maze to escape multiple antagonists. The walls of the maze in both games consist of line segments mounted on pivot points; the protagonist can reshape the maze by swinging wall segments on their pivot points and—after developing a certain proficiency at the game—can trap antagonists, thereby escaping capture.

For purposes of IBM's summary judgment motion, and therefore for purposes of the appeal, the defendants had conceded that Frybarger owned a valid copyright in Tricky Trapper, and that Gebelli had had access to Tricky Trapper before writing Mouser. The only issue for the appellate court to decide, therefore, was whether Judge Schwartz had correctly concluded that there was insufficient similarity in the expression of the two programs for the case to go to a jury.

The panel of the Court of Appeals for the Ninth Circuit reviewed the evidence, including the videotapes. In an opinion written by Judge Dorothy Nelson, it concluded that the decision turned on the difference between the ideas in Tricky Trapper's user interface (i.e., the play of the game) and the expression in that interface. Frybarger had to show substantial similarity in both ideas and expression, but to the extent that the only similarities demonstrated were similarities in ideas, he had not made out a case. Judge Nelson wrote:

Those features of Frybarger's work that are ideas are not protected . . . against even directly copied identical ideas in Gebelli's works. Thus, to the extent that the similarities between Frybarger's and Gebelli's works are confined to ideas and general concepts, these similarities are noninfringing.

The court reviewed all the similarities it could find between the user interfaces of the two programs. Its list was as follows:

1. The display screen of each game is filled with straight rows of pivot points on a solid colored background.

2. Between some of the pivot points are solid lines, connecting two pivot points.

3. There is a single protagonist.

4. The single protagonist has legs and a face.

5. The single protagonist moves vertically and horizontally between rows of pivot points.

6. The single protagonist may cause one end of a line to come unattached from one pivot point and attach to a different pivot point by bumping into the line as the protagonist moves between rows of pivot points.

7. There is more than one antagonist.

8. Each antagonist moves toward the general location of the protagonist.

9. If an antagonist bumps the protagonist, the progress of play stops.

10. An antagonist will be immobilized if it is surrounded on three sides by lines and the protagonist bumps a line across the fourth side, closing off the only remaining avenue of exit.

11. The player may obtain points by causing the protagonist to elude and "trap" antagonists.

12. The speed at which the protagonist and antagonists move increases as the game progresses.

The Court of Appeals concluded that each of these similar features represented a basic idea of the two games, and that to the extent that such features were expressive, the expression in them was, as a practical matter, indispensable or standard in the treatment of the particular idea. The notion of "indispensable" expression derives from the so-called *scenes à faire* doctrine, under which stock circumstances or transitions in plays, movies, novels, or the like are commonly susceptible of expression only in terms that are going to be inherently similar. ("The outlaw drew his gun. 'Stick 'em up,' he growled.") Such circumstances or transitions have been left explicitly unprotected, Judge Nelson observed, in order to encourage their individual expression in original works of authorship.

In an echo of the *Whelan* language to the effect that structural similarities essential to the purpose of a program may not be protected by copyright, the Court ruled that

the mere indispensable expression of these ideas, based on the technical requirements of the videogame medium, may be protected only against virtually identical copying. . . . Indispensable expression is accorded only this slight protection because it is so close to the nonprotectible idea itself that "the expression provides nothing new or additional over the idea."

Since the "indispensable expression" in the twelve listed features of Mouser was not "virtually identical" to that in Tricky Trapper, since the twelve features were in themselves ideas, not expression, and since there were no other similarities between the two games, the Court of Appeals agreed with Judge Schwartz. This was not an infringement situation. More recently, the same approach used in *Frybarger* was used in analyzing similarities between screen displays in two computer karate games. In *Data East v. Epyx*, the defendant was held by the trial court to have infringed the plantiff's copyright in visual displays. On appeal, the decision was reversed. The Court of Appeals undertook its own review of the two games, including their modes of play. Despite finding similarities not only in the overall idea of a computer game based on karate (analogous, in the *Whelan* context, to the overall idea of auto-

mating dental laboratory accounting) but in at least fifteen specific elements of the two games, ranging from colors of uniforms and scoring
methodologies to the changing of geographic backgrounds for succeeding rounds of play, the Court of Appeals held that there was no substantial similarity in expression beyond the similarities inherent in the
game of karate itself. That holding is completely consistent with the
Whelan rule that expression necessary to the purpose or function of a
program is not protectable.

Frybarger and *Data East* are examples of judicial parsing of the idea-
expression dichotomy that I have put forward to help the reader appreciate that this principle is the basis for an adequately administrable,
if highly fact-dependent, rule in software cases. These cases also demonstrate that the administration of the idea-expression dichotomy will
produce results that are reasonable and need not result in overprotection
of authors of original programs. Arguments to the contrary are not well-
founded.

What can we say, then, about the two examples propounded earlier
in this chapter? In the first of those, translation, clearly entails close
conformance to the detailed design of the original work. This is not a
gray-area question—it is clearly infringement under the traditional copyright rule. Questions of administrability of that rule do not therefore
arise in our first example.

As to the second example, we cannot yet assess the administrability
of the traditional rule. That is because, as clearly as the example seemed
to be stated, it was riddled with ambiguity. There is no fixed boundary
to compatibility, and there is no definition of what is "necessary" to be
copied in order to achieve compatibility within any particular arbitrary
boundary. Even so, traditional copyright law provides a number of useful principles, and as we examine them in succeeding chapters, we shall
see that courts have provided ample guidance through the factual thicket
in cases involving software clones.

Let's move on, then, to consider the other policy issues relating to
copyright law as applied to computer programs.

14

The "Dissemination" Argument: *Broderbund v. Unison World*

I think that the judges themselves have failed adequately to recognize their duty of weighing considerations of social advantage. The duty is inevitable, and the result of the often proclaimed judicial aversion to deal with such considerations is simply to leave the very ground and foundation of judgments inarticulate, and often unconscious. . . . I cannot but believe that if the training of lawyers led [judges] habitually to consider more definitely and explicitly the social advantage on which the rule they lay down must be justified, they sometimes would hesitate where they now are confident, and see that really they were taking sides upon debatable and often burning questions.

Oliver Wendell Holmes, Jr.,
"The Path of the Law," *Harvard Law Review*, 1897

The judiciary is rather more conscious today than it was in Holmes's time that the effect of their decisions on the social order of the country should be taken into account in formulating those decisions. In addition to trying to sort out right from wrong as between the feuding parties before them, judges try to use language in their opinions that will clearly articulate right from wrong so that others will not find themselves feuding over the same legal issues in the future. The reason that judicial decisions affect the social order is that they are written and published and, in common law countries like the United States and the U.K., at least, serve as precedent for later judicial decisions. By way of contrast, arbitration rarely has any significant effect on the social order, because arbitrators' decisions are normally not published (in fact, arbitrators hardly ever write opinions at all), and their decisions are binding only on the parties to the arbitration. In the *Apple v. Franklin* and *Whelan v. Jaslow* opinions, we find language explicitly recognizing that the courts were deciding matters of social advantage, not just resolving private disputes. Thus, Judge Becker in *Whelan:*

Precisely because the line between idea and expression is elusive, we must pay particular attention to the pragmatic considerations that underlie that distinction and copyright law generally. In this regard, we must remember that the purpose of the copyright law is to create the most efficient and productive balance between protection (incentive) and dissemination of information, to promote learning, culture and development.

In both *Whelan v. Jaslow* and *Apple v. Franklin,* the courts felt that the social advantage belonged to the copyright owner.

One of the arguments against extending full copyright protection to computer programs, however, avers that the copyright law is for the benefit of the public, not the author, and such rights and privileges as are granted to authors must always be subordinated to the public interest. In the case of software, it is said, the public interest includes the interests of competitors in the relatively free appropriation of others' work, in order that there may be a rapid proliferation of equivalent programs. That argument is, at present writing, being strenuously advanced in Japan, where the debate over the scope of copyright protection for software is front-page news, due in part to the IBM-Fujitsu dispute, to which we are coming shortly, and due in part to the commonly—and somewhat unfairly—held view, even in Japan, that the Japanese are poor programmers and can only advance their domestic computer industry if Japanese computer suppliers are relatively free to appropriate the contents of software written in the United States and elsewhere.

The same argument was also advanced by Rand Jaslow and his codefendants in their unsuccessful petition for certiorari before the Supreme Court, and by others held to have infringed software copyrights. It is not an argument that falls with grace from the lips of persons so situated, however, because of their intense personal interests in avoiding liability.

The "public interest" argument is also advanced in certain academic circles in the United States, by persons whom one would expect to be more dispassionate than copyright defendants. In one formulation, advanced by Pamela Samuelson among others, the academic argument asserts that the purpose of the copyright grant is to promote dissemination of ideas, and that since the texts of computer programs are unintelligible to most people, full protection for those texts does not further the purpose of the law.

There are several crucial factors that the Samuelson argument intentionally or inadvertently ignores. Firstly, it ignores the fact that computer programs, while unintelligible to most, are intelligible to many. The author has sat awestruck in the presence of software writers who were able to read even the seemingly incomprehensible strings of ones and zeros in an object code dump of a program. The numbers of such persons are assuredly not large. However, the numbers of persons who can read Esperanto are not large either, and the law does not for that reason provide less than full protection for works of imagination written in Esperanto. The fact that it requires a certain competence to read a computer program with appreciation merely puts computer programs in company with foreign language texts and other specialized literature: the ideas in them are not unintelligible; they simply do not yield themselves up to those untrained in the language in which the ideas are expressed.

Second, and far more important, all those competitors who are so eager to benefit the public by writing "equivalent programs" would have nothing to be equivalent to if there were not sufficient incentive for authors of original programs to publish their works in the first place. It is a cheap trick, but a legitimate cheap trick, to ask, for example, where Rand Jaslow would have been without Elaine Whelan. Obviously there would have been no Dentcom program at all without Dentalab. Now turn the question around. What if Elaine Whelan had been told before she wrote Dentalab that Rand Jaslow could freely create a competitive program with the same data structures, data flow, logic flow, and user interfaces. Would she have invested the time and modest resources of her company in the development of the structures, flows, logic, and user interfaces of Dentalab? Now increase the scope and scale of the question: would the world's suppliers of original software have invested the billions of dollars that to date have been poured into the writing of programs for profit if they had believed that those programs could not be protected against translation or close paraphrasing by others? Because the cost of paraphrasing (i.e., developing a program by copying the structure, logic, and flow of someone else's program) is so much less than the cost of starting from scratch, and the schedule is so much shorter, the answer is "No." The innovator's economic calculus, discussed in Chapter 2, comes up with red ink. The investment will not promise to produce a return justified by the risk of making it, because "knock-off" products can quickly reach the market. Returning to our analogy to Bertolucci's *The Last Emperor*, is there any question that the producers of that film would have withheld the several tens of millions of dollars that went into its making if the rule as to movies was that the structure, logic, and flow of Bertolucci's interpretation of the life of the last Chinese emperor could freely be copied by any other filmmaker?

The concern is no different for software. Permitting paraphrasing or translation would eliminate the competitive lead time that is a major incentive for investment in new programs.

The question that must be asked of the free appropriationists is what is meant by "equivalent." If what is meant is a program that achieves the same purposes as an original program, then only extremists in favor of broad protection would say the copyright law should prevent "equivalence." No such rule is necessary to protect the original investment, and there is certainly no indication that the copyright law is moving toward that level of protection. If, on the other hand, "equivalent" means identical in text or in detailed design, then the incentive to innovate is substantially removed by the proposed limitation on copyright protection.

Public interest considerations relating to investment incentives were of dominant importance to the Court of Appeals for the Seventh Circuit in the case of *Atari, Inc. v. North American Philips Consumer Electronics Corp.*, in which Philips was preliminarily found likely to have infringed the copyright in Atari's PAC-MAN game, not by literal copying but by copying elements of the structure (i.e., the appearance of the "gobbler" and "ghost" characters) and the flow (i.e., the roles of those characters in the play of the game) of the PAC-MAN user interface. In assessing the effect of allowing Philips to continue marketing its K. C. Munchkin game just during the period between this preliminary finding and the full trial, Judge Harlington Wood, Jr., gave the following analysis:

By marketing K. C. Munchkin, North American jeopardized the substantial investments of Midway [the owner of rights to the arcade version of PAC-MAN] and especially Atari [owner of rights to the home version of PAC-MAN]. The short-lived nature of video games further underscores the need for a preliminary injunction. . . . Moreover, the Atari and Odyssey game cartridges are not interchangeable. To play K. C. Munchkin, the purchaser must also buy North American's ODYSSEY[2] game console. The impact of North American's infringement therefore extends even beyond the PAC-MAN game to the whole Atari system.

The balance of hardships and public interest factors do not weigh against the entry of a preliminary injunction. North American's only alleged hardship is the profits it would lose if enjoined from marketing K. C. Munchkin. This argument, however, "merits little equitable consideration." . . . "Advantages built upon a deliberately plagiarized make-up do not seem to give the borrower any standing to complain that his vested interests will be disturbed." . . . This is also not a case in which the plaintiffs' harm would be *de minimis* in comparison to that of the defendants. Finally, a preliminary injunction is necessary to preserve the integrity of the copyright laws which seek to encourage individual effort and creativity by granting valuable enforceable rights. . . . Defendants point to no competing public interest that would be harmed. [Citations omitted.]

Thus investment even in a program the social value of which has been the subject of considerable debate is to be preferred over investment in a close and unauthorized derivative of that program.

A final problem with the "dissemination" argument is that it is simply not true that the purpose of the copyright grant is to promote dissemination of ideas. The purpose of the copyright grant (at least in the United States, as the reader will recall from the historical discussion that opened our inquiry) is explicitly stated in the constitutional clause from which the copyright law springs: "to promote the Progress of Science and the useful Arts." While it may be that one means of achieving that purpose is to arrange for the dissemination of ideas, that is by no means the only means. In particular, it was not the means sanctioned by the Founding Fathers. Rather, the means sanctioned by the Founding Fathers, and the only means permitted to be enacted into law by Congress, was to grant exclusive rights for limited times to authors. Explaining the basis of the exclusive grant, James Madison wrote, "The public good fully coincides in both cases [i.e., copyrights and also patents] with the claims of individuals." The Framers had decided that the purpose of promoting progress in science and the useful arts would best be achieved by allowing authors to control public use of their writings. That decision reflects a judgment that dissemination of ideas, as well as other indicia of "progress," will occur in most desirable fashion if authors as a class are able to pursue their self-interests. In particular, free dissemination would only occur under the constitutional scheme after the "limited time" of the exclusive copyrights had expired.

The academics who propose that, as to software, copyright coverage should reflect only a purpose to disseminate ideas, are thus ignoring the fact that their proposals would require a constitutional amendment. "Dissemination" is not a principle that flows naturally from the grant of "exclusive rights," rather it is an unbounded deprivation of exclusivity. At its limit, a law based solely on the principle of dissemination would encourage piracy, and that is certainly not what the Framers handed down to us.

Those academics are also ignoring the fact that the copyright law simply does not require dissemination of the copyrighted work, whether it is a program or any other form of literary work. Copyright attaches as soon as the work is fixed in a tangible medium of expression, whether or not the work is ever published. (That is why the author J. D. Salinger was able to sue the publisher Random House in copyright to prevent the publication of his private letters.) Copyright also attaches even if the work is never registered and deposited with the Copyright Office. Indeed, even for programs that are registered and deposited, the Copyright Office permits deposit of as little as the first twenty-five and last twenty-five pages of the program, which in most cases is substantially

less than complete dissemination. Moreover, Copyright Office procedures allow for registration by deposit of identifying materials only, in
appropriate cases, so the registered work itself need never be available
for public inspection. It is manifest that dissemination is not the purpose
of the copyright law; rather, it is but one of the anticipated consequences
of that law.

In sum, one must view with considerable skepticism the appeals to a
"public dissemination interest" in "equivalent programs" as an excuse—
not for the independent writing of competing programs—but for access
to and copying of the detailed design of an original program. Fortified
with that skepticism, let's examine the first progenitor of the look and
feel cases.

In the summer of 1983, David Balsam and Martin Kahn brought a
quirky program they had developed to Broderbund Software, Inc., a
California software house specializing in personal computer programs,
in the hope that Broderbund would market it for them. The program
created greeting cards on diskette. The idea was that people would send
diskettes to one another through the mail, exchanging birthday, sea-
sonal, and other greetings with one another via their computer screens.

Broderbund's reaction was that the program would, to put it charit-
ably, appeal to only a limited audience. Broderbund recommended that
Balsam and Kahn rewrite their program so that it would prepare printed
greeting cards and other graphic documents such as signs. In exchange
for an exclusive marketing license, Broderbund worked with Balsam and
Kahn for almost a year to redevelop the program, which it began marketing as "Print Shop" for Apple computers in May, 1984.

In that same month, the president of Broderbund met the president
of a company called Unison World, Inc., Mr. Hong Lu. Unison had
made a business of converting programs from one machine environment
to another. Unison rarely, if ever, developed programs of its own, but
rather adapted programs written by others so that they would run successfully on computers other than those for which they were designed.
In the discussions that resulted from that meeting, Unison made it clear
that it was interested in creating a version of Print Shop for the IBM PC,
a project that Broderbund had not only contemplated but had even
attempted itself, thus far without success. Lu claimed that Unison could
produce an IBM version of Print Shop in three months, an assertion that
Broderbund greeted with substantial doubt as a result of its own diffi-
culties with the same project.

Broderbund told the Unison personnel that if the IBM rights to Print
Shop were to be licensed, it would only be for development of an exact
reproduction of the original work. Accepting the challenge, Unison personnel went to visit Balsam and Kahn to verify that a faithful reproduction could be developed in three months. Balsam showed a Unison
programmer, MacDuff Hughes, the source code for Print Shop, and

gave Unison several copies of Print Shop diskettes to show to Japanese software producers with whom Unison might subcontract the development work.

For the next four to six weeks, Hughes worked incessantly to develop an IBM PC version of Print Shop. He met from time to time with Balsam and Kahn to discuss his progress. His orders from Lu were to recreate Print Shop as closely as possible, which would have been fine had the license from Broderbund been consummated.

Unfortunately, that's not what happened. Negotiations for the license broke down while Hughes was in mid-project. Unison wanted a larger advance payment against future royalties than Broderbund was willing to offer, and the parties stopped talking. Hughes did not stop working, however. Instead, under instructions from Lu, he continued to develop a graphic printing program. Although he was told to stop copying Print Shop, he was not told to remove whatever copying he had already done. Instead, he was directed to enhance the product, incorporating such improvements as he could, but finishing the project as soon as possible. Truth be told, Hong Lu had intended from the outset that Unison would develop an enhanced version of Print Shop, whether licensed by Broderbund or not.

In a hurry both to finish the project and get back to Stanford University where he was a math student, Hughes retained what he had already copied, which comprised a generous portion of the Print Shop screen interface. The copied screens included the menu screens from which users selected the functions to be performed, plus another ten screens from the specific "greeting card" and "sign" functions, and the "picture editor" screen interface. As to the latter, Hughes had had a totally different idea for a picture editor interface, but used the Print Shop interface because it was much further along. Once Hughes was finished, other Unison programmers added new functionality and enhanced usability features, but otherwise did not change what Hughes had done. The Unison program was released as Printmaster in March, 1985. Broderbund's lawsuit was filed two months later.

The suit alleged audiovisual copyright infringement, textual copyright infringement, trademark infringement, and unfair competition. It was assigned to District Judge William Orrick, who separated the case into pieces and took the liability portion of the audiovisual copyright claim to trial first. The facts of the case as found by Judge Orrick are substantially as stated above, so the reader need not suffer any suspense as to whom the judge favored in his decision. It's not so much the result that should interest us, but the reasoning.

The first question Judge Orrick had to ponder was whether screen interfaces to computer programs are protected by copyright. The reader might wonder why there was such a question at all; why the judge could not take as a first principle that the screen displays of a program are protectable by copyright. The practical answer is that, since the defendant had clearly copied the screen displays, his lawyers had nowhere else to run for an argument. Their argument was framed in terms of what has now become an old chestnut for us: merger of idea and expression. Unison argued that the Print Shop screens expressed nothing different from the idea that underlay them. They contended that any menu-driven program for printing cards, signs, and the like would have screen interfaces substantially similar to Print Shop's, because there is no other conceivable way of structuring such a program.

That was a reasonably risky argument. To deflate it completely, all Broderbund had to do was to demonstrate the existence of another functionally similar program with screen interfaces that weren't substantially similar to Print Shop. Not surprisingly, Balsam, Kahn, and Broderbund were not the only people in the world to have come up with the idea of a printer program. Broderbund put before Judge Orrick a program with the cheerful name Stickybear Printer. After examining it, Judge Orrick concluded that while the functions of Stickybear Printer were substantially the same as those of Print Shop, its screen interfaces were not at all substantially similar. Therefore, he reasoned, there were multiple and quite different ways of expressing the ideas in Print Shop, and there was no merger.

The defendant argued, however, that the screen interface was nothing other than a structured sequence of layouts, the very type of thing held by Judge Higginbotham to be unprotected by copyright in *Synercom*. (Plaintiffs argued, on the other hand, that the structured sequence of screen layouts in a user interface are protected for the same reason that *Whelan* held nonliteral aspects of a program to be protected.) Judge Orrick agreed that the input formats at issue in *Synercom* served essentially the same purpose as the menu screens in Print Shop: They told the user what type of data to enter, where to place it, and how to enter it. He agreed that Synercom had argued unsuccessfully for the protectability of the "sequencing and organization" of the formats. He accepted that Judge Higginbotham (also a trial judge at the time of *Synercom*, but in a different Federal Circuit, and therefore not necessarily a judge whose opinion Judge Orrick had to treat as binding precedent) had held that there was a merger of idea and expression in the input formats, and that therefore they could be freely copied.

Judge Orrick was simply not persuaded to Judge Higginbotham's view, however. Instead, "[n]otwithstanding Judge Higginbotham's excellent opinion in *Synercom*," he wrote, "this Court is persuaded by the reasoning of *Whelan*." He agreed with the *Whelan* court (the first and, at the time, the only appellate court to consider the question) that the ideas in a computer program are its purposes and functionality. The idea of Print Shop, accordingly, was the creation of greeting cards, banners, posters, and signs that contain infinitely variable combinations of text, graphics, and borders.

A rival software publisher is completely free to market a program with the same underlying idea, but must express it through a substantially different structure. . . . Applied to the facts of the present case, *Whelan* compels the rejection of defendant's argument that the overall structure, sequencing and arrangement of screens in Print Shop fall outside the ambit of copyright.

In so deciding, Judge Orrick rejected two further arguments advanced by Unison. One was that the screens were purely utilitarian, and copyright does not protect utilitarian pictorial or graphic works. The other was that the screens were simply "rules and instructions," and the copyright law does not protect rules and instructions. The court swept aside both arguments on the grounds that the screens contained artistic and aesthetic elements, and therefore were not just utilitarian or instructional.

In the present case, it is clear that the structure, sequence, and layout of the audiovisual displays in "Print Shop" were dictated primarily by artistic and aesthetic considerations, and not by utilitarian or mechanical ones. Repeatedly, the testimony of David Balsam showed that, in creating the screens of "Print Shop," he based textual and graphic decisions on the basis of aesthetic and artistic preferences. On the "Now Type Your Message" screen of "Print Shop," for instance, no mechanical or practical constraint forced Balsam to make the "Stencil" typeface smaller on the display than the "Alexia" typeface. The choice was purely arbitrary. On the "Choose a Font" screen, no mechanical or practical factor compelled Balsam to use those exact words. He could have written "Select a Font," or "Indicate a Typeface Preference," "Which Typestyle Do You Prefer," or any combination of those terms. Another example is the "Magic Screen" function—Balsam considered calling this "See Animation." He could have called it "Kaleidoscope." The bottom line is that the designer of any program that performs the same functions as "Print Shop" had available a wide range of expression governed predominantly by artistic and not utilitarian considerations.

As to the "rules and instructions" argument, the judge merely observed that it applies only in cases where the idea can be expressed in only a limited number of ways, so that affording a copyright on rules or instructions would be tantamount to protecting a game or process itself. Here, he had already found that there were many ways to express the ideas in Print Shop.

The legal issues under his belt, Judge Orrick went on to consider whether Unison had in fact copied the structure, sequence, and layout of Print Shop's user interface. He of course found that they had. In order to nail the point home, he took the unusual and completely unnecessary step of finding both that there was sufficient direct evidence of Unison's copying efforts to hold them accountable, and sufficient circumstantial evidence (access plus substantial similarity) to find them liable. He found worthy of mention the following example:

In the "Custom Layout" screen of "Print Shop," the user is instructed to press the "Return" key on the Apple keyboard. Similarly, in the "Custom Layout" screen of "Printmaster," the user is instructed to press the "Return" key on the IBM keyboard. Actually, the IBM keyboard contains no "Return" key, only an "Enter" key. Lodge [a Unison official] admitted that Unison's failure to change "Return" to "Enter" was a result of its programmers' intense concentration on copying "Print Shop."

As in *Whelan*, although there seems to be no question that Judge Orrick reached the correct result based on the case before him, some have expressed the view that in doing so he used language that defines the idea in a program too narrowly. Frankly, it is difficult to see how he could have defined Print Shop's idea more broadly and still have reached a sustainable result. Implicit in his decision is the notion that it was not improper for Printmaster to have screens that performed the same functions as Print Shop's "Now Type Your Message," "Select a Font," "Magic Screen," and "Custom Design" screens (and, presumably, others as well), so long as the structure, sequencing, and layout of the entire suite of Printmaster screens and each individual screen was independently developed. The identification of individual screens to particular functions of a program is an element of intermediate design. In effect, the judge was deciding that in the gray area it was acceptable for "equivalent programs" to have copied Broderbund's design, but that Unison had stepped beyond the gray area and copied the detailed design of Print Shop. This can be said to be a reasonably balanced determination, in the sense that it should make both followers and innovators equally unhappy. While it may have been appropriate in the case of Print Shop to hold, by implication, that the decision which screens to include in the program was part of (or necessary to) the idea of the program, however, the same will clearly not be true for all programs. Where the decision as to what screen displays there should be in a program is an assertion of creativity or imagination rather than necessity, we would expect a rule that would not stifle the efforts of the original author.

For completeness' sake, I should mention a side issue in *Broderbund* that is a matter of unsettled law. One of the ancillary determinations that Judge Orrick made on his way to deciding for the plaintiff was that a computer program's display screens are protected by the copyright in the program. No separate audiovisual copyright need be obtained for the screens. In a later case protecting a screen interface from copying, *Digital Communications Associates, Inc. v. Softklone Distributing Corp.*, the court declined to follow Judge Orrick's ruling in that regard, and held instead that a separate audiovisual copyright must be registered for the screens in order to sue for infringement of them. The Copyright Office, aghast at the thought of the flood of applications for audiovisual registrations that it would face under the *Softklone* rule, has adopted the position that, not only are the screens protected by the copyright in the program, as Judge Orrick decided, but the office will simply not accept separate applications for display screens. The Copyright Office's views of the law are not at all binding on the courts, but given that office's new procedure, one can only hope that the *Broderbund* rule and not the *Softklone* rule will prevail. Otherwise, program authors will face a Catch–22 worthy of Bogdasarian: In order to sue for infringement of display screens, they must prove that they have registered a copyright in the screens, not just in the program, but the Copyright Office will not register copyrights in the screens because it believes the screens are protected by the copyright in the program.

15

Clean Rooms and Fright Wigs: The *Plains Cotton* Case and Some Principles for Software Clones

Property is founded upon occupancy. But how is possession to be taken, or any act of occupancy to be asserted, on mere intellectual ideas? . . . The occupancy of a thought would be a new kind of occupancy indeed.

Opinion of Justice Yates in *Millar v. Taylor*,
4 Burr. 2303, 2357 [King's Bench 1769]

There was one respect in which Judge Orrick did not felicitously state the law in his *Broderbund* opinion. It was something of an oversimplification for him to say, "A rival software publisher is completely free to market a program with the same underlying idea [as Print Shop], but must express it through a substantially different structure." A more accurate statement of the law would be, "A rival software publisher is completely free to market a program with the same underlying idea as Print Shop, but must express it without copying Print Shop's structure."

In particular, a rival supplier who developed a user interface identical to Print Shop's but who did so entirely serendipitously and without ever having seen Print Shop would not be an infringer and would be perfectly free to market his or her program in competition with Print Shop. That is because the copyright law does not provide a monopoly of the copyrighted text; it provides only the exclusive right to copy the text produced by the author thereof. One who, without copying, produces a similar or even identical text has not violated the copyright owner's exclusive right.

In such a circumstance, there may of course be problems of proof. If two texts are identical, the law tends to presume that the later text was copied from the earlier one. Indeed, if a text of some complexity is absolutely identical to an earlier work, it may not even be necessary for the copyright owner to demonstrate that access to his or her work was resorted to in writing the later work. Access will be presumed, as no other explanation is plausible. The burden, therefore, would be entirely on the author of the second work to prove a negative: that he or she did not copy.

The hope of establishing a record that will prove that negative is what lies behind the so-called "clean room" concept. "Clean room" procedures are procedures for isolating persons who are developing software intended to be competitive with existing software offered by others, and for maintaining records that will establish that their work was done without copying. In some cases, such procedures are designed to insure that personnel in the clean room will simply not have access to the target program or any information about it whatsoever. In theory, such procedures should satisfy the defendant's burden of proof. In practice, though, the defendant is still trying to prove a negative, and if the level of resulting similarity is very high, the inference that the "clean room" procedures were somehow circumvented may be very difficult to overcome.

In other cases, clean room procedures are used to assure that personnel in the clean room have access only to certain information about the target program; for example, its purpose and functionality. In those cases, other personnel typically extract the permitted information from the documentation or code of the target program and pass it into the clean room. The process of running a clean room for clone software is exemplified by the practice at the California company Western Digital.

In order to establish that the Western Digital programmers' expression is original, and that only the ideas have been taken from the target program, a "double-blind method" is employed. A group of experienced analysts study the target program to determine its functions. The analysts then write a detailed specification explaining how a compatible program must perform, but not indicating how the code should be written. To ensure that the compatible program will not be "contaminated" with knowledge of the expression in the target program, Western Digital hires programmers who have not had any previous contact with the target program. The recruits are made to sign affidavits testifying that they have never had access to the target program. They work entirely from the specifications given to them. If they have any questions about the specifications, they must submit them to the analysts in writing. Western Digital retains all documentation created in the course of the project, including documentation of all the mistakes made along the way, as evidence they hope will prove that the programmers' work is original.

Where a clean room is used in this way, if a highly similar program does result from the development effort, the developer has two problems. First, once again the inference of circumvention works against him or her, and second, in this scenario, he or she cannot deny that personnel outside the clean room who are in contact with personnel inside the clean room have had access to the code and documentation of the target program. Such access clearly presents the opportunity for circumvention, and therefore strengthens the adverse inference.

Obviously, our first Consolidated Computer example, translation, does not lend itself to clean room treatment at all. Translation is too complete a taking of the substance of the original work to be accomplished through double-blind methodologies. The clean room process, and its problems, are thought to be relevant to developers who wish to clone the target program, as in the second of our Federated Computer/ Consolidated Computer paradigms described above. It is to that paradigm that we now turn, as it presents the remaining policy arguments in their sharpest relief.

At the outset, I should note that there is a certain peculiarity about the "software clone" concept. *Wall Street Journal* reporter Michael Miller has likened it to the concept of cloning the record album *Meet the Beatles*: a task that one must despair of doing without infringing someone else's copyright (in this case, probably musician Michael Jackson's, since he now owns much of the Lennon/McCartney portfolio). As already noted, the idea of producing a cheap look-alike of someone else's protected work is not greeted sympathetically in most developed countries. In fact, so unsympathetically is it looked on that there are several different legal grounds for attacking the producer of the look-alike: for example, unfair competition, passing off, trademark infringement, theft of trade secrets, patent infringement, and copyright infringement. Particularly where the product is pure intellectual property such as a literary work or a piece of music, the clone strategy seems not only socially undesirable but nonsensical. For example, Tom Clancy is a "hot" author of thrillers at the moment. At this writing, he had one title on the *New York Times* hardcover best-seller list and two on the same publication's paperback best-seller list. If someone wanted to enter the thriller business with a cloning strategy, Clancy's books would be good targets. Take *The Hunt for Red October*. Would we find it offensive for our clone supplier to use the same title? How much would he or she have to change it to avoid giving offense? Is *Another Hunt for Red October* all right, or *The Hunt for Red November*? How different must the cover art be? More importantly, how different must the plot be? Can the characters be the same? Can they do the same things? The reader can see that, for traditional copyrighted works, cloning is simply not within the realm of reasonable contemplation.

Nonetheless, when it comes to software, many people have a different attitude. Among those people, one has to count Rand Jaslow and the principals at Unison World and Franklin Computer Corp., to be sure, and their views cannot be given much weight. However, there are also students of copyright law, software experts, and executives of large computer companies who believe that in some sense it *makes* sense to talk about cloning software. Why is this?

Some say it is because software is utilitarian or functional—like a hammer—and one expects there to be a certain commonality among tools designed for the same purpose. That is not a particularly satisfying explanation, however. The constitutional mandate, after all, relates to promoting progress in "Science and the *useful* Arts" (emphasis added). It plainly meant to extend exclusive rights to authors of utilitarian works, not just aesthetic works. We have already demonstrated that in terms of range of expression, software is more like poetry than like a phone directory. Why, then, is it said that a computer program is like a hammer? The argument appears to be that in addition to being a writing, and unlike other writings, a computer program produces results in the real world. But so did Upton Sinclair's *The Jungle* and Rachel Carson's *Silent Spring*. Moreover, not all programs produce results in the real world. Some do not accomplish a utilitarian result at all, but rather serve as entertainment, and the code of entertainment programs is not different in nature from the code of utilitarian programs. It is not the fact that software is functional that should determine the extent of cloning that is lawful or socially acceptable. That determination should be based on the consequences that can be expected to flow from the drawing of the line at one place versus another.

The issue, simply put, is whether a computer program that appropriates the look and feel, including the user interface and program-to-program interface, of another program infringes the copyright in the latter. Around this issue dance two sets of masquers in two very different kinds of fright wigs. If the answer is "Yes," the masquers who favor compatibility or clone business strategies warn, the result will be to grant patent-like protection to nonpatentable items for periods of time that extend far beyond the life of a patent, to eliminate a vital element of competition in the computer industry (i.e., software clones), and to prohibit the incremental enhancements that have marked progress in the industry since its inception. If the answer is "No," say the masquers who do not favor compatibility or clone business strategies, there will be no economic incentive to innovate, and a premier high-tech industry will be brought to its knees by copycat jackals.

Between the extremists in their fright wigs sit a large number of program owners and authors who occupy a middle ground. On the one hand, they are not particularly interested in having their programs cloned, and even less interested in having their copyrights infringed.

On the other hand, they recognize that from time to time the market value of their own programs can be significantly enhanced by adding the capability for those programs to behave to a certain extent like programs written by others. Indeed, as customers pressure for computers of disparate manufacture and computer programs of disparate authorship to work together, it is to be expected that more and more suppliers will find themselves on this middle ground. That group, as much as the masquers in the fright wigs, is anxious to know what the law is, because they may find themselves in court, one day as copyright plaintiffs and the next day as copyright defendants. Furthermore, they are anxious to have a law that is protective of their interests, but not overprotective because their interests may on occasion collide with others' interests. Having spoken with executives and other representatives of numerous suppliers of computer programs, I believe it not hyperbole to say that the uncertainty resulting from the activities of the masquers is having a substantial chilling effect on that area of human expression known as computer programming.

There is, of course, no black-and-white statement of the law in this area. Asking what acts taken to achieve software compatibility constitute copyright infringement is not the same as asking what acts must be taken to effectuate a valid conveyance of real property in Connecticut. The latter question may be answered crisply and definitively on the basis of existing law over a broad range of factual situations. In the case of the former question, there is not a long history of precedent. In that connection, it has been said that in this arena the technology is ten years ahead of the law. In a sense, that is so; but in another sense, that assertion is just a fright wig of a different color. Technology has always led the law, and enough is now known from the vast corpus of copyright law already extant with respect to literary works to give the thoughtful observer the ability to articulate several quite reliable principles about the way copyright law will be applied to software compatibility.

The first of these principles is that *there are substantial benefits to be derived from deciding questions about the conflict between software compatibility objectives and intellectual property rights on the basis of copyright law, rather than making up a separate set of legal rules to govern that conflict.* Copyright law is a stable, well-understood body of law that is reasonably consistent among the developed countries, and under which reciprocal privileges are granted in foreign countries pursuant to international compact. It is desirable for commercially distributed intellectual property to be governed by such an internationally accepted and predictable regime. Recent experience with specialized legislation, specifically the Semiconductor Chip Protection Act of 1984 in the United States and similar laws rapidly enacted in other countries, demonstrates that untested laws can increase substantially the level of commercial uncertainty at the same time that they attempt more closely to define rights and obligations.

The second principle is that *the mere fact that a supplier adopts a compatibility strategy does not give that supplier carte blanche to copy whatever it wants from the target program of another supplier*. We have fully discussed this principle already.

The third principle is that *the compatible supplier may copy the ideas in the target program and any expression essential to implementing those ideas*. Copying anything else is risky, as we have seen now in several different contexts.

The fourth principle, which follows from the discussion earlier in this chapter, is that *compatibility achieved completely independently of the target program does not constitute copyright infringement*.

To understand the power of the latter principle, consider the case of *Plains Cotton Cooperative Association of Lubbock, Texas v. Goodpasture Computer Service, Inc.* Plains Cotton is a cooperative association of cotton farmers in Texas and Oklahoma. To assist members in the growing and marketing of cotton, Plains Cotton developed a computer program, called Telcot, that would provide members, in communication by terminal with the co-op's central computer, with information about cotton prices and supply, accounting services, and the ability to consummate sales transactions. Telcot was first marketed by the co-op in 1975.

Four years later, the co-op's general manager quit in order to start a company that would adapt Telcot for the personal computer. This was not an acrimonious departure. His company, CXS, entered into an agreement with the co-op for the development and marketing of a personal-computer version of Telcot, which would be jointly owned by CXS and the co-op. Four years after that, however, CXS had not yet produced the program.

On April 13, 1985, CXS hired away four of the co-op's programmers who had helped develop Telcot, and one of those programmers left the co-op with a complete machine-readable copy of the Telcot source code. On April 18, the co-op terminated its contract with CXS.

The four former co-op employees continued to work at CXS and within a year produced a comprehensive design specification for a personal-computer version of Telcot. Paying the programmers and meeting its other obligations, however, proved too much for CXS, and it filed for bankruptcy in March 1985. The "Gang of Four" that had worked for the co-op found themselves on the job market. As fate would have it, a Brownsville, Texas, firm called Goodpasture Computer Service, Inc., was interested in the PC-Telcot project, and hired them all. Although each of the four signed an agreement promising not to breach any confidences of their former employers, one of them (Fisher) brought to Goodpasture a diskette containing Telcot design specifications.

Less than a month after joining Goodpasture, the four programmers had completed the design of GEMS, a PC version of a cotton exchange program. By November 1985, Goodpasture was marketing GEMS.

On January 15, 1986, the co-op filed suit against Goodpasture and the Gang of Four, and quickly moved for a preliminary injunction barring the marketing of GEMS pending trial of the case. As in *Apple v. Franklin*, among the things that Plains Cotton had to prove in order to succeed in its motion was that it had a substantial likelihood of succeeding in the ultimate trial of the case. After a two-day hearing, Judge Halbert O. Woodward, chief judge of the Federal District Court for the Northern District of Texas, concluded that the co-op was not reasonably likely to succeed in proving copyright infringement, and denied the co-op's motion. The co-op appealed to the U.S. Court of Appeals for the Fifth Circuit, and it is the opinion of that court, written by Judge Jerre S. Williams, that we will now consider.

The Court of Appeals described the factual situation as follows:

GEMS is very similar to Telcot on the functional specification, programming and documentation levels. . . . The main difference between the two systems is that Telcot is designed to work on a mainframe computer, whereas GEMS is designed for a personal computer.

This sounds like a scenario not unlike that in *SAS* or *Whelan*. However,

[Defendants] allege that, with one exception, they did not copy programs used for Telcot, but instead "drew on their knowledge of the cotton industry and expertise in computer programming and design gained over a number of years." The exception is [defendant] Fisher's admission that he did copy one Telcot subroutine in programming GEMS. When Goodpasture discovered the copying on February 6, 1986, the subroutine was replaced, and Fisher was discharged.

The posture in *Plains Cotton* was therefore different from that in either *SAS* or *Whelan* in one crucial respect. Here, while there was evidence of substantial similarity at some levels of the program, there was also credible evidence of independent development. In *SAS*, while there was similar evidence of independent development, to wit the testimony of the S&H employees, the court found that those employees were simply not credible. In *Whelan*, there was no evidence, credible or incredible, of independent development. The defendants basically admitted copying what they copied, and rested their defense instead on the presumed nonprotectability of structure, logic, and flow, and on their supposed contractual rights to copy.

In its argument to the Court of Appeals, the co-op argued that Judge Woodward had applied the wrong standard for determining copyright infringement. The co-op asserted that the district judge decided only that there was no evidence of line-by-line or literal copying, and failed to consider evidence of "organizational" copying; further, that the district judge failed to apply the *Whelan* precedent to the facts of this case.

The Court of Appeals disagreed. In its view, Judge Woodward was presented with ample testimony of organizational similarity, and clearly based his opinion on all the testimony presented. The defendants' evidence was that they did not refer to any Plains Cotton or CSX materials in writing GEMS. Their expert testified that Telcot, a mainframe program, was simply too large to modify into a PC program in the time it took the Gang of Four to write GEMS, and that GEMS was written based on the knowledge and experience of the Gang of Four as programmers in the cotton industry. Judge Woodward was entitled to rely on that evidence.

As to *Whelan*, Judge Williams wrote that the Fifth Circuit was not ready to "embrace" that opinion, for two reasons. First, the appeal in *Plains Cotton* was based on a preliminary injunction hearing rather than a full trial. Therefore, the record was less than fully developed, and the appellate review was "one step removed from the merits of the case." Second, there was evidence that many of the similarities between GEMS and Telcot were "dictated by the externalities of the cotton market." There was uncontradicted testimony, for example, that GEMS was designed to present the same information as that contained on a "cotton recap sheet," a standard industry report. Given that the record supported the inference that market factors play a significant role in determining the "sequence and organization" of cotton marketing software, the Fifth Circuit felt that the facts of *Plains Cotton* fell squarely within Judge Higginbotham's "powerful analogy" to the hypothetical development of gear stick patterns in the *Synercom* opinion.

In other words, like the input formats in *Synercom*, the portions of GEMS that produced "recap report–compatible" output, and other portions of GEMS, were sequenced and organized in a way in which there was no expression separate from the ideas they embodied. In *Synercom*, that conclusion was based on Judge Higginbotham's opinion, grounded in his gearshift pattern analogy, that the sequencing and ordering of STRAN's input formats couldn't constitute expression because the sequencing and ordering didn't express any idea separate from sequence and order themselves, and you'll recall that we have questioned the underpinnings of that opinion. In *Plains Cotton*, the conclusion has a different basis altogether, and one that seems rather sounder. The basis for Judge Williams's conclusion was that the similar sequence and organization of GEMS and Telcot might reflect the fact that the market factors that both programs were designed to address could be ideas expressible in only one way. That possibility could not be assessed without a full trial, and therefore Judge Woodward was right not to award an injunction at this preliminary stage of the proceedings.

Was there a third reason why the Fifth Circuit was not ready to embrace *Whelan*? Judge Higginbotham, author of the *Synercom* opinion, had by now been elevated to a judgeship on the Fifth Circuit Court of Appeals. He did not participate in the *Plains Cotton* decision, but there was no reason for his brethren on the bench to reach to embrace an opinion from another circuit that was arguably critical of his earlier work.

In any case, the Fifth Circuit probably overstated the power of Judge Higginbotham's gearshift pattern analogy. Judge Higginbotham himself recognized that "there are many more possible choices of computer formats" than there were choices of gearshift patterns, and that the decision as to what formats to use was more arbitrary than the decision as to what gearshift pattern to use. In his view at the time (eight years before the *Whelan* opinion), the wider range of choice and greater arbitrariness available to programmers than to gear-shift-pattern designers did not detract from the force of the analogy. With the benefit of hindsight, however, we can see that the infinite potential for alternative structure, sequence, and flow in the detailed design of original programs that accomplish the same result is the principal reason for concluding that the detailed design of a program constitutes expression. We can also see that the availability of alternative modes of expression at the detailed-design level assures a socially desirable balance between the interests of innovators and those of followers.

It has been argued that *Plains Cotton* is inconsistent with *Whelan* and demonstrates that American law is unsettled as to whether structure, logic, and flow of computer programs are protected by copyright. (Among the people making that claim, of course, was the co-op, which petitioned the Supreme Court for certiorari on the basis that there was now a conflict among the Circuit Courts on this issue. The Supreme Court declined to take the case.) That claim is hollow. There is no conflict whatever between *Plains Cotton* and *Whelan*. Both cases recognize the relevance of assessing "organizational" copying. Both cases recognize that the structure, logic, and flow that are essential to a program's ideas are not protected by copyright. Faced with the *Plains Cotton* facts, there is no indication that the *Whelan* court would have decided the Texas case any differently than did the Fifth Circuit. Faced with the *Whelan* facts, there is no indication that the *Plains Cotton* court would have decided the Philadelphia case any differently than did the Third Circuit.

The *Plains Cotton* opinion is a demonstration of our fourth principle. Its lesson is that similarities in expression that result from environmental factors—other than the design of the target program itself—cannot serve as proof of infringement. This principle should give substantial comfort to authors who wish their programs to be compatible with the same environmental factors as those that underlie target programs.

16

Rights of Copyright Owners:
The *Softklone* Case

I was hungry enough for literature to want to take down the whole paper at this one meal, but I got only a few bites, and then had to postpone, because the monks around me besieged me so with eager questions: What is this curious thing? What is it for? . . .

"It is a public journal; I will explain what that is, another time. It is not cloth, it is made of paper; some time I will explain what paper is. The lines on it are reading matter; and not written by hand, but printed; by-and-by I will explain what printing is. A thousand sheets have been made all exactly like this, in every minute detail—they can't be told apart." Then they all broke out with exclamations of surprise and admiration:

"A thousand! Verily a mighty work—a year's work for many men."

"No—merely a day's work for a man and a boy."

Mark Twain, *A Connecticut Yankee in
King Arthur's Court* (1889)

There are some other principles by which the software clone supplier may guide his life. These are related to the most important policy consideration surrounding the question whether and how the copyright law ought to be applied to computer programs: Does the extension of traditional copyright protection to computer programs give authors of original programs a monopoly? That view is repeatedly expressed by the narrow protectionists. It usually takes the form of an assertion that, because of software's utilitarian nature, protecting its structure, logic, and flow is tantamount to providing patent-like protection to unpatentable items, a situation that does not arise in the case of other kinds of literary works. Unlike the copyright, the patent is indeed a monopoly grant: patent holders may, if they so choose, bar anyone from using their inventions. If copyright holders may bar anyone from using the design of their programs, it is said, they can carve out technological feifdoms in particular areas of commerce.

There is a short answer and a long answer to this argument. The short answer was given by Judge Reed in the Canadian *Apple* case mentioned in Chapter 11:

[T]he purpose of the Copyright Act is and always has been to grant a monopoly. No distinction is made therein as to the purpose of the work created—for entertainment, instruction or other purposes. The legislation historically, in my view had two purposes: to encourage disclosure of works for "advancement of learning," and to protect and reward the intellectual effort of the author (for a limited time) in the work. A book is an article of commerce, as is a map or a chart. The interpretation of the legislation which the defendant urges, based on a view that the Act was not intended to interfere with commerce, is both not accurate and would add a gloss to the statute which its wording does not bear.

In other words, carving out fiefdoms in areas of commerce is what copyright law is about.

The long answer is rather more benign than this view from the frosty North. In point of fact, the copyright grant is not like the patent grant. The copyright holders may not bar others from using either the ideas or—in many circumstances—the expression in their work. As we have just seen, if someone arrives at a substantially similar, or even identical, expression by completely independent means, he or she is free to market the program embodying that expression in competition with the original author's program. Moreover, whether arrived at independently or by copying, the author of a second program is free to include in his or her work the ideas from the original author's program. The patent grant does not freely permit analogous behavior.

Copyright law is properly viewed, then, as providing either no monopoly or a very weak monopoly. In the case of programs, it does not prevent the copying of the processes or methods of operation that underlie the program; nor does it inhibit in any way the independent creation of expression. All it does in fact is to prohibit exercise by others of the limited exclusive rights reserved to the copyright owner. Those rights are:

1. The right to reproduce the copyrighted work;
2. The right to prepare derivative works based on the copyrighted work (derivative works being defined as any form into which the copyrighted work may be translated or adapted);

3. The right to distribute by sale or other transfer of ownership, or by rental, lease, or lending;

4. The right to perform the copyrighted work publicly; and

5. The right to display the copyrighted work publicly.

Obviously, the listed rights do not constitute a grant of monopoly over the information in the copyrighted work.

I referred earlier to the case of *Digital Communications Associates, Inc. v. Softklone Distributing Corp.* That case was the second look and feel case. Both *Softklone* and *Broderbund* involved visual displays, the program elements at the heart of the controversy over software cloning. In *Broderbund*, a sequenced suite of screen images was copied; in *Softklone*, only a single screen. That single screen, however, had been separately registered with the copyright office as an audiovisual work. The defendants were held to have infringed the copyright in that work. Did the result in *Softklone* give Digital Communications Associates a monopoly? Hardly. The program that generated the copyrighted screen was a successful program for managing communications over phone lines between personal computers or between a personal computer and a mainframe. In March 1987, the time of the decision in that case, there were a substantial number of competing suppliers of functionally equivalent programs. There still are.

Considering the evidence in Softklone, the result is unexceptional. The defendants set out to write a clone of Crosstalk XVI, the plaintiff's data communication program. They obtained legal advice to the effect that, while the source code of Crosstalk was protected by copyright, the status screen was not. That advice, if indeed it was given, did not serve Softklone particularly well. The defendants proceeded to develop a program called Mirror that performed virtually the same suite of functions as Crosstalk and had virtually the same status screen. Here is a reconstruction of the status screens of the two programs:

```
        |--------- CROSSTALK - XVI Status Screen ------------|     Off line
NAme   Crosstalk defaults                    LOaded    C:STD.XTK
NUmber                                       CApture   Off

|-------- Communications Parameters ------|   |------ Filter Settings ---------|
   SPeed   1200 Parity  None  DUplex Full       DEbug  Off  LFauto    Off
   DAta    8    STop  1       EMulate None       TAbex  Off  BLankex   Off
   POrt    1                  MOde  Call         INfilter On  OUtfilter Off

|------------ Key Settings --------------|   |---- SEnd control settings -------|

   ATten   Esc          COmmand  ETX (^C)      CWait   None
   SWitch  Home         BReak    End           LWait   None

|---------------------- List of Crosstalk Commands ----------------------|
   NAme     NUmber    ANswerback  APrefix   ATten     BReak     DEbug
   DPrefix  DRive     DSuffix     EDit      EMulate   EPath     Filter
   DPort    PWord     RDials      RQest     SCreen    SNapshot  SWitch
   Timer    TUrnaround Video      ACcept    CWait     DNames    FKeys
   GO       INfilter  LFauto      LOad      LWait     MOde      QUit
   RUn      SAve      SEnd        XDos      BKsize    BLankex   BYe
   CApture  CDir      COmmand     CStatus   DAta      DIr       DO

More to come...   press ENTER: _

   DUplex   ERase     FLow        GKermit   HAndshak  HElp      KErmit
   List     NO        OUtfilter   PArity    Picture   PMode     PRinter
   RCve     RKermit   RXmodem     SPeed     STop      TAbex     TYpe
   UConly   WRite     XKermit     XMit      XXmodem
For more information on a command, type "help xx" where "xx" is the command
name (for example, "help LO" for information on the LOad command).
If you need more general help, type "help general" or "help call".


Command? _
        |------------Mirror Status Screen ---------------|     Off-line
NAme   Mirror Default Settings               LOaded    STD.XTK
NUmber                                       CApture   Off

|-------- Communications Parameters ------|   |------ Filter Settings ---------|
   SPeed   1200 PArity  None  DUplex Full       DEbug  Off  LFauto    Off
   DAta    8    STop  1       EMulate None       TAbex  Off  BLankex   Off
   POrt    1                  MOde  Call         INfilter On  OUtfilter Off

|------------ Key Settings --------------|   |---- SEnd control settings -------|

   ATten   Esc          COmmand  ETX (^C)      CWait   None
   SWitch  Home         BReak    End           LWait   None

|---------------------- List of Mirror Commands ----------------------|
   ABort    ACcept    ALarm       ANswerback APrefix   ASk       ATten
   BAckgrnd BKsize    BLankex     BReak      BYe       CApture   CDir
   CLear    COmmand   CRc         CStatus    CWait     DAta_bits DEbug
   DIr      DNames    DO          DPrefix    DRive     DSuffix   DUplex
   EDit     EMulate   EPath       ERase      Filter    FKeys     FLow
   GKermit  GO        HAndshake   HElp       IF        INfilter  JUmp
   KErmit   LAbel     LFeed       List       LOad      LWait     MEssage
More to come...   press RETURN: _

   RDial    REply     RHayes      RKermit    RQuest    RUn       RWind
   RXmodem  SAve      SBreak      SCreen     SEnd      SKip      SNapshot
   SPeed    STop_bits SWitch      TAbexpand  Timer     TUrnarnd  TYpe
   UC-only  WAit      WHen        WRite      XBatch    XDos      XHayes
   XKermit  XMit      XXmodem

For help on a particular command, enter HE followed by the command
name (e.g., HE LW for help on the LWait command).


Command?
```

The court separated the protected elements of the Crosstalk screen from the unprotected elements in a way that makes it clear why the copyright grant cannot lead to monopolies. "Idea," the court said,

is the process or manner by which the status screen . . . operates and the "expression" is the method by which the idea is communicated to the user. As indicated by the evidence presented at trial, the status screen operates by the user typing on the bottom line of the screen two symbols, which correspond to a particular command, usually followed by a value. The computer then effects a change in the operation of the program based upon the particular command and value involved and reflects the changed status of the program on the upper portion of the status screen. As an example, if the user wishes the program to operate on a certain speed, e.g. 1200, the user can type on the bottom line of the status screen the two symbols "SP" followed by "1200." The computer will then operate at a speed of 1200 and that fact will be reflected by the appearance on the upper portion of the status screen of "1200" next to "SPeed."

Certain aspects of the example noted above are clearly "ideas" which any other party, including the defendants, could legally copy. The use of a screen to reflect the status of the program is an "idea"; the use of a command driven program is an "idea"; and the typing of two symbols to activate a specific command is an "idea." All of these elements relate to how the computer program receives commands or instructions from the user and how operationally the computer program reflects the results of those commands. Certain aspects of the status screen, however, are unrelated to how the computer operates and are "expression." The arrangement of the parameter/command terms has no relation to how the computer operates. That is to say, the computer allows for any sequence of commands, e.g., first entering a "SPeed" command and then entering a "DAta" command has the same effect as first entering a "DAta" command and then entering a "SPeed" command. Likewise, the highlighting and capitalizing of two specific letters of the parameter/command terms listed on the status screen has no relation to how the status screen functions, i.e., the user need not type in two highlighted, capitalized symbols to effectuate a command.

Within the framework established by the *Softklone* court, there is clearly ample maneuvering space for competitors.

One might properly ask, then, what is the source of the narrow protectionists' concern? Apparently they feel that, despite the modest protection afforded by traditional copyright coverage, in the specific case of a supplier of "compatible" software, the copyright law inhibits competition. It must be conceded that competition based on "knocking off" someone else's literary work is indeed inhibited by the copyright law. Not all attempts to achieve a degree of software compatibility are "knock-offs," however. The inhibition of the copyright law runs to the competitor who would replace an original program with one that, to all external appearances was not significantly different.

17

IBM v. Fujitsu

We must be aware that there are images and images. Pygmalion made the statue of Galatea in the image of his ideal beloved, but after the gods brought it to life, it became an image of his beloved in a much more real sense. . . .

Thus, besides pictorial images, we may have operative images. These operative images, which perform the functions of their original, may or may not bear a pictorial likeness to it. Whether they do or not, they may replace the original in its action, and this is a much deeper similarity.

Norbert Weiner, *God and Golem, Inc.* (1964)

IBM v. Fujitsu is a most unusual proceeding. As I've already mentioned, arbitrations are usually private matters in which no written opinions are issued. In *IBM v. Fujitsu*, although the decision would have no weight as legal precedent, the arbitrators felt it best to publish explanations of their decisions. Aside from brief press statements, the parties themselves, including their lawyers (of whom I am one), were not and are not permitted to comment on the results. The arbitrators in this ongoing matter are John L. Jones, formerly executive vice president of the Norfolk and Southern Railway and a distinguished data processing executive, and Robert F. Mnookin, professor of law at Stanford Law School and director of the Stanford Center on Conflict and Negotiation. What follows is what they had to say about compatibility in the context of this dispute between an author of original programs (which happens to be the world's largest computer company) and an author of compatible programs (which happens to be the world's third largest computer company and the largest in Japan) in their opinions and related materials released on November 29, 1988.

In October 1982, IBM first confronted FJ [Fujitsu] with allegations that FJ operating systems programs and manuals contained IBM programming material in violation of IBM's intellectual property rights. By that time, FJ had already developed and committed itself to offering an IBM-compatible line of operating systems and FJ customers had become dependent on FJ's IBM-compatible software.

After eight months of negotiations, the parties executed an Agreement of Settlement, dated as of July 1, 1983 ("1983 Settlement Agreement") and an Agreement on External Information, also dated as of July 1, 1983 ("1983 Externals Agreement"). Neither 1983 agreement contains any admission or acknowledgement of guilt by FJ with respect to IBM's claims of copyright infringement.

Pursuant to the 1983 Settlement Agreement, and in exchange for the payments specified [in the Settlement Agreement], IBM granted FJ immunity and waived all claims with respect to past and future distribution or other use of certain FJ programs designated by FJ for immunity ("Designated Programs"). With respect to its future sales of each designated program, FJ agreed to pay IBM, on a semiannual basis, an amount equal to the license fee for each functionally similar "IBM Corresponding Program."

The 1983 Settlement Agreement allowed FJ to continue marketing its IBM-compatible Designated Programs and protected FJ customers that had already installed such programs.

The 1983 Settlement Agreement and Externals Agreement required that IBM and FJ each provide the other party with "External Information," a term that was never adequately defined but that related to interface information provided to customers to utilize licensed programming material. These 1983 agreements permitted either party to copy, reproduce, distribute and use the other party's "External Information" in exchange for compensation to be determined by the parties.

The parties' 1983 agreements were unsuccessful. These agreements failed to define clearly what IBM information FJ could use in its software development or to specify what FJ should pay IBM for such use. The agreements also failed to establish a common understanding between the parties about the extent to which FJ could use its original Designated Programs as a base for future software development.

As a result, the parties' fundamental disagreement concerning FJ's use of IBM programming material, unresolved by the 1983 agreements, became exacerbated and new disputes emerged concerning FJ programs (including successor versions of Designated Programs) released after the execution of the 1983 agreements. These disputes involved claims that FJ had included infringing portions of its original Designated Programs in the new FJ programs and versions. These disputes did not involve claims that FJ infringed IBM's intellectual property rights with respect to IBM programs released after 1983. . . .

[The arbitrators' earlier opinion, dated September 15, 1987, describes the positions advanced by the parties at the outset of the arbitration:]

During the months prior to the commencement of this arbitration, the parties

attempted to negotiate a resolution of disputes through voluminous correspondence and numerous meetings of technical and business personnel. None of these
attempts was successful. Finally, in June of 1985, IBM invoked the formal dispute
settlement process under the 1983 Settlement Agreement by issuing a "Final
Report" setting out its claims against FJ. Thereafter, IBM filed a demand for
arbitration with the AAA.

IBM's Final Report alleged that FJ had "systematically and pervasively" copied
from IBM programming material, including portions of the Designated Program
base, enhancements contained in new versions and releases of IBM programs,
and "IBM External Information." IBM alleged that FJ, in so copying, breached
its covenant under the 1983 Settlement Agreement to refrain from infringing
IBM's copyrights and other intellectual property rights and to develop additional
programming material in compliance with those rights and with the Protective
Procedure set out in that agreement. IBM alleged that FJ had obstructed IBM's
review efforts in violation of the 1983 Settlement Agreement. Throughout this
arbitration IBM has also alleged that FJ's internal guidelines and procedures for
the use of IBM information in FJ software development provide inadequate
safeguards.

In a December 15, 1985 "Response to IBM's Final Report," FJ set out the basic
position which it has continued to assert throughout this arbitration: that FJ's
use of IBM's programming material does not violate IBM's rights under the 1983
agreements or under applicable intellectual property law. FJ has maintained that
all such uses fall into one or more of the following categories: (1) FJ's use of
IBM material dating to uncopyrighted versions of IBM programs and therefore
in the public domain; (2) FJ's use of IBM material which does not constitute
protected expression under the copyright laws of the United States or Japan; (3)
FJ's use of "External Information" within the intent of the 1983 Settlement
Agreement and Externals Agreement; (4) FJ's use of material subject to immunity
under the 1983 Settlement Agreement; (5) research or high-level architectural
design authorized under the 1983 Settlement Agreement Protective Procedures;
and (6) standard programming techniques. FJ has restated each of these arguments and IBM has disputed each such argument.

FJ has also sought to frame the dispute in a broader competitive context. It
has repeatedly argued that it has the right under the 1983 Settlement Agreements
and applicable intellectual property law to use IBM information necessary for
FJ to independently develop IBM-compatible operating system software. FJ has
argued that certain design and functional characteristics of IBM operating system
software have become, in effect, industry standards which FJ must utilize in
order to compete with the IBM mainframe operating system. According to FJ,
IBM has pursued a deliberate strategy effectively to "lock in" users to the IBM
operating system environment.

IBM has consistently rejected all FJ arguments that any alleged need to maintain "compatibility" entitles FJ to *any* IBM information. IBM has maintained that
(1) U.S. federal judges have consistently ruled not only against plaintiffs who
have raised antitrust claims against IBM but specifically against plaintiffs who
have previously litigated claims that they were entitled to information necessary
for "compatibility"; (2) the information that FJ claims is indispensable to create
"IBM-compatibility" goes far beyond the information necessary to connect with,

communicate with, and interchange data and instructions with, IBM systems; (3) because of the history of the parties' conduct, IBM had no continuing obligation to provide "External Information," which in all events should be narrowly defined. . . .

[Returning to the 1988 opinion, we see that, after the preliminary skirmishes, the arbitrators actually became, in part, mediators. Whereas the job of arbitrators is to sit in judgment, the job of mediators is to forge an agreement between parties who cannot themselves come to agreement.]

In July of 1985, IBM filed a demand for arbitration with the AAA [American Arbitration Association] and in November, 1985, FJ filed various counterclaims. The Panel held its first hearing in December, 1985. The hearings and meetings held by the Panel during 1986 are described in the 1987 Opinion. After summary judgment rulings in October of 1986, the parties authorized the Panel to attempt mediation of their disputes. . . . The Panel's mediation efforts between November, 1986 and February, 1987, led to an agreement dated February 23, 1987 ["the Washington Agreement"] which set out a framework for the resolution of all disputes between the parties concerning the past and future use by FJ of IBM programming material. . . .

The parties in the Washington Agreement empowered the Panel to create detailed rules implementing the Secured Facility regime, rather than simply adjudicate past disputes on a program-by-program basis. . . .

[For a description of the so-called "Secured Facility regime," we turn again to the 1987 Opinion.]

The Secured Facility regime described in the [Arbitrators'] Order is founded on several basic principles:

First, *access in exchange for adequate compensation*. Specified personnel of a party, not otherwise engaged in software development, will have access in a Secured Facility to programming material of the other party (including source code whether or not generally available to customers) from which they may derive, and place on survey sheets, only such interface specifications and any other information specified in the Instructions. A party will have to pay the other party, fully and adequately, for its access to such information. The Arbitrators will determine the amount of such compensation.

Second, *independent compliance monitoring*. A party's examination and use of the other party's deposited programming material, and compliance with the Instructions, will be strictly monitored and policed by an independent and technically expert Facility Supervisor under the guidance and authority of the Arbitrators.

Third, *immunity*. A party may use information placed on approved survey sheets in its subsequent development of operating system software and the other party may not challenge such use.

Fourth, *limited duration*. A party's right to examine deposited material of the other party, and to extract information specified in the Instructions, will end after the completion of a limited Contract Period, lasting five to ten years, as determined by the Arbitrators.

The Order (and the Instructions, rules, guidelines and procedures established and implemented pursuant to it) will exclusively define the rights and obligations of each party with respect to the use of the other party's programming material during the Contract Period. In effect, the Order, and the Arbitrators' subsequent decisions pursuant to the Order, will constitute the applicable intellectual property law until the end of the Contract Period, notwithstanding copyright decisions of U.S. or Japanese courts or previous agreements of the parties. . . .

[Because the Instructions established pursuant to the Arbitrators' Order "define IBM FJ compatibility," they are central to the Secured Facility regime. Together with appendices, they comprise eighty pages of typewritten text. To summarize the Instructions for interested readers, the Arbitrators issued an Overview of the Instructions and an Instructions Fact Sheet. The following questions and answers from the Instructions Fact Sheet will give the reader a general feel for what the Instructions contain:]

- What are the instructions?

  The Instructions describe and limit the information Fujitsu may derive from IBM programming material. This information may be used by Fujitsu to independently develop and maintain its own IBM-compatible operating system software.

- What kinds of information do the Instructions contain?

  The Instructions define interface specifications only. Generally, these specifications describe what the program does, not how it does it.

  Fujitsu will not be able to use IBM's internal design information.

- What areas of compatibility are covered by the Instructions?

  . . . The Instructions define compatibility primarily in terms of *application program interfaces*. Application program interfaces provide the ability for customers to run application programs intended for IBM operating environments in Fujitsu operating environments.

  The Instructions also provide for a *limited* kind of *multi-vendor* compatibility. Multi-vendor compatibility relates to the ability to combine both companies' mainframe processors and operating system software.

- What Instructions apply to application program compatibility?

  The "Instructions for User Interfaces and Application Program Interfaces" ("API Instructions") define interfaces necessary for Fujitsu to have a reasonable opportunity to maintain and develop operating systems that will run application programs originally written for IBM environments. . . .

- What Instructions apply to "multi-vendor" compatibility?

  The "Instructions for Multi-vendor Interoperability" ("MVI Instructions") are divided into two parts. The first part describes the information provided for *multi-vendor networking*. The second part describes the information provided for *multi-vendor data sharing*.

- What do the MVI Instructions provide for networking compatibility?

  For *networking compatibility*, the MVI Instructions provide information that will allow Fujitsu a reasonable opportunity to independently develop and maintain operating systems products that permit, with full 1988 function and reasonable efficiency and reliability, "any-to-any" connection with IBM SNA networks. With "any-to-any" connections any terminal or application program in one party's network can access any terminal or application in the other party's network.

  [The term "SNA" refers to IBM's Systems Network Architecture, presently the most popular set of proprietary formats and protocols for communication within and among large computer networks in the world.]

  Fujitsu may use IBM's SNA Network Interconnection or SNI protocols to achieve these connections. Fujitsu may not, however, use these protocols in its backbone network architecture. Rather, Fujitsu is to use these protocols to develop a gateway between its networks and SNI gateways in the IBM networks, thereby preserving the autonomous operation of the two networks. (SNI is a set of protocols that allow communication between two SNA networks.) The Instructions prohibit Fujitsu from otherwise attempting to share control of the IBM network . . . .

- What do the MVI Instructions provide for data sharing?

  For *data sharing*, the Multi-vendor Instructions provide information that will allow Fujitsu a reasonable opportunity to independently develop and maintain operating systems products that permit limited Direct Access Storage Device (DASD) sharing compatibility using simple, stable IBM file structures only.

- For how long will Fujitsu be able to derive program information for application program compatibility? For multi-vendor compatibility?

  Fujitsu may extract information relating to application program compatibility contained in IBM programs released up to June 25, 1997. Fujitsu may extract information relating to multi-vendor compatibility contained in IBM programs released up to January 1, 1994.

[What happens after June, 1997? As Arbitrator Jones put it, "After that time, then-current copyright law or subsequent agreements between these companies will govern such information access."

The second major determination of the arbitrators' 1988 opinion was the fixing of the amounts to be paid by Fujitsu both in terms of access fees for "use of new IBM programming material" and in terms of a paid-up license for "continuing and future use of Fujitsu programs that were developed in the past and were covered under the 1983 and 1987 agreements." Dealing with the latter set of figures first, Arbitrator Mnookin described them this way:]

Under the 1983 agreements, Fujitsu initially paid IBM $65,000,000 for the *pre-1983* use of the designated Fujitsu programs.

Between 1983 and 1987, Fujitsu paid an additional $406,186,000 in semi-annual fees which we have concluded should be reduced by an overpayment credit of $33,865,000.

Fujitsu's paid-up license fee is $395,930,000 towards which they have already paid $124,824,000.

If you have kept up with the math here, you will have discovered that, in total, Fujitsu will have paid $833,251,000 for the past and future use of these Fujitsu programs, some of which may contain pre-1983 IBM material. . . .

[As for access fees for use of new IBM programming material, Professor Mnookin explained the Arbitrators' computation as follows:]

We decided that an access fee should not be set for the entire duration of the regime. Rather, we decided to set the access fee for an initial one year period and then reevaluate this amount annually. For 1989, Fujitsu will pay IBM an amount between $25,671,000 and $51,342,000. The precise amount will depend on the extent to which Fujitsu seeks to review particular IBM programming material in a Secured Facility. For each IBM program that Fujitsu reviews in a Secured Facility, it will make an additional payment beyond a base amount. . . .

[In terms of what IBM programming material Fujitsu may access outside a Secured Facility, and what IBM programming material it must access inside a Secured Facility, Mr. Jones gave this summary:]

Under this regime either company will be able *outside* a Secured Facility to review the *unlicensed* manuals and to perform machine analysis of object code programs belonging to the other. They will be allowed to derive and must document the interface information they extract. This information will be reviewed to assure that it is within the established instructions. . . .

In addition, if either company wishes to derive interface information through the examination of the other's *licensed* manuals and source code, it may only do so *inside* a Secured Facility subject to strict and elaborate safeguards. Before this extracted information may be used in software development, it must be reviewed to assure that it is within the established instructions.

The point of this extended exposition, aside from giving the reader a view into the granddaddy of all the silicon epics so far, is to demonstrate the considerations taken into account, decisions made, and controls put in place by independent decision-makers who were attempting to produce a dispute-free regime for compatible software development. As elaborate as the foregoing exposition is, it only scratches the surface of *IBM v. Fujitsu*. Readers interested in more detail can obtain the full opinions and associated documents from the American Arbitration Association, 140 West 51st St., New York, N.Y. 10020.

18

An Introduction to Compatibility

There is much difference between imitating a good man, and counterfeiting him.

A countryman between two lawyers is like a fish between two cats.
Benjamin Franklin, *Poor Richard's Almanack*, 1737, 1738

Perhaps I was wrong earlier about Franklin and Jacquard. Poor Richard seems very nicely to have captured the spirit of the compatibility issue. In any case, the reader is hopefully no longer a "countryperson" when it comes to questions of software and copyright.

Critics of full copyright protection for software claim that compatible program development unsupervised by independent decision-makers would be too uncertain a business unless protection is limited to literal text only. As we continue our inquiry into the question of whether extending traditional protection to software tends to create monopolies, it is important to keep in mind that what the suppliers of compatible software want to know is how closely they can copy various elements of someone else's program without being held as infringers. It is a fair policy question to ask ourselves as a preliminary matter, however, why society should be at all solicitous of persons whose aim is to make a profit by testing the boundaries of other people's property rights. Why not deal with more pressing problems of the social order, and let the clones suffer the consequences of whatever risks they choose to take?

What I hope we have seen in these pages is that both the clones and the innovators need reasonable guidance as to what those boundaries are, because of the sums of money and the breadth of economic activity at stake. IBM and Fujitsu may have worked out with their arbitrators a resolution of their particular dispute, but the rest of the industry needs to know how the law is likely to apply to efforts to "be compatible." A committee of the software trade association ADAPSO has developed an "Openness Guidebook," in which they propose to record information about the extent to which a program author allows competitors to (a) freely connect to his or her program with their programs, or (b) implement a program that uses the same interfaces and performs the same functions (i.e., a compatible replacement product).

ADAPSO's objective in this regard is to obtain and distribute sufficient information about software products so that its members can determine whether an investment in developing complementary or replacement products for a particular target program will have reasonable or unacceptable risks.

This is a noble, but blissfully naive, endeavor. What matters, after all, is not what an author asserts his or her property rights to be, but what in fact they are. True, an author who publicly abandons the right to protect certain aspects of a program will probably not be able to change his or her mind at a later point in time. However, an author who claims copyright protection for the ideas in a program does not thereby obtain protection for those ideas.

We've already articulated several principles that help define the boundaries of a program author's rights. In this chapter, we will complete that articulation. To do so, we are going to have to descend into a netherworld of technobabble demons. Although novelists like John Gardner and Ann Rice have eloquently demonstrated that conversations with demons need not be unpleasant, I fear that the demons we must confront are rather primitive and flat in comparison to Grendel and the vampire. Ours are the conceptual demons of software compatibility.

When a computer system is operating under the control of a given program, that program's instructions are interacting in various ways with entities other than the program itself. Such interactions might be:

—With the processor,
—With various other hardware devices,
—With various other programs in the processor's memory,
—With various other programs being executed by other processors, or
—With human beings.

The term *compatibility* does not refer to a clearly-defined correspondence between a program and the entities with which it can communicate. Compatibility has many meanings. When we say that two people are compatible, we usually mean that they relate well to one another. When we say that two programs are compatible, we *may* mean that they relate well to one another, in terms of exchanging data or sharing tasks. That sense of compatibility connotes complementarity. One program "attaches" to the other, and the two programs work well together as a team.

We may also mean, however, that the first program relates to a third (or fourth or *n*-th) program in the same way that the second one does, and/or that the first program relates to the end user or items of computer hardware in the same way that the second one does, and therefore is to a greater or lesser extent a replacement for the second program. That sense of compatibility connotes competition. One program is designed to displace the other.

In general, the more relationships between the target program and other programs, users, or hardware that the author of a competing program wishes to replicate in order to achieve displacement, the more demons he or she must confront.

We can think of these demons as being, generically, either *formats* or *protocols*, and I will now endeavor to describe them for you. As we saw early on, most programs do not have the capability of dealing meaningfully with unstructured interactions. Program authors design their programs to recognize a limited range of incoming communications—which must be in exactly the form the author designs the program to receive—and to issue communications in a limited number of ways and in a very specific form. In a way, the program is a conversation between author and user, but a peculiar conversation in which the author's contributions are prewritten, and are given when the proper cues are received from the user, from another program, or from a hardware device.

Interactions with a computer program, to be successful, must have two attributes: (1) they must be in a format that the program is capable of accepting (e.g., consistent with the data structure of the program or in the form of one of the words from its command set); and (2) they must occur in accordance with rules that the author had in mind when the program was written. These rules, or protocols, prescribe the range of circumstances under which successful interaction may occur. Thus, even though the format of a communication to a program is proper, the interaction will not succeed unless it proceeds according to the program's protocols as to what information is exchanged under what circumstances.

An example of an interaction between a program and its end user will illustrate what we mean by formats and protocols. Imagine that you are seated at a keyboard and have been working with your computer for a while. You're hungry, and you want to go out for junk food. You type the single character *q* and press the Enter or Return key (depending on what make of computer you've imagined), thereby transmitting the char-

acter q to the processor, where the program you've been working with
resides. The program causes the following message to appear on the
tube at which you are staring: "Do you want to quit now? Y/N." This
is the "quit" verification, and it drives you crazy, because you just
indicated that you want to quit by typing q, and because you realize that
the program author anticipated that klutzes might type q by mistake and
that their intentions would have to be verified, and because you are not
a klutz.

In any case, the quit verification message is always in the same, fixed-
content format, "Do you want to quit now? Y/N," and is always sent
after a message in the fixed-content format q is received. That sequence
is part of the protocol of the quit verification routine. Obviously, at this
point the program author expects you to type either a Y or an N. If
instead you type S for Sure, the program does not respond, because the
author did not intend for its protocol to "support" a message in that
format at that point in the proceedings. You enter Y. The program then
flashes the following message: "Do you want to Save or Erase the file?
S/E." At this point in its protocol, we see that the program will accept
a message of format S, and in fact will not accept a Y or an N any longer.
You enter an S, and the program responds, pursuant to its protocol,
with a message of fixed-content format: "Please enter a name for the
file. (Six alphabetic characters)." What the author is asking you to do at
this point is to type in a message that is not in fixed-content format but
rather in variable-content format. The name you type in will have a fixed
length, a variable content, and a limited range of permissible symbols
(i.e., twenty-six).

The foregoing example involved messages in alphabetic formats readable by or written by humans. To each of those messages, however,
there is a corresponding machine-language image presented to the processor, which is indifferent whether the message comes from a human
or from a program. The same principles apply to interactions that occur
entirely in machine language, as in the case of exchanges of data or
commands between two programs, or between programs and hardware.
In fact, we are now starting to see the emergence of programs that
automate tasks heretofore carried on by computer operators and programmers in large computer installations. Some of these programs interact with other programs in those installations by pretending to be
people; that is, by issuing the responses that the other programs expect
to receive from human operators or programmers when they see particular messages on the display screen.

The suite of formats required by a program will have some determinate
attributes. For example, the content of certain messages, the length of
certain messages, or the meaning ascribed to specific characters at specific positions in a message (e.g., the first six characters are the date,
the next eight are the user's Social Security Number, etc.) may be in-

variant. Other formats in a program may be variable in content, length, or meaning, usually within some sort of limiting boundaries: for example, "Enter your name (up to 13 characters)." A program's protocols are the rules for permissible sequences of exchanges of information in prescribed formats.

Formats and protocols are the key to compatibility. The author of the target program will usually identify for the users, in the documentation that accompanies the program, or in the documentation—such as help screens—that is in the program itself, what the formats and protocols of the user interface are. The problem is that formats and protocols are unfortunately also the key to the detailed design of the program. Just as there are formats and protocols for exchanges between two programs, there are formats and protocols for exchanges between one part of a program and another. For instance, when one part of a program passes control to another part, it may do so by calling a subroutine. The subroutine call is a fixed-format message. If the program is delivered to customers only in object code form, customers may never see that call. If, however, it is delivered in source code form, they will see it if they read the source code. Once having found it, they may use that call in their own programs, so that when running with the original author's program, the customers' programs can invoke the same subroutine. This they may do whether the original author intended the subroutine call for customer use or not. In the extreme case, which we saw in *Apple v. Franklin*, so many different customers had written programs linking to internal regions of Apple's operating system that Franklin claimed not to be able to achieve 100 percent compatibility without exactly duplicating Apple's software.

Those of us who can read source code will find that a program's fixed-content formats typically appear as such in the code of the program itself. In our quit verification example, both "Y" and the phrase, "Do you want to Save or Erase the file? S/E" will actually appear in the program, perhaps in an instruction of the form

IF "Y," THEN PRINT "Do you want to Save or Erase the file? S/E."

On the other hand, variable-content formats and protocols will typically not be explicitly written in the source code of a program. For example, we never find, in executable lines of code, a statement saying specifically

"The 'quit' protocol is invoked by entering the character 'q.' The program responds by asking, 'Do you want to quit now? Y/N.' "

Such a statement might or might not appear in the comments to the source code, depending on the author's style of commenting. Even though variable-content formats and protocols are not explicitly rendered in the text of a program, however, a qualified reader would be able to infer them from a careful study of the executable code in which they are implemented.

Thus, a qualified reader could easily ascertain that our quit protocol consists in part of a message of the form q sent by the user, just as such a reader would be able to ascertain from the source code of a particular sorting program what algorithm was used for alphabetizing. Protocols may also be disclosed by things other than the source code. Screen formats can hint at the protocols used by the program. For the protocols of the user interface, some description will normally be found in the program's manuals. Internal protocols not otherwise documented to users may be ascertained by translating the object code of the program into a more readable form.

We can thus distinguish between the messages a program can generate or receive and the instructions in the program that cause those messages to be generated. For example, there is no output format more rigid than alphabetization, but there are many different ways to write programs that can alphabetize. Protecting the authorship in a program does not result in granting a monopoly over a particular format or a particular protocol. On the other hand, since a program's formats and protocols are a part of its detailed design, one who wishes to copy all or a substantial subset of them must understand that he or she is copying someone else's intellectual property.

To see how this distinction works in practice, let's put ourselves in the place of a would-be supplier of compatible software and joust with a couple of the demons of compatibility.

19

Compatibility Demons: *Johnson v. Uniden* and Further Principles for Software Clones

"But why," pursued the summoner, "track your game
In various shapes? Why don't you stay the same?"
"Just to appear," he said, "in such a way
As will enable us to snatch our prey." . . .
"Tell me," the summoner said, "—I'm just a dunce—
But do you make new bodies as you go
Out of the elements?" The fiend said, "No;
We just create illusions, or we raise
A corpse and use it; there are many ways."

Chaucer, *Canterbury Tales* (cir. 1390)

As I've just said, compatibility means different things to different people in the software industry. One definition of compatibility is that it is the condition whereby two programs will work together. For that condition to obtain, the second program must conform to the formats and protocols that the author of the first program prescribed for communication with that program. The two programs will then be complementary.

Another definition of compatibility is that the second program will replace the first program. Here, there are a range of possibilities, depending on how "compatible" the follower wants to be. The second program might duplicate all the functions of the first program. It might duplicate all the functions of and run on the same hardware as the first. It might do those things and also duplicate the formats and protocols of the application program interface of the first. It might do all those things and also duplicate the formats and protocols of the end user

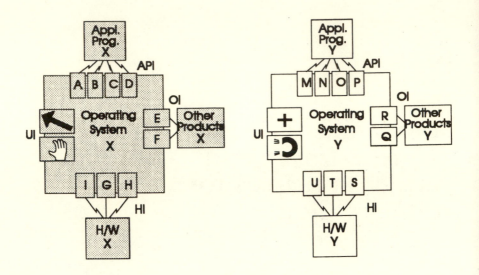

API = Application Program Interface

UI = User Interface

HI = Hardware Interface

OI = Other Interfaces

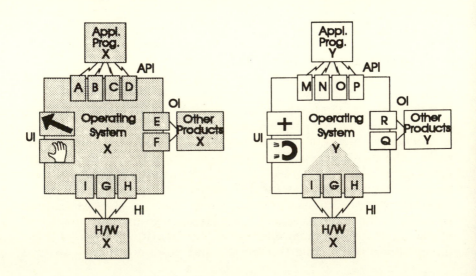

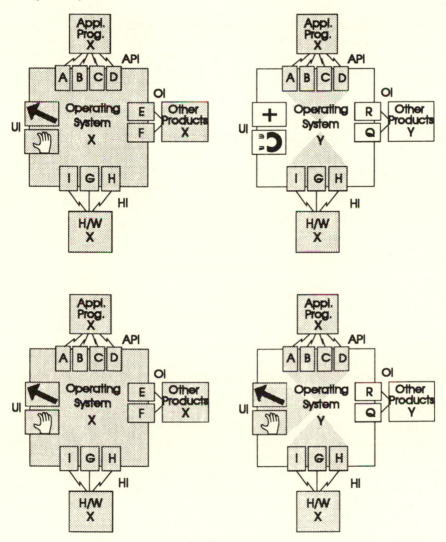

interface (screens, messages, operator commands, and the like). Finally, it might do all those things and duplicate the internal formats and protocols of the first program in order to be certain to work in exactly the same way as the first program with every single piece of hardware and software with which the first program works. (Reproducing the internal elements of an original program in the name of "compatibility" starkly illustrates why there cannot be a black-and-white rule excepting "program interfaces" from copyright protection: almost any expression in a program can be used as part of an interface, whether the author intends for that to happen or not. As a result, removing copyright protection

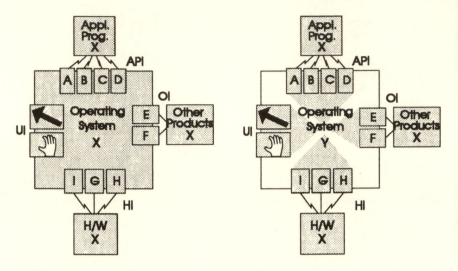

for "interfaces" that anyone might assert were needed for compatibility, would effectively vitiate all copyright protection for the program.)

The latter formulations of compatibility strategies are obviously the most aggressive and risky business strategies for a clone supplier to adopt, because the more attributes of an original program that are duplicated, the greater the risk of going beyond the taking only of ideas. That is particularly true in the case of a competitor with an aggressive cloning strategy who has access to the original program during the design of the compatible program. A literary analogy makes the reason clear. If I decide to write a murder mystery, there is no infringement in that decision. If I decide to set the mystery in a medieval abbey in Italy, that decision does not portend infringement either. If I then decide that my protagonist will be an English monk, and that the narrator will be his youthful assistant, those who have read *The Name of the Rose* will immediately recognize the similarity. Were I to tell you that I, too, have read *The Name of the Rose*, you would immediately conclude that I had gotten my idea from Umberto Eco's novel. So far, though, all I've taken is idea, not expression. Now, suppose that my plot involves a series of comico-grizzly murders in the abbey. Suppose that it pits the English monk against the papacy. Suppose that the plot implicates a mysterious, apocalyptic document, includes the fiery razing of the abbey and . . . Well, you get the picture. Clearly there comes a point at which the author who has had access to *The Name of the Rose* and who sets out to clone it will properly find himself burdened with the obligation of rebutting a prima facie case of copyright infringement.

There are reportedly seven levels of Hell for human souls. For writers of compatible programs, there are only three, represented by the three different classes of relationship that a target program may have with the outside world: relationships with other programs, relationships with hardware, and relationships with humans. The task we are going to set for ourselves as hypothetical compatible software suppliers is to replicate as many of those relationships as we can without infringing the copyright in the target program.

At the outset, we cloners must ask ourselves as responsible business-people—indeed, as responsible citizens—whether there are ways to eliminate or substantially reduce the risk we are running. One such way would be to obtain a license from the author of the target program. In the domain of intellectual property, one who sets out to copy the externally perceptible characteristics of someone else's creation is well-advised—and normally prepared—to obtain a license from that someone else. It is not a good idea to rerecord *Meet the Beatles*, to copy a Dior dress, to duplicate the artistic style and messages of a line of Snoopy greeting cards, or to remake *The Last Emperor* without a license. This will not surprise the reader. A vendor who wishes to contend for shelf space with the fashion item, book, record, video, or other creative product of another vendor by offering a product highly similar in design and realization to the original is expected to pay for the privilege of appropriating the design and realization, or to be barred from having the privilege. That is what intellectual property rights are all about. They are rights in intangible property, the benefits of which may be enjoyed either by licensing others to reproduce the property or by keeping that right to oneself. It is one of the great curiosities of the computer industry that in the context of software a number of suppliers, among them some perfectly upstanding corporate or individual citizens, feel free to reproduce without license the intellectual property represented by the external characteristics of another supplier's program, and cry foul if the other supplier attempts to assert its rights against them.

Let's assume, nonetheless, that we have decided not to seek a license because we think that one will not be granted or because we'd rather that the target competitor not know what our product strategy is until our product appears on the market. Is there any other way to reduce the risk of this software cloning business? Our lawyer mumbles something about a clean room. If we set up a clean room for our compatible design team, and only send into that room information about the target program that is unprotected by copyright, he or she feels capable of defending us. Consequently, we set up a clean room. All the development of the compatible program is done inside, by people who have not previously had any access whatever to the target program. Any access may be too strong a statement . . . but they haven't had access to the particular release of the target program which they are cloning, only to prior releases. Actually, that's not quite right either, because one of them has sat at a terminal and observed the user interface of the new release. Nonetheless, they haven't studied the code or even read the user manuals for the latest release. Finding true "virgins," as they are called in the lingo of compatible software development, is not easy. On the other hand, other aspects of the clone's job are easy: There is no need to do market research or to worry about what the functional specifications of our program will be. We simply pick a successful target program and duplicate its functions (as well as whatever else our lawyer lets us send into the clean room).

There's a computer in the clean room, of course, but it's not connected to any computers outside the clean room. There are no telephones in the clean room, no fax machines, and no other ways of receiving information electronically from the outside. A security guard prevents access to the clean room to anyone who is not part of the compatible development team. All information that comes in arrives in the form of hard copy or magnetic media, and is logged in by a librarian. Likewise, any information or requests for information that come out of the clean room must be in writing. It's pretty unwieldy, and don't ask us yet what happens when it comes time to test the program developed in the clean room or to fix bugs in its compatibility features, but for now, those people in the clean room are *isolated*.

The action, of course, is outside the clean room, where our other employees have liberal access to the target program and all its documentation. Their job is to extract from those materials the unprotected elements of the target program and to send that information into the clean room. Will those unprotected elements be sufficient to allow us to pursue an aggressive cloning strategy? Will our employees outside the clean room be able to distinguish idea from expression? Will they be under pressure to err on the side of providing more information? The answers are fairly obvious, but we plunge along anyway.

Rather than go through each and every format and protocol of the target program and show you what our employees have to do to satisfy their management's aggressive cloning strategy, I've selected four examples that should give you an adequate feel for the risks that we face, even with a clean room. We'll look at two kinds of program-to-program interface (command languages and macros), one kind of program-to-hardware interface (instruction sets), and one kind of user interface (screen formats).

One of the demons we have to conquer as suppliers of clone software is the set of commands that the target program provides for use by application programs. The target program offers a convenient suite of commands for customers to use in writing their own programs that utilize the services of the target program. Ordinarily a program author has broad latitude in the choice of commands that the program is allowed to recognize, and there are numerous considerations that the author with complete freedom of action might weigh in making such choices. That was true for the author of the target program. We are not in that position, though. We wish our program to replace the target program in customer installations, and work just as it works with customer-written programs. Therefore, we want to adopt the syntax and semantics of the target program's commands.

One of the commands that our hypothetical target program offers, for example, is SCRNFMT [a, b, c, d]. SCRNFMT is used by customer programs to request that the target program format the computer's screen display in a particular way. The parameters a, b, c, and d are, respectively, the foreground color, background color, font size, and line length. By inserting specific values for those parameters, the customers, through their programs, ask the target program for specific screen set-ups. The target program's syntax requires that screen format requests be presented to it exactly as described: first, the keyword SCRNFMT, then a series of four one-digit numbers separated by commas. We want our clone programs to (a) interpret the character string SCRNFMT as a screen format command, (b) interpret each of the four parameters the way the target program interprets them, and (c) issue an appropriate series of detailed instructions to the processor in order to accomplish the screen set-up.

Temptations abound in Hades. We know that the target program already includes perfectly satisfactory instructions to do these things, and it would be so easy for us simply to read the target program, photocopy those instructions, and send them into the clean room. Our programmers then would not have to think about how such code might best be written. However, we know that infringement lies in that direction, so instead we have our employees outside the clean room create a different kind of document. For SCRNFMT and the sixty other commands in the target program's application program interface, we create a vocabulary list with sixty-one entries, together with a definition for each entry that states the purpose of the command and what responses the target program gives to the command under various circumstances, plus a set of grammatical rules for the use of each command and associated parameters. The document is thirty pages long, and we are left with the question of whether the document itself, and as a result the program written in the clean room, infringes the copyright in the target program. Let's hold that question until we finish our thought experiment.

The second demon I will confront our team with is the macro. Macros, you'll recall, are small, self-contained programs, usually delivered as part of a larger program, that can be called to the fore by name and thereby inserted into a customer's program. The target program offers

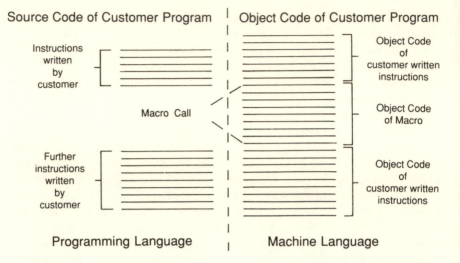

a number of macros. Some of them, when the customer's program first calls them by name, become permanently inserted in the object code of the customer's program. Once they are so inserted, those macros define parts of the interface between the customer's program and the target program. In other words, what at the source-code level was a clean interface consisting of a series of macro calls, becomes at the object level a more complex interface consisting of all the relationships the author of the target program had envisioned between each macro and the rest of the target program. Where the customer whose program calls the macro is itself a software house, these target program's macros become part of the programs that are themselves distributed commercially to other customers.

There are other macros in the target program that don't become permanently integrated into customers' programs. Instead, they are imported into the customers' programs each time the latter are run on a computer in which the target program also resides. The customer writes his or her program so that when it commences execution, it calls by name (and also, where necessary, by specifying the requisite parameters) the macro it desires. We can think of such macros as being transient additions to customer programs.

The benefit obtained by calling macros is that the functions they provide do not need to be written individually by the customer's programmers. For example, by calling the PRNTMAC macro in our hypothetical target program, a customer can take advantage of a macro that organizes the computer's resources to achieve printing of output reports on the computer's printer.

Macros present compatible program developers like us with some interesting challenges. Where the customer has not written the code that provides certain facilities that his or her program needs, but instead has written a call to a macro in the target program, our strategy requires us to provide a macro in our program that has the same name, the same parameters, and the same facilities as the macro in the target program. Therefore, among the inputs to the clean room must be the names of all the target program's transient macros, the specification of each parameter of each macro, and a description of each facility provided by each macro. When completed, this document also turns out to be about thirty pages long.

For those macros that become permanently integrated into customer programs, there is another dimension of difficulty. Think of each such macro as having a single head and a multiplicity of tails. The head is the macro's name, the single identifier by which the macro is summoned and imbedded in the customer's program. The tails are the various strings of instructions by which the macro communicates with each part of the target program with which it must communicate in order to achieve its purpose. When such a macro is inserted into the customer's object code, it multiplies by many times the complexity of the interactions to which we need to conform in pursuit of our business strategy.

This demonic transformation is particularly maddening for us. While the target program's macro calls are neatly and completely described in the user manuals sold with the target program, the connections between the macro's tails and the rest of the target program are not described anywhere except in the macros themselves. These connections include connections to internal subroutines in the target program, and they also include references to internal data areas. How can we specify all these design elements for our clean room developers without infringing the copyright in the target program?

Of course, if we had chosen a slightly less aggressive cloning strategy we wouldn't have this problem. If we were willing to tell our customers to recompile their source code using one of our compilers, we would not need to copy any of the target program's internal design. The customer's source code would contain the same macro calls, but when our compiler "saw" those calls in the course of converting the customer's source code into object code, it would summon from our clone program a macro that we have written, which would serve in place of the target program's macro. Then, the macro tails could be defined by us in any way we wished. This is a particular instance of a general truth: the less aggressive the compatibility strategy, and the greater the conversion effort the clone supplier is willing to undertake (or have the customer undertake), the lower the infringement risk. For example, there is no need even to conform to the target program's macro calls imbedded in the customer's source code. The customer (or we) can rewrite the customer's programs to substitute calls to the clone program for the calls to the target program.

We conclude, though, that we're willing to take the risk of infringement in order to be able to tell our customers that they can run their programs with our clone program without the need for recompilation. We tell our employees to document all the connections between macro tails and the rest of the target program in sufficient detail for our clean room developers to create a program that will look, to the macro tails imbedded in customer programs, just like the target program. When completed, that documentation takes up 150 pages.

Two hundred ten pages so far. There are other program-to-program relationships that we want to copy as well, but let's turn now to program-to-hardware relationships. Basically, this is the relationship of the target program to the processor on which it is designed to run. If our clone program is effortlessly to replace copies of the target program in the marketplace, it must use the hardware's instruction set in exactly the same ways as the target program does. In other words, it is not enough for us to know what the instructions in the processor's instruction set are. There are roughly a hundred of those instructions, and we can of course learn what they are from the hardware and its documentation, without looking at the target program at all. The performance of the target program, however, depends in large measure on the particular combinations of hardware instructions that it issues in the course of performing its various functions. Although we might develop a faster program by independent research into efficient use of the hardware instruction set, the easiest way to assure that our program achieves at least the same performance is to have it issue the same hardware instructions to accomplish the same purposes as the target program. It may be that here and there the programmers in the clean room can improve our performance by altering the sequence in which those instructions are issued, but if we don't start with the target program's sequences as a baseline, we run the risk of ending up with a slower product, which is unacceptable strategically. We tell the people outside the clean room to send in a document listing the sequences of hardware instructions issued by the target program for various purposes. This adds another 150 pages.

To complete the picture, we turn to the program-to-user interface. This consists of end-user screens, operator messages, and formats of printed output. We'll confine our attention to end-user screens. There are dozens of these, each one signifying a different phase of the program. Users of the target program are accustomed to working with these screens. They understand what the content of each screen means, how the target program "expects" them to react to each screen, and how the screens relate to one another. We don't want those end users to have to learn a new set of screens. We want to be able to advertise "No Retraining!" Regrettably, there's only one way to achieve that level of compatibility. We instruct our people to send into the clean room copies of each screen and a description of how the user interacts with each and how the screens relate to one another. We do not feel terribly comfortable about this, as our lawyer has read the *Softklone* case, but it is better than the other alternative we considered: sending the object code of the target program into the clean room so our developers could run it and get the look and feel of the screens first-hand. The documentation of the screens consumes one hundred pages.

It's nerve-wracking being a supplier of software clones, isn't it? The clean room in our hypothetical situation so far contains some 460 pages describing just the four elements of the target program that we've specifically considered in this chapter. There's much more to send in if we wish to achieve our goal of full compatibility. Do the 460 pages describe ideas or expression? Each individual element of the description could be argued to be a detailed idea, in the sense that every element of a program is to some degree conceptual; but taken together, what the documentation comprises is a detailed outline of major elements of the design of the target program. At some point, like the fellow who sets out to clone his way into Tom Clancy's shelf space, we are going to cross the line. The screens, of course, present a special problem, as these were not even abstracted before being provided to the clean room.

A further principle that we can state about compatibility and copyright, then, is that clean room strategies are only as good as what is put into the clean room. The clean room can serve to prove lack of access to the target program by developers of the clone program, but it will only serve that purpose if there is in fact no detailed design information about the target program inside the clean room. In the *Intel* case, what went into the litigation clean room was what NEC was licensed to copy and what Intel did not contend that NEC could not copy. In the real world, operators of clean rooms have not normally had either licenses or permission to copy what they send into the clean room. Conservatism is therefore very important.

A final principle that should now be clear to the reader is that there is no special dispensation to copy interfaces. Software interfaces are simply parts of the program's design that are convenient connection points. They are not like sockets in a wall. They are all contained in the text of a program. The interfaces in an original program can take as much creativity to generate as the other elements of the program, and they can be as arbitrary. Indeed, programming interfaces may not be intended as interfaces at all by the program's author. They may be "created" after the fact by someone other than the program's author who determines that an internal subroutine call is a convenient place to attach. Here, the concept of "interface" vanishes, as there is no difference between such interfaces and the internal design of the program. At the ultimate, for instance, there are classes of programs—typified by the performance monitor, a program that provides statistics on how efficiently another program executes its work inside a processor—that attach probe points deep inside the other program in places never intended to be interfaces. In order for such programs to run in conjunction with a clone of the program for which they were designed, the clone program must be identical in internal detail at all the anticipated probe points, and identical in its operation in connection with all the parameters measured at those probe points.

Moving from programming interfaces to end-user interfaces, we find that end-user interfaces in particular can be a highly valuable feature of an original program. Programming interfaces are, after all, only of interest to programmers. End-user interfaces are of interest to what the Apple advertisements call "the rest of us." "The user illusion," says Alan Kay, "is theater."

Are there times when interfaces are dictated by the environment in which a program operates? The answer is, "Yes, always," in the case of clone programs. In the case of original program, the answer is, "Yes sometimes." An original program may have some interfaces that conform to international standards, or to customary documentation in the industry at which the program is directed. An example of the latter situation was found in the *Plains Cotton* case, wherein the cotton recap report was a standardized output format that both plaintiff's program and defendant's program had to duplicate. Obviously, where the environment dictates the interface, the foregoing discussion of creativity does not apply. In such cases, just as obviously, it is unnecessary for the clone to refer to the target program in order to achieve compatibility.

Do you have a phone in your car? I don't. Nor a fax machine. But then I don't live in Silicon Valley. Before mobile phones and mobile faxes, there was mobile radio. Mobile radios were and are widely installed in police cars, taxis, and delivery vehicles. Where there are mobile radios, there are "repeaters," base stations that communicate with the radios. Inside the repeaters and inside the radios there are computers, controlled by the programs that manage the communications between the former and the latter. Now this begins to sound relevant, doesn't it? The reader can already conjure up the scenario: an innovator sells base stations and radios with substantial success, until a follower begins selling low-priced "compatible" radios and taking away some of the business.

The innovator was the E. F. Johnson Company of Waseca, Minnesota. Johnson made "logic-trunked" mobile radio systems. "Logic trunking" allowed all available frequencies in the network to be shared by all users. The software in the radios and in the repeaters was what kept pandemonium from erupting in Johnson's networks. It controlled access to a particular channel at a particular time so that conversations would not bleed into one another. That software was imbedded in ROM, and controlled an Intel 8049 microprocessor. In the market for trunked mobile radio systems, Johnson's logic-trunked units were in great demand. By the mid–1980s, the size of that market in the United States was on the order of $200 million in annual retail sales. The size of Johnson's annual sales at retail was about $40 million.

The follower was the Uniden Corporation of Indiana, a subsidiary of Uniden of Japan. In 1984, Uniden commenced development of a Johnson-compatible radio. The development effort entailed gaining access to and studying Johnson's software. Uniden engineer S. Katsukura "disassembled" the software in the Johnson ROM. Disassembly is a process of translation. Katsukura first "dumped" Johnson's object code program, or caused it to be read out of the ROM in which it was stored. Then he translated the object code into assembly language. Then he and another Uniden engineer, S. Uwabe, analyzed the program and prepared flow charts detailing its logic. One of the things they discovered in analyzing Johnson's program was that it contained a notice of copyright, a discovery that was reinforced when Johnson, on hearing rumors of Uniden's project, wrote to Uniden warning them not to copy its logic trunking program.

Undaunted, Uniden completed its project and introduced its radios at a trade show in April 1985. Johnson of course bought one, and its engineers promptly disassembled the Uniden code for comparison with the Johnson program. They concluded that the data areas were identical and that a line-by-line examination demonstrated copying of the Johnson program. Not long thereafter, Uniden found itself before Judge Harry H. MacLaughlin in the U.S. District Court in Minnesota arguing why its radios should not be barred from the market and impounded pending trial.

Uniden's principal argument was that it had only copied what was necessary to make it compatible. The focus of the court's opinion was therefore on whether the similarities between the two programs were "necessary to compatibility" or not. Along the way, the court made several other relevant observations:

—Uniden's software was substantially similar to Johnson's.

—Uniden had the right to develop compatible software, so long as it did not copy the expression in Johnson's program. The mere fact that Uniden wanted to be compatible did not give it any larger right to copy Johnson's program than anyone else had.

—If there were ideas in Johnson's program that could only be expressed in a single way, Uniden was free to copy that expression.

—Ruling against Uniden would not allow Johnson to monopolize the market. There were other suppliers of Johnson-compatible radios, and Uniden was free to pursue a compatibility strategy, too. [Although the court did not mention it at this point in its opinion, the "market," for purposes of determining whether Johnson had a monopoly or not, would doubtless have included Johnson's noncompatible competitors, too. In the market properly measured for antitrust purposes, Johnson's share was 25 percent, hardly a monopoly, and not even within striking distance of one.]

The real question, the court felt, was whether it was necessary for Uniden's program to be substantially similar to Johnson's in order for Uniden to achieve compatibility. Judge MacLaughlin assessed the principal similarities one by one to answer that question.

The first of these related to synchronization between the radio and the repeater. In order to be sure the two were synchronized, Johnson's radios sampled incoming data and compared the sample against a "lookup table." The incoming data always included a particular pattern of eight bits, called a "Barker word," specifically transmitted for synchronization purposes. The Johnson program was designed to take eight samples of seven bits each, or fifty-six bits altogether, for comparison to the table entries. If eight or fewer errors were detected, the radio and the repeater were assumed to be synchronized. Uniden's program operated the same way. The court found that the only necessary similarity was that, given the eight-bit error-checking pattern in the incoming data stream, the Uniden program would have to search for that pattern. The selection of a fifty-six bit sample, the use of a table-lookup technique to check for errors, and the assumption that synchronization had succeeded if there were eight or fewer errors in the sample were all discretionary design choices that could easily have been changed without loss of compatibility. Indeed, since the Uniden radio utilized a Hitachi microprocessor with an architecture quite unlike that of the Intel microprocessor, one would have expected different design choices if the capabilities of the Hitachi chip were to be best utilized.

The second area of similarity examined by the court had to do with error checking. Johnson's radios and repeaters used an "H-matrix" and an "inverse H-matrix" for this purpose. These matrices are simply patterns of ones and zeros arranged in rows and columns, which are checked periodically during transmission to make sure they are being accurately received. Uniden used the same H-matrix and inverse H-matrix. Johnson's program loaded the H-matrix in inverse order; so did Uniden's. The court found that, while Uniden would not have been compatible had it not used some form of H-matrix for error checking, it could have used any one of thirty-two patterns for this purpose. It did not have to have the same pattern as Johnson. Further, there was no necessity whatsoever to utilize an inverse H-matrix, a feature which had only been included in Johnson's program because of a miscommunication between Johnson's designer and its coder. Finally, the reverse-order loading of the H-matrix in the Johnson program was done because of a particular design constraint of the Intel chip. That constraint did not exist in the Hitachi chip, nor was reverse loading necessary for compatibility.

The third similarity assessed by the court was a tiny but telltale fingerprint. There were three lines of code in the Johnson program whose presence was completely superfluous. They were not put there specifically to catch infringers, but were a vestige of a duplexing feature that had been written into the Johnson program and later removed. By mistake, Johnson's coder had left three inoperative statements in the program. The same three statements appeared in the same part of the Uniden program. Uniden engineer Uwabe testified that the three statements were written by him to accommodate a duplexing feature, should Uniden choose to offer one in the future. Not surprisingly, Judge MacLaughlin didn't believe him.

The fourth similarity was an error in the "busy signal" routine of the two programs. In the Johnson code, when a single call dispatcher was transmitting to a single radio, all radios that attempted to communicate, not just with that dispatcher but with any dispatcher on the system, received a busy signal. That error was corrected in later releases of the Johnson program, but not before it appeared in Uniden's program. The court found it more likely that the error found its way into the Uniden program as a result of copying than as a result of serendipitous inadvertence.

There were a number of other similarities between the two programs, including similarities in stylistic idiosyncracies, in subroutine organization, and in design decisions. Judge MacLaughlin found the Uniden program infringed the copyright in the Johnson program and that, until a full trial could be had, Uniden should be barred from selling or distributing its Johnson-compatible program in any form, or from infringing the copyright in Johnson's program in any way.

Johnson v. Uniden serves as an interesting and instructive example of a parsing of a clone program to determine which similarities were dictated by a compatibility objective and which were not. Based on his analysis, Judge MacLaughlin concluded that:

Copying plaintiff's code was not the only and essential means of creating an LTR [Logic Trunked Radio]-compatible software program. Defendant was required to copy plaintiff's Barker word, as discussed above. Virtually all other aspects of defendant's program could have been independently created, however, without violence to defendant's compatibility objective.

What Judge MacLaughlin's opinion suggests is that if Uniden had had a clean room, the only explicit information from Johnson's program that would need to have been sent into that clean room would have been the Barker word. For the rest, abstracted descriptions of what the Johnson program did would have sufficed.

More problematically, the opinion also suggests that if copying Johnson's program were the "only and essential means" of achieving compatibility, then such copying would be lawful. That suggestion, which may have been appropriate in the factual situation facing Judge Mac-Laughlin—and in any case was completely unnecessary to the judge's decision—is far too simplistic to be reliable in other contexts. As we've seen, an aggressive compatibility strategy entails creating a series of optional similarities between the clone program and the target program, which are by no means the "only and effective means" of competing effectively with the target program. Rather, these similarities are simply strategic business decisions designed to make it as easy as possible to replace the target program in the field and reduce the clone supplier's marketing costs. For example, while it may be convenient for customers to see screen formats in the clone program that are identical to those in the target program, the clone supplier is in no way compelled to achieve that level of similarity in order to compete with the supplier of the target program, and, as the *Broderbund* case showed us, there is no assurance whatsoever that such a degree of compatibility will be permitted. The only reliable teaching from *Johnson v. Uniden*, and the final principle in our litany, is that for clone suppliers, Le Corbusier's rule is paramount: "Less is more." Cloning should be limited to the elements of a target program that can be emulated without copying.

20

The "Look and Feel" Cases

Men always prefer to walk in paths marked out by others and pattern
their actions through imitation. Even if he cannot follow other people's paths in every respect, or attain to the merit of his originals, a
prudent man should always follow the footsteps of the great and
imitate those who have been supreme. His own talent may not come
up to theirs, but at least he will have a sniff of it.

N. Machiavelli, *The Prince* (1513)

I don't know about the "sniff" of it, but we certainly come to the end of
our Odyssey ready to take on the question of the "look and feel" of it.
Armed now with the basic principles of copyright, we can make informed judgments about the legal merit of look and feel cases, and apply
our policy analyses to them. We cannot, of course, predict the outcome
of any particular case, for one thing that the reader should have learned in
assessing copyright cases is, in Dickens' words from *Hard Times*:

Now, what I want is Facts. Facts alone are wanted in life. Plant nothing else,
and root out everything else. You can only form the minds of reasoning animals
on Facts: nothing else will ever be of any service to them.

That is, a firm understanding of whether a particular activity constitutes
infringement can be foretold only if all the circumstances are known.
What is proposed to be copied from the target program; why and how?
When these things are revealed in detail, the copyright law provides a
reasonable, stable, and predictable indication of the outcome to be expected. Subject to the caveat that different facts may well lead to different

results, we should be able to assess the wisdom or the folly of attempting to clone the "look and feel" of a popular program.

Earlier, I referred to a kind of copying called "comprehensive nonliteral similarity." That is the kind of copying that was done in the *Whelan* case. It is usually the result of an attempt to do simultaneously two things that can't be done simultaneously: evade an infringement charge while capturing the essence of someone else's copyrighted work. This is like trying to whistle while eating soda crackers, and usually produces just as messy a result.

Comprehensive nonliteral similarity has long constituted infringement, except in cases where idea and expression merge. In the caselaw, achieving comprehensive nonliteral similarity is often referred to as copying the "total concept and feel" of another's work. The phrase "total concept and feel" comes from a twenty-year old copyright case involving the copying of thematic and stylistic features of a line of greeting cards. It is commonly thought that the phrase that interests us, "look and feel," derives from "total concept and feel." Whether that is etymologically accurate or not, it is certainly true that, at least in the United States, copying the total concept and feel of the original and protected elements in someone else's program is not permitted. It is also beyond doubt that, factually, the user interface of a program is primarily responsible for giving that program its total concept and feel. Is "look and feel" the same thing as "total concept and feel"? To the extent that it is, the legal principles that apply to the look and feel cases are well known. The complaint filed by Ashton-Tate Corporation against Fox Software, Inc., accuses Fox of copying "the novel and highly successful application development and data management environment of the dBase programs and duplicat[ing] their unique look and feel to the program user." Attached to the complaint are several exhibits comparing dBase screen displays and FoxBase screen displays. Here is one of the comparisons:

<u>dBase III</u>:

```
. display structure
Structure for  database:  C:travel.dfb
Number of data records:     49
Date of last update      : 11/14/05
Field  Field Name    Type       Width    Dec
    1  FIRSTNAME     Character     20
    2  LASTNAME      Character     20
    3  PHONE         Character     13
    4  TRAVELCODE    Character      4
    5  TRAVELPLAN    Character     40
    6  DEPARTURE     Date           8
    7  COST          Numeric       10      2
    8  PAID          Logical        1
    9  AGENT         Character      2
```

```
    10  RESERVDATE  Date        10
    11  NOTES       Memo        10
  **Total**
  ,
Command Line  | <C:> | TRAVEL |         Rec: 1/49 |     |

             Enter a dBase III PLUS command,
----------------------------------------------------------
                         FoxBase
, display structure
Structure for database: C:\TRAVEL.DBF
Number of data records:    49
Date of last update     : 11/14/05
Field Field Name  Type      Width   Dec
     1 FIRSTNAME  Character   20
     2 LASTNAME   Character   20
     3 PHONE      Character   13
     4 TRAVELCODE Character    4
     5 TRAVELPLAN Character   40
     6 DEPARTURE  Date         8
     7 COST       Numeric     10     2
     8 PAID       Logical      1
     9 AGENT      Character    2
    10 RESERVDATE Date        10
    11 NOTES      Memo        10
  **Total**
  ,
Command Line  | <C:> | TRAVEL |         Rec: 1/49 |     |

             Enter a FoxBase+ Command
```

Apple's complaint against Microsoft and Hewlett-Packard accuses the defendants of copying the "fanciful displays and images appearing on the computer screen" of the Macintosh. Apple asserts that millions of dollars of creative effort had gone into the creation of "artistic, aesthetically pleasing" visual displays and graphic images that enhance the value and appeal of Apple's products, and that the distinctive displays and images generated by the Macintosh programs are "widely recognized as a hallmark of the Macintosh computer system." Attached to Apple's complaint were a series of photographs comparing of the screen displays of the Macintosh with those generated by Hewlett-Packard's New Wave software operating in conjunction with Microsoft's Windows 2.03 software. One such comparison appears in the figure on the next page.

On first blush, the similarities demonstrated by both plaintiffs are visu-

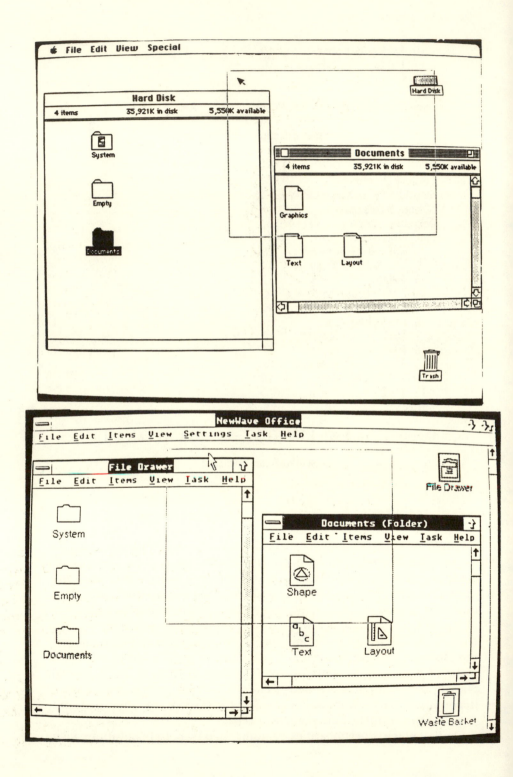

ally arresting. However, when, like Sergeant Joe Friday, we ask for "Just the facts, Ma'am, just the facts," a somewhat more complicated picture begins to emerge. In both Apple's case and Ashton-Tate's case, for example, the hypothetical users created some of the similarities. Thus, in the Ashton-Tate illustration, the field names and field widths are items normally entered by the user. That they are identical in the dBase and FoxBase illustrations has little bearing on whether Fox Software's screen display is a copy of Ashton-Tate's. Similarly, in the Apple photos, the wastebasket icon shown in the defendants' display is not an invariable part of that display. It is an option that may be selected from the Hewlett-Packard program by the user, and if it is, it then will reappear each time the system is booted up.

Furthermore, in both cases, other similarities on the screen are due to the use of typical industry conventions. Calling field types "character," "numeric," or "logical," for instance, is not particularly original; nor are rectangular windows.

Moreover, some of the similarities did not originate with the plaintiffs. dBase III relies on a query language, SQL, that originated at IBM and is now an official industry standard. Apple's file icon is visually similar to the Star system created at the Xerox Palo Alto Research Center in the 1970s.

There are other complications as well. For example, in settlement of an earlier infringement dispute, Microsoft was licensed by Apple to reproduce the user interface of Windows 1.0 program in subsequent versions of Windows, and although that license has been found not to immunize Windows' newer version, Version 2.03, from charges of infringement, it does apparently immunize the elements in Version 2.03 that were also part of Version 1.0, with the result that the principal matter at issue is Microsoft's implementation in Windows 2.03 of overlapping application windows.

In other words, the courts that are handling these cases have to sort out the original elements of the plaintiffs' user interfaces from the non-original elements, determine whether the arrangement of nonoriginal elements is in itself original, separate the similarities that the user can create from those that the plaintiff's program creates, identify the aspects of the original elements that are necessary to the purpose of the plaintiffs' programs and those that are not, and deal with other factual complications that may arise out of the relationships between the litigants. (In addition, in the *Apple* case, the court must deal with such animation or audio visual effects as are not immunized by the license agreement.) At the end of the day, those courts may indeed find that there is some original expression in the selection of items on the screen, in the arrangement of those items, in their placement and in other aspects of their appearance. They are certainly likely to find, for whatever it is worth, that a great deal of thought and effort was put into creating the Apple and Ashton-Tate "user illusions." (The existence of the table displayed in the Ashton-Tate illustration is, after all, an illusion. dBase III can create the table on command and display it on the screen of a personal computer, but the table does not exist as such in the code of the program. Of course, there is no physical trash can in the Macintosh operating system; nor does a file physically disappear from diskette when its icon is dumped in the trash can. The icon is an illusion, a metaphor used for making conversation with a human being.)

What if the courts do reach such conclusions? What will be the fate of the defendants?

Broderbund teaches us that the structure, logic, and flow of a suite of screen displays is protectable subject matter. *Softklone* affirms that the arrangement and design of even a single screen display is protectable subject matter. A third case, *Manufacturers Technologies, Inc. v. CAMS, Inc.*, affirms that the flow of a related sequence of display screens is protectable, to the extent not dictated solely by functional considerations; and that the selection, arrangement, and organization of the content of individual screens is protectable, although such things as the "method of navigation" (movement of the cursor) within or among screens are not. These cases set a baseline for the "look and feel" question. Literal knock-offs of original screen displays will not be rewarded by society.

At the opposite end of the spectrum, the *Frybarger* and *Data East* cases set another baseline. Conventional elements common to programs having the same idea (in *Frybarger*, the array of pivot points and lines that constituted the maze) and the program elements necessary to convey the idea of the program (in *Frybarger*, the presence of a protagonist and antagonists and the ability of the protagonist either to evade or trap the antagonists) are not protectable subject matter.

Fox Software, Microsoft, Hewlett-Packard, and the *Lotus* defendants, Mosaic Software and Paperback Software will be spared liability if, when everything is eliminated except the expression that may not be copied in the plaintiffs' user interfaces, it is found that they have not copied that expression. Without knowing what will be left after the boiling-away exercises, one cannot predict the outcome of any particular case. It is safe to say, though, that the law will protect original elements of a user interface the expressive content of which rise above the level of "blank forms," and will not protect either ideas as to how to convey information on a screen or the expression necessary to convey those ideas, i.e., the expression that "merges" with the ideas.

Between those two baselines lies the gray area, the playing field on which the general principles set out in the preceding chapters provide the rules of the game. For convenience, those principles are summarized below:

1. There are substantial benefits to be derived from deciding questions about the conflict between software compatibility objectives and intellectual prop-

erty rights on the basis of copyright law, rather than making up a separate set of legal rules to govern that conflict.

2. The mere fact that a supplier adopts a compatibility strategy does not give that supplier carte blanche to copy whatever it wants from the target program of another supplier.

3. The compatible supplier may copy the ideas in the target program and any expression essential to implementing those ideas.

4. Compatibility achieved completely independently of the target program does not constitute copyright infringement.

5. The exclusive rights of the copyright owner do not constitute a grant of monopoly over the information in the copyrighted work.

6. Clean room strategies are only as good as what is put into the clean room.

7. There is no special dispensation to copy interfaces, since they are a part of the program's design.

8. Less is more.

The rules of the game as articulated above should lead suppliers of compatible software to conclude that cloning must be limited to the elements of a target program that can be emulated without copying. When it comes to the user interface, that conclusion presents some hard choices. Consider the clean room. If we, as compatible suppliers, wish to clone the user interface of an original program to the extent permitted by law, what may we send into the clean room that will convey the look and feel of the target program but still allow us to claim lack of access to it? Is the Macintosh trash can an idea or an expression?

Hopefully, the reader has learned how to answer such questions by now. The trash can alone is not what is at issue. It's easy enough to use a different icon: a black hole, as Steve Jobs has done, or a shredder, as IBM has. It is also not infringement to copy just the trash can if everything else on the screen is different. The issue is whether there is qualitative substantial similarity of the two user interfaces. Assuming for the sake of simplicity that all the elements of the Macintosh visual displays originated entirely with Apple—which is said by Microsoft and Hewlett-Packard not to be true in fact—it would be risky to send a picture of each of Apple's user interface elements and a description of the way each is used into the clean room as elements that can be duplicated in the name of compatibility. In contrast, it would not be risky to ask the developers in the clean room to permit users to express by means of icon manipulation their desire to reuse space on a diskette occupied by an existing file, to copy a file from one disk to another, to page through a document, to print a document, and to perform the other functions common to personal computer use.

Why should competitive suppliers be required to go to such trouble? There are three reasons.

First, it is because, as Alan Kay pointed out in his 1984 *Scientific American* article, the user interface is "primary." The user interface or "illusion" is often the most important feature of a program, and is almost always very important. Kay put it this way:

The user interface was once the last part of a system to be designed. Now it is the first. It is recognized as being primary because, to novices and professionals alike, what is presented to one's senses *is* the computer.... The software designer's control of what is essentially a theatrical context is the key to creating an illusion and enhancing its perceived "friendliness."

A program's screen displays are an "illusion" and a "theatrical context" because they reflect a wholly imagined conversation between the program author (acting through the program) and the user, a conversation that will be different every time but that will (every time, if the interface is well designed) guide users, through a series of constructs that will allow them to achieve their goals in using the program.

Those constructs may, but need not, have something to do with the way the program itself actually works. Thus, if, late one night, you boot up a copy of the game Deja Vu on your personal computer, you will find that the user interface allows you to instruct the computer to drive cars, open doors, climb stairs, shoot guns, read labels, and splash cold water on your face. The program itself naturally does none of these things physically. That is true of any program, game or not. As noted above, there is no real trash can offered as an accessory to the Macintosh, and the file that a user throws into the trash can on the screen does not physically disappear from the user's disk. (In a different "theatrical context," that of IBM's office-automation system PROFS, the world discovered along with Oliver North and Fawn Hall the difference between the user illusion that one can erase a file with the push of a function key and the real-world fact that all that is erased is an index pointer to the file. The file itself remains on the disk unless or until it is overwritten with other data, and then only to the extent of the overwriting.)

The user interface simulates an environment familiar to the user in order to make communication with the user more "friendly." The application of imagination to the design of user interfaces, a task that until recently was relegated to a position of afterthought in software design, is activity that should be encouraged in order to expand the usability of programs by people who are not computer scientists. What the user sees on a screen or in printed output and what the user must do to communicate with the program dictate the usability of the program and, ultimately, its popularity. It would be perverse not to protect the factor that provides the most value in a program.

Second, as Kay also points out, programming "has not yet had its

Galileo or Newton, Bach or Beethoven, Shakespeare or Molière." It is still early days in terms of the evolution of user interfaces, and we need to encourage investment in that evolution. In not too many years, icon manipulation and macro calls will be obsolete as user interface paradigms, having been replaced by the spoken word, interactive video, natural language sentences, or other technologies not yet imagined. Because the look and feel of a program is the part of the program with which the user most closely identifies, and the part of the program that cannot be hidden from competitors, there would be absolutely no point in investing in development of innovative user interfaces if the results of those investments could be freely copied by others.

Third, of all the elements of a program, the user interface represents the feature that is most obviously comparable to works traditionally protected by copyright. Even the narrow protectionists cannot argue that the user interface is not intelligible to humans. (Actually, I have seen some user interfaces that really are almost unintelligible, but obviously that is not the goal of sensible design.) To deny them protection would run against strong expectations in society.

Clone suppliers have argued that once large numbers of customers become accustomed to a particular user interface, it is difficult to coax them away. That will probably only be the case if those users are not just accustomed to the interface, but both accustomed to and content with it. What can the clone offer such a user? A lower price? The original program will usually already have been paid for by the users whom the clone wishes to coax away. Besides, the clone could offer a lower price yet if society permitted copying of the entirety of the original program. The price competition argument therefore leads into logical absurdity. Better performance and an improved interface? Yes, but if I can think of a better ending for Arthur C. Clarke's *2001*, should I be allowed to copy the rest of the novel and market it with my ending? The difficulty in coaxing customers away from the old and toward the new is a particularly weak argument in the context of the computer industry, where radically new products emerge every year. Better performance and improved interfaces have arrived at dizzying speed despite the absence of industry-wide clone software. And, moreover, precisely because of the rapid advances in price-performance, customers are quite used to retraining and quite willing to do so, particularly since, if they are engaged in business, they know that their competitors can easily retrain and become more efficient thereby. The assertion that, for example, customers have investments of a thousand dollars per user-employee in Lotus 1–2–3 training, therefore, not only fails to inform the debate over whether the Lotus 1–2–3 user interfaces are protectable as a matter of copyright doctrine, it fails to put forward a meaningful social-policy justification for denying traditional protection to those interfaces.

At this juncture, the academic critics intervene in the debate. As we have seen, their principal policy argument is that if we don't allow user interfaces to be copied, the originator of a particular look and feel will have a monopoly. The response to this argument is the same as it was to the argument that extending copyright to the structure, logic, and flow of software would create monopolies: Copyrights are simply not strong enough to exclude competition. There is ample empirical proof that this is true, and not a single instance where a copyright owner has been able to avoid competition by exercising the exclusive rights granted under the copyright law. Does the Apple Macintosh face substantial competition despite its particular user interface? Indeed it does. For most of its history, the Macintosh has been struggling to establish a place in the pantheon of personal computers. It is by no means the only icon-based, mouse-controllable multiple-window operating system. There are many others now, and the number is growing rapidly. Does Lotus 1–2–3 have a stranglehold on the spreadsheet business? The sales success of Microsoft's Excel would indicate not; and if you don't like Excel, try Trapeze, Wingz, Full Impact, Ragtime 2, or some of the other commercial spreadsheet programs. Likewise, dBase III has not managed to exclude other data base programs from the market. (Ashton-Tate didn't even try.) For programs running on larger computers, the story is the same. The user interface of the IBM System/360, System/370, 9370, and 30XX mainframes has evolved from a common base established in the 1960s, and yet IBM faces vigorous competition from systems with different look and feel. Indeed UNIX, a relative upstart operating system originated at AT&T, is challenging the IBM user interface for prominence in the 1990s. The story is the same for Digital Equipment Corporation, the world's second largest computer company and the most successful competitor in mid-range computers. DEC both faces competition from systems with diverse user interfaces and provides substantial competition to others, including IBM, with its own VAX system's look and feel.

There are some academics who have a fairly myopic view of competition. Dennis Karjala, for instance, has argued that Rand Jaslow's program did not compete with Elaine Whelan's program "because it was designed to run on an incompatible computer," and that S&H's statistical analysis program didn't compete with SAS, presumably for the same reason. In the real world of the computer industry, however, most competition occurs among products that are not clones; and to judge by the results in terms of price-performance improvements realized by customers, that competition has been and remains very vigorous indeed.

Most academics who worry about the risk of monopolization would concede, I think, that the availability of copyright protection for screen displays is not the real source of their concern. Human beings are, after all, relatively flexible, and can adapt from one set of screen displays to a competing set without a great deal of difficulty. What they are really worried about are the program-to-program interfaces, the look and feel of a program to someone writing complementary programs. A successful program that provides facilities for others to write programs of their own may result in the creation of a large body of user programs written to a specific program-to-program interface. User programs are not as flexible as human beings, the argument goes, and the economic friction induced by the inability to run user programs with programs that replace the underlying successful programs is what creates the monopoly situation. This argument is used most frequently with respect to operating systems, but applies equally to application programs, such as Lotus 1–2–3 and dBase IV, that allow user programs to be written on top of them.

This is an interesting theoretical argument, but one that bears little relation to the facts. In 1980 there were tens of thousands of commercially available application programs written for the Apple II personal computer. The number of application programs written by users themselves may have been in the millions. Did that situation give Apple a monopoly on personal computers, or on operating systems for personal computers? If so, it was a peculiar kind of monopoly, about which we need not be terribly concerned, since in less than a decade it has completely vanished. Since 1980, the number of suppliers of personal computers and personal computer operating systems has gone up, not down, and innovational competition has brought dramatically improved price-performance and dramatic new functionality to customers. That is so even though Apple has vigorously enforced the copyrights in the Apple II operating system.

In 1980, there were tens of thousands of commercially available application programs written for the IBM System/370 operating environment. Did that situation give IBM a monopoly on large computers, which might at that time have been described as having more than ten megabytes of minimum storage and processing speeds of more than ten million instructions per second? Did IBM have a monopoly on operating systems for such computers? Again, if so these were not monopolies that need have concerned policymakers. Since 1980, the number of suppliers of computer systems of that size and of operating systems for those computers has gone up, not down, and the price-performance improvements and new functional capabilities provided to users of those computers has been nothing short of spectacular. That is the case even though IBM has vigorously enforced the copyrights in its operating systems.

Monopoly power is the power to exclude competition and raise prices. Neither capability is manifest in the computer industry. The facts are so wildly out of line with the academic concerns over monopolization as to recommend that we give those concerns little weight in determining whether providing traditional copyright protection for software is consistent with balanced social policy, particularly since there already exists an entirely separate and powerful body of law, the antitrust law, that serves as a means of attacking the exercise of monopoly power.

Another argument originating in academe is that society is best served by standardizing user interfaces for software. The basis for that assertion is not clear. Standardization is of great value when technologies are mature, but it is stultifying when technologies are in rapid evolution. As I've already noted, user interfaces to computer programs have their history still ahead of them. Standardization is in fact coming to this area of endeavor, slowly and as appropriate. It began years ago with programming languages, like FORTRAN and COBOL, that users employ in writing complementary software. The SQL language for formulating data base queries, mentioned above in connection with the *Ashton-Tate* case, is now an official standard user interface. The International Standards Organization and national standards bodies are actively pressing forward on the user interface features of OSI (Open System Interconnection), an elaborate set of protocols for communication among compatible and noncompatible systems. Finally, there are various movements in industry to standardize certain graphical symbols used in icon-based visual displays. These are but examples of a broad range of governmental and industry standardization activities in the area of user interfaces. An industry that has had a consistent record of responsiveness (in some cases, it might be argued, overresponsiveness) to customer requirements, can surely be relied on to meet customer requirements for standardized user interfaces, to the extent that there are such requirements.

It is well to have in mind how standards are created. There are basically two ways. A supplier who has written a program having a particular user interface may wish to see that interface adopted by others, and may therefore offer his valuable intellectual property to the world. On the other hand, a multilateral standards committee may labor and debate for a period of time and create a user interface of its own. Neither of these activities are what the narrow protectionists of academe contemplate. What they have in mind is a kind of eminent domain process, a taking by condemnation of popular user interfaces, so that the fruits of their popularity may be shared by competitors who contributed nothing to the achievement of that popularity. There is nothing constructive in that suggestion, except in a case that has never yet presented itself; a case of an entrenched monopolist who because of unlawful behavior must be deprived of rights that others commonly enjoy. If such a case ever did present itself, the antitrust laws, and not the copyright laws, would be the source of the appropriate remedy. In the absence of such a case, a practice of eminent domain seizure of popular user interfaces would bring to a screeching halt the lively and supremely healthy process of innovational competition that is fueling the evolution of user interfaces that make computers increasingly user-friendly.

21

Into the Corrida

In bull-fighting, they speak of the terrain of the bull and the terrain of the bull-fighter. As long as the bull-fighter stays in his own terrain he is comparatively safe. Each time he enters into the terrain of the bull he is in great danger. Belmonte, in his best days, worked always in the terrain of the bull. This way he gave the sense of coming tragedy. People went to the corrida to see Belmonte, to be given tragic sensations, and perhaps to see the death of Belmonte. Fifteen years ago, they said if you wanted to see Belmonte you should go quickly, while he is still alive. Since then he has killed more than a thousand bulls. When he retired the legend grew up about how his bull-fighting had been, and when he came out of retirement the public were disappointed because no real man could work as close to the bulls as Belmonte was supposed to have done, not, of course, even Belmonte.

Ernest Hemingway, *The Sun Also Rises*, (1927)

Bullfighting is an activity in which it is required at some point to enter the terrain of the bull. Writing software is not such an activity. Entering the gray area, offering programs that mimic aspects of someone else's program, is an option, not a necessity. Those who do so enter that arena with their eyes open, and with the extremists on either side of the spectrum shouting at them from the stands either to get closer or to pull farther back.

The copyright law imposes on competitors in the software corrida a set of civilizing rules. Those rules balance the rights of the bull—the innovator—and those of the bullfighter—the follower—so that the bar-

barism of the traditional bullring does not leak into this large and important area of socioeconomic activity. When the rules of the game are followed, the bull's blood is not drawn, and the bullfighter is not gored.

Ideas from an original program, including those reflected in its structure, logic, and flow, and in its user interface, are made available for free appropriation by the follower. The expression chosen by the innovator remains their exclusive property to exploit, unless it is necessary to the idea or unless without access to the original the follower serendipitously arrives at the same expression. This formula has worked to order humankind's affairs for over two hundred years in relation to written expression. No good reason has been advanced for departing from it in the case of computer programs.

We have seen that the silicon epics that give life and personality to the computer are works of authorship in which the range of expression can be both broad and deep. That is not always so. Some programs exhibit no great creativity and by their nature cannot do so. For programs in that category, traditional copyright protection will be as thin as it is for recipe books. Generally speaking, though, programs of any significant size and complexity are works of authorship that exhibit all the attributes of those kinds of imaginative literary works of the type with which the general public—and the copyright law—are already quite conversant. Despite the fact that—today—they are written in languages unfamiliar to most of us, they are not qualitatively different from traditional works of imagination in ways that should affect the protection available for their detailed internal and external designs.

Copyright is not only an appropriate form of protection for computer programs, its application is critical for their continued commercial availability. Other forms of protection do not provide adequate coverage. The principal additional forms of preserving the asset value of original software are patent and trade secret. Neither of these is sufficient to the purpose.

Patent protection is only available for software that contains inventions, which is only a small proportion of the software written in a given year. Moreover, when a program does embody an invention, protection is only available for the portions of that software that comprise the invention. IBM has a patent, for instance, on a particular method for checking a text for spelling errors by computationally matching the words in the text against candidate words from a stored dictionary. "Spell-checking" is offered as part of many word-processing systems. The patent covers only small parts of some of IBM's word-processing programs.

Moreover, the patenting process is expensive. Unlike copyrights, which arise automatically as soon as the program is written down or otherwise "fixed in a tangible means of expression," patent rights do not accrue until the patent is issued by the patent office, and for that to happen the inventor must prepare, submit, and prosecute an application.

Neither would the industry be well-served if all or most programs could be patented. The patent grant, as I pointed out earlier, is a true monopoly grant. It is not in the interests either of innovators or of followers for the software industry to be carved up into a series of program-specific fiefdoms. A simple example will illuminate the point. Suppose that an innovator patents a new technique for sorting data. A clone is thereby blocked from implementing that technique. (So is a noncompatible competitor.) However, a clever clone might rush to devise a series of improvements on the innovator's program, and patent those. Then the innovator would be blocked from making those improvements. (So would the noncompatible competitor.) Unless this sort of face-off results in mutual licenses, innovational competition would be deep-frozen, a highly undesirable result. Fortunately, the patent system protects only implementations that contain the degree of novelty recognized as invention; even so, it is easy to see that in comparison to software patents, software copyrights are a relatively weak form of protection.

(The foregoing discussion relates to what are called "utility patents." There is another type of patent, called a "design patent," that protects the ornamental features of an "article of manufacture." Although there is some question whether a computer program is an "article of manufacture," the Patent Office has granted Xerox design patents for ornamental designs of certain screen displays. Design patent protection, if available for visual displays of software, is in most cases more like copyright protection than like utility patent protection.)

Trade secret protection is another mode of protection for software, and is commonly used in conjunction with copyright. Trade secret protection is only good so long as the code of the program is kept secret. For software distributed commercially, that may not be very long. Once competitors can acquire a copy of the program, even an object code copy on diskette, the process of unravelling the secret begins. Software suppliers commonly try to protect themselves against loss of secrecy by contract. Software is commonly licensed rather than sold, and license agreements typically contain clauses prohibiting some or all of the activities known as "reverse engineering." It is not clear how effectual such provisions are. For one thing, they are not necessarily binding on those who have not signed the license agreement, and it is not uncommon for a customer who is a licensee to invite onto his or her premises a software supplier to do contract programming, which contractor will not have signed license agreements with respect to the other suppliers' software on the premises. For another thing, the narrow protectionists

have moved beyond copyright and have begun agitating for legislation
that would render unlawful contractual prohibitions on "reverse engineering."

I put the term "reverse engineering" between quotation marks because, in the context of computer programs, it is a misnomer. Reverse
engineering, as traditionally understood, is the process of analyzing,
disassembling, and testing a constructed physical device in order to
determine its engineering specifications, usually for purposes of con-
structing a similar product. There is no physical device to deconstruct
in the case of software. There are no engineering specifications, toler-
ances, chemical compounds, operating speeds, or mechanical linkages
to deduce, measure, assay, or calibrate; there is just text. What does it
mean to speak of reverse engineering a text? First, if one could read and
understand a text, one would not have to reverse anything in connection
with it. One would simply assimilate it. Problems of assimilation arise
when the putative reader cannot understand the text. For software, this
generally occurs when the text of the program is delivered in object form
only, as sequences of ones and zeros on a magnetic recording medium.
Reverse engineering that text means one of two things: either running
the progam through its hardware player, the processor, and deducing
its meaning by observing its interactions with the user, with data, with
other programs, or with the hardware; or simply translating it into a
more readable language. The former activity may entail "dumping" the
contents of the processor's memory onto paper while the target program
is running in order to see how it has organized that memory and what
actions are underway as a result of the program's control of the processor. It may also entail "tracing" the program's instruction sequences
as they move through the processor, or the program's communications
as they emanate from the processor over communications lines. The
latter activity normally consists of inputting the object code of the target
program into a computer as text to be decompiled by a program that
does the reverse of what a compiler does; a program, in other words,
that translates from machine language into high-level language. Although most authors of commercial programs distribute their products
in object code form only, specifically in order to preserve the source
code as a trade secret, dumping, tracing, and decompiling are all activities that vitiate that secrecy. Accordingly, most software suppliers license their software under terms explicitly prohibiting such activities.
Again, the terms of those license agreements may not prevent dumping,
tracing, decompilation, or other translation activities by persons who
legitimately have access to the object code of the target program without
being obligated under those agreements.

Copyright is thus a critical mode of protection for the asset value of
software despite the availability of patent or trade secret protection. It

protects original expression, whether that expression is an invention or not, and therefore covers software writing more generally than does patent protection. On the other hand, it does not provide the exclusory powers that patents do, and therefore its broad applicability does not risk freezing progress. Unlike trade secret protection, copyright protection does not vanish if the work in question is made public. In addition, since dissemination is not required in order to obtain copyright protection, a nice balance is struck in respect of "reverse engineering": while competitors are allowed to read and understand the target program, using mechanical aids for that purpose if necessary, the activities of dumping, tracing, and decompiling may only be carried on—even if the competitor is not prevented by contract from undertaking them—to the extent that they do not result in making unauthorized translations of the target program.

The software protection question is international in scope. The innovators and the clones—and their respective supporters in government and academe—jet around the world to seminars and meetings, trying to drum up support for their points of view. At such a seminar in Phoenix, Arizona, early in 1989, there were lawyers and businesspeople from Japan, a functionaire from the European Commission, and a judge from Taiwan. Not long ago, I received notice of a seminar on "reverse engineering of software" sponsored by Japanese computer manufacturers but to be held in Berlin with speakers from the United Kingdom and the United States as well as West Germany and Japan. Articles on American copyright law as it applies to software appear in European legal periodicals. Articles on Japanese copyright law as it applies to software appear in American legal periodicals. The subject receives a lot of attention, and deserves it.

The Commission of the European Community has recently had occasion to consider the various forms of protection available for computer programs, in connection with a study of the need for harmonizing the laws of the Common Market countries regarding legal protection for software. It concluded, in a *Proposal for a Council Directive on the Legal Protection of Computer Programs* detailing its proposed harmonization, that it was

essential to create a legal environment which will afford a degree of protection against unauthorized reproduction to the computer program which is at least comparable to that given to works such as books, films, musical recordings or industrial designs, if research and investment in computer technology are to continue at a sufficient level to allow the Community to keep pace with other industrialized countries.

In the commission's view, the "overwhelming weight of evidence . . . indicated that protection by copyright is the most appropriate measure to adopt." The commission further opined that "within the framework of copyright, protection as a literary work is desirable" since a program "has all the characteristics of a literary work, namely that it is the expression in language and in a perceivable form from which it can be reproduced of an idea or series of ideas, created by the expenditure of human skill and labour."

In terms of the balance between innovators and followers, the commission found the traditional formulation salutary. On the one hand, "Without such a legal environment, the intellectual effort and financial resources employed to devise computer programs are put at risk by the ease with which the programs can be reproduced, imitated or counterfeited. If the level of protection given to computer programs in Member States should fall below that accorded to programs created in other countries it is evident that the work of European innovators in this fast moving and highly competitive field will be easily appropriated by predatory activities from outside the Community." On the other hand, "Where the specification of interfaces constitutes ideas and principles which underlie the program, those ideas and principles are not copyrightable subject matter." While the singling out of interfaces for special mention in connection with the idea-expression dichotomy is a political compromise that I believe can only work substantive mischief if it finds its way into the final directive, the general conclusions of the Eurocrats, as they have begun to call themselves, echo those of CONTU members in the United States a decade ago, and confirm that traditional copyright protection for computer programs is the appropriate course to follow.

In Japan, the picture is mixed. The Japanese Ministry of International Trade and Industry (MITI) tried a few years ago to have a special law of software protection adopted in place of traditional copyright protection. The special legislation would have limited fairly substantially the scope of protection for software in Japan. The attempt failed, but MITI has not given up. Meantime, an amendment to the Japanese copyright law that did pass the Japanese Diet excluded from protection "algorithms, rules and programming languages." Though it seems probable that this exclusion is only the idea-expression dichotomy dressed in modern clothes, some argue that, due to the statutory exclusion, interfaces are not protected by Japanese copyright law. Again, this is a mischievous gloss on traditional copyright protection, because the unbounded terms "algorithms," "rules," and "programming languages" will be read by some to excuse copying of elements essential to the expression of a computer program, thereby undercutting the very notion of copyright protection. At the limit of credibility, or perhaps beyond, for example, a Fujitsu representative argued during an international seminar in Tokyo in 1987 that the following program elements should be considered unprotectable: "For example, and not by way of limitation, program structures, pattern of a program or of part of a program, data structures, file structures, sequence of processing, a set of codes, programming languages such as COBOL, etc., interface, protocol and algorithm . . . [and] routines that are staple, commonplace or familiar." What, if anything, would be left protected in such a Clone Heaven?

Even in Japan, however, where one after another of the world's industries has been overtaken by a strategy whose early phases have consisted of slavish copying, there is a new recognition that—at least in the case of software—a different strategy is necessary. In major part, that realization is the result of the pressures put on Japan's industrial base by competition from the newly industrialized nations of the Pacific Rim, such as Korea, Taiwan, and Singapore. Products from those nations are now not only eating into Japan's share of the American market, they are invading Japan itself. A remarkable article by Yukuo Takenaka, head of Peat Marwick's "Project Japan," in the Japanese magazine *Biz Trend* for January/February 1989 signals the new thinking engendered by those pressures. Mr. Takenaka points out that providing protection to intellectual property rights will have the effect not only of stemming the inroads of suppliers from the newly industrialized nations, but also of increasing the influence of those Japanese suppliers who invest substantially in research and development. On the other hand, government policies that downplay intellectual property rights will lead to the de-emphasis of research and development and consequent stagnation of Japanese industry. Strong intellectual property laws, in Mr. Takenaka's view, promote development of technology and rejuvenation of industries. He argues that while Japan has so far managed to succeed industrially using technologies developed in the advanced nations, it now finds itself in a position where it must develop independent technologies in order to be a worldwide industrial leader.

With specific reference to software, Mr. Takenaka believes that Japan can become a global leader, but only if the Japanese government changes its attitude toward intellectual property protection. He asserts that this is not just a short-term business issue; rather, it is "a moral issue which demands that Japan adopt a global point of view in its truest sense. In other words, intellectual property rights have now become 'global business etiquette.' " Whether Takenaka-san's views will be more widely adopted in Japan remains to be seen.

In the United States, the state of the law is clear. Computer programs are eligible for traditional copyright protection. As the body of caselaw expands, the paths through the gray area of the idea-expression dichotomy become easier to see. An orderly unfolding is underway, providing a balanced legal environment for the further development of a vital industry.

As a medium of expression, software is evolving quite rapidly. The force behind that evolution is innovational competition. Copyright protection both induces and facilitates innovational competition by protecting original expression while simultaneously permitting the free use of ideas. Narrowing that protection, or carving out artificial exceptions to it for certain classes of competitors, threatens the engine of progress, and should not be encouraged.

Given the appropriate statutory framework, it is desirable to allow detailed principle to evolve, along with technology, through consideration of individual fact situations. The judicial system is designed for just that purpose. Not long ago I was sitting on a sunny terrace in Palo Alto discussing with a highly respected computer lawyer whether in fact the judiciary has the capacity to handle software copyright cases. My luncheon companion argued that the complexity of the cases was too great, and also that judicial salaries are too low to attract the quality of intellect to the bench that is required to decide such cases. I didn't find either argument compelling. As we've seen, there is no complicated technology involved in programming. There *is* arcane language to learn. Usually that language is a stilted variant of Basic English, highly laced with names and labels that may on first glance appear to be gibberish, but once the language is mastered, the rest is simply logic. No skills that a competent federal judge does not already possess are required to deal with software copyright cases. The burden is on the lawyers in these cases to provide the necessary education. Both of the District Court judges involved in the *NEC v. Intel* litigation have praised the lawyers on each side for their educational efforts in advance of trial. If sufficient forethought and effort is put into tutorial presentations and expert testimony, the problem is tractable. Indeed, I hope that this book demonstrates that point.

As to the assertion that the federal judiciary is underpaid, I agree that relatively speaking this is so. Whether the root of that problem is that judges are underpaid or that lawyers appearing before them are highly overpaid is an interesting point to debate, but it is unarguable that high-quality lawyers can earn far more in private practice than on the federal bench. The ramifications of that observation go far beyond software copyright cases, though. All litigation is affected thereby, if one takes as given that it is desirable to have as judges persons whose principal motivation is pecuniary. There is no reason to single out a particular class of dispute for removal from the federal courts on these grounds, and even if software copyright cases were removed from the federal courts, where would they be decided?

I submit that there is no cause for concern. While the trial of software copyright cases can present challenging problems of proof, the courts have succeeded so far in coming to grips with the facts and applying the well-known principles of copyright to those facts. A useful and, one might say, fascinating body of precedent is developing. Companies active in supplying software to users in the United States and elsewhere in the world know—or can know—what is expected of them when they choose to refer to their competitors' products in developing their own products. There is every reason to believe that the judiciary will continue to succeed in adapting copyright doctrine to the arcane epic poetry of the Computer Age.

Notes and References

Regarding the annotation convention used below, see the last paragraph of the Introduction.

Introduction

0.1. The claims brought by Apple, Ashton-Tate, and Lotus are found respectively in: Complaint, *Apple Computer, Inc. v. Microsoft Corp and Hewlett Packard Co.*, No. C88 20149 RPA, (N.D. Cal. 1987); Complaint, *Ashton-Tate Corp. v. Fox Software, Inc.*, No. 88–6437 TJH (Tx) (C.D. Cal. 1988); Complaint, *Lotus Development Corp. v. Mosaic Software, Inc.*, No. 87–0074K, (D.Mass. 1987); Complaint, *Lotus Development Corp. v. Paperback Software, Inc.*, No. 87–0076K, (D.Mass. 1987). For a sampling of the hundreds of trade press articles on these cases, see, e.g., Rachel Parker, " 'Sequence and Flow' Ruling Could Clarify Interface Copyright Issues," *Infoworld*, March 13, 1989, p. 1; Roberta Furger and Rachel Parker, "Software on Trial," *Infoworld*, January 9, 1989, p. 31; Mark Tebbe, "This New Year's Resolution: No More Lawsuits," *PC Week*, December 26, 1988, p. 19; Ron Eggers, "Ashton-Tate Sues Fox, SCO Over dBase," *Computer and Software News*, November 28, 1988, p. 1; Brenda D. Lewis, "Copyright Issue Blurs," *Computerworld*, July 18, 1988, p. 25.

0.2. Insights as to the way programmers' minds work may be found in: Ben Schneiderman, *Software Psychology* (Cambridge, Mass.: Winthrop Publications, 1980); Gerald M. Weinberg, *The Psychology of Computer Programming* (New York: Van Nostrand Reinhold, 1971).

0.3. "The Life of the law is not logic...": O. W. Holmes, Jr., *The Common Law* (Boston: Little, Brown, 1881), p. 1.

Chapter 1

1.1. As to the Jacquard Loom, see: Herman H. Goldstine, *The Computer from Pascal to von Neumann* (Princeton: Princeton University Press, 1972), pp. 20–22.

1.2. The doctrine of original intent explained (and criticized): L. W. Levy, *Original Intent and the Framers' Constitution* (New York: Macmillan, 1988).

1.3. " . . . machines of loving grace": Richard Brautigan, "All watched over by machines of loving grace," *The Pill versus the Springhill Mining Disaster* (New York: Delta Publishing, 1968), p. 1.

1.4. Copyright being "the area of intellectual property law most affected by advances in communications and information technologies": U.S. Congress, Office of Technology Assessment, *Intellectual Property in an Age of Electronics and Information* (Washington, D.C.: U.S. Government Printing Office, 1986), p. 25.

1.5. Historical development of copyright law through 1976: Harry Hunt Ransom, *The First Copyright Statute* (Austin: University of Texas Press, 1956); *Donaldsons v. Becket*, 4 Burr. 2303, 98 Eng. Rep. 257 (K.B. 1774); M. Nimmer, *Nimmer on Copyright*, §1.01[A] (New York: Matthew Bender, 1988); *Goldstein v. Calif.*, 412 U.S. 546, 555–56 (1973).

1.6. Formation of CONTU: Pub. L. 93–573, 88 Stat. 1873 (1974).

1.7. CONTU's final recommendations are found in: National Commission on New Technological Uses of Copyright, *Final Report of the National Commission on New Technological Uses of Copyrighted Works* (Washington, D.C.: U.S. Government Printing Office, July 1978).

1.8. CONTU recommendations adopted as 1980 amendments to the Copyright Act: Act of Dec. 12, 1980, Pub. L. No. 96–517 §10(a), 94 Stat. 3028(1980), codified at 17 U.S.C. §§101, 117 (1982). See H.R. Rep. No. 1307, 96th Cong., at 23 (1980).

1.9. Importance of copyright in encouraging software development: Yale M. Braunstein, Dietrich M. Fischer, Janusz A. Ordover, and William J. Baumol, "Economics of Property Rights as Applied to Computer Software and Data Bases," in George P. Bush and Robert H. Dreyfuss, eds., *Technology and Copyright* (Mt. Airy, Md.: Lomond Publications, 1979), pp. 237–38.

Chapter 2

2.1. Size and scope of the U.S. software industry: National Research Council, *The Competitive Status of the U.S. Electronics Industry* (Washington, D.C.: National Academy Press, 1984), pp. 29, 58; U.S. Dep't. of Commerce, *A Competitive Assessment of the U.S. Software Industry* (Washington, D.C.: U.S. Government Printing Office, 1984), p. 5.

2.2. The importance of software to national economies: National Research Council, p. 63; Ulrich Weil, *Information Systems in the 80s* (Englewood Cliffs: Prentice-Hall, 1982), p. 307; William H. Davidson, *The Amazing Race* (New York: John Wiley & Sons, 1984), p. 113.

2.3. Growth rates for software revenues: John Soat, "Megabucks and Megadeals: Software and Service Industry Growth," *Computer & Communications Decisions*, September 1988, p. 53; *Software Industry Report*, June 27, 1986, p. 10.

2.4. For a description of CASE methodologies: see, articles collected in "Product Spotlight: CASE Tools," *Computerworld*, March 27, 1989, p. 65.

2.5. Software industry exhibits the attributes of authorship: U.S. Department of Commerce, *Competitive Assessment*, pp. 7, 11, 27.

2.6. Successes of individual authors and garage shops: see, Robert Levering, Michael Katz, and Milton Moskowitz, *The Computer Entrepreneurs* (New York: New American Library, 1984), pp. 115–33, 145–53, 155–63, 189–94, 205–12.

2.7. Computer programs may be *ported* from one type of computer to another: Bruce MacLennon, *Principles of Programming Languages: Design, Evaluation and Implementation* (New York: Holt Reinhart and Winston, 1983), pp. 157–59; Jean Sammet, *Programming Languages: History and Fundamentals* (Englewood Cliffs: Prentice-Hall, 1969), pp. 36–48.

2.8. *The Last Emperor*: see, Jenny Lenore Rosenbaum, "Bertolucci Found by Critical Searchlight," *Christian Science Monitor*, July 22, 1988, Arts & Leisure Section, p. 19.

2.9. Dynamics of competition in the computer industry: U.S. Congress, Office of Technology Assessment, *Intellectual Property*; Arthur A. Thompson, *Economics of the Firm* (Englewood Cliffs: Prentice Hall, 1973), pp. 464, 469–79; Franklin M. Fisher, James W. McKie, and Richard B. Mancke, *IBM and the U.S. Data Processing Industry* (New York: Praeger, 1983), pp. 353–55; Montgomery Phister, *Data Processing Technology and Economics* (Santa Monica: Santa Monica Press, 1979), pp. 54–73.

2.10. Software as a non–capital intensive industry: Capers Jones, *Programming Productivity: Issues for the Eighties* (New York: Institute of Electrical and Electronic Engineers, 1981), p. 3; J. K. Buckle, *Managing Software Projects* (London: Macdonald and Jane's, 1977), p. 4.

2.11. There are two forms of competitive response to software innovation: see, Fisher, McKie, and Mancke, *IBM*, p. 471; Christopher Freeman, *The Economics of Industrial Innovation* (Cambridge: MIT Press 1982), pp. 179–82.

2.12. Software innovator's profits are dependent on the lead time provided by copyright: Braunstein, Fischer, Ordover, and Baumol, "Economics of Property Rights," pp. 237–38; Peter S. Menell, *Tailoring Legal Protection for Computer Software*, 79 *Stan. L. Rev.* 1329, 1337 (1987).

Chapter 3

3.1. The basis for the discussion of *Apple v. Franklin* in this chapter is drawn from the court opinions in the case, *Apple Computer, Inc. v. Franklin Computer Co.*, 545 F. Supp. 812 (E.D. Pa. 1982), *aff'd* 714 F.2d 1240 (3rd Cir. 1983), *cert. dismissed*, 464 U.S. 1033 (1984), and on discussions with counsel for Apple.

Chapter 5

5.1. Computer programs are written to be read by humans: Richard C. Linger, Harlan D. Mills, and Bernard I. Witt, *Structured Programming: Theory and Practice* (Reading, Mass.: Addison-Wesley, 1979), pp. 147–48; see also, Sammet, *Programming Languages*, pp. 14–17.

5.2. Academic opinions that software should be narrowly protected by copyright: Paul Goldstein, "Infringement of Copyright in Computer Programs," 47 *U. of Pitt. L. Rev.* 1119, 1125 (Summer 1986); Dennis S. Karjala, "Copyright, Computer Software and the New Protectionism," 28 *Jurimetrics* 33, 50 (Fall 1987); Pamela Samuelson, "Is Copyright Steering the Right Course?" *IEEE Software*, September 1988, pp. 78, 83.

5.3. On Luddites: see Thomas Pynchon, "Is It O.K. to Be a Luddite?" *New York Times Book Review*, October 28, 1984, p. 1.

5.4. Argument that the range of expression for software is narrow: see, e.g., P. Samuelson, "Creating a New Kind of Intellectual Property: Applying the Lessons of the Chip Law to Computer Programs," 70 *Minn. L. Rev.* 471, 527 n. 259 (December 1985); N. Monya, "The Scope of Legal Protection for Computer Programs," paper presented at the International Symposium on Legal Protection of Computer Software, Tokyo, Japan, October 28–30, 1987.

5.5. As to whether computers can "understand," see generally John Haugeland, ed., *Mind Design* (Cambridge, Mass.: MIT Press, 1981).

5.6. Setting the switches in early computers: Goldstine, *The Computer*, pp. 149–84.

5.7. All modern computers are stored program computers: C. W. Gear, *Introduction to Computer Science* (Chicago: Science Research Associates 1973), pp. 49–50; Matthew Mandl, *Fundamentals of Electronic Computers: Digital and Analog* (Englewood Cliffs: Prentice-Hall, 1967), pp. 6–8.

5.8. Functions and elements of processors: Harry L. Helms, ed., *The McGraw-Hill Computer Handbook*, §2.8 (New York: McGraw-Hill Book Co., 1987); Anthony Ralston, *Encyclopedia of Computer Science and Engineering*, 2d ed. (Englewood Cliffs: Prentice-Hall, 1983), pp. 102–6.

5.9. Parallel processing: R. Colin Johnson and Chappel Brown, *Cognizers: Neural Networks and Machines That Think* (New York: John Wiley & Sons, 1988); David J. Evans, ed., *Parallel Processing Systems* (Cambridge: Cambridge University Press, 1982).

5.10. Computer instruction sets: Helms, *McGraw-Hill Computer Handbook*, §6.16.

5.11. Processors read only binary numbers, and use of numeric notation systems by early programmers: Helms, *McGraw-Hill Computer Handbook*, §1.7; A. Gillie, *Binary Arithmetic and Boolean Algebra* (New York: McGraw Hill Book Co., 1965), pp. 1–14.

5.12. Use of blocks of binary numbers to represent alphabetic and other characters: Martin H. Weik, *Standard Dictionary of Computers and Information Processing*, 2d ed. (Rochelle Park, Md.: Hayden Book Co., 1977), p. 49.

5.13. The correspondence between binary arithmetic and formal logic: S. Adelfio and C. Nolan, *Principles and Applications of Boolean Algebra* (New York, Hayden Book Co. 1964), p. 51.

5.14. Electronic circuits that perform binary arithmetic functions: Helms, *McGraw-Hill Computer Handbook*, §5.2; Adelfio and Nolan, *Boolean Algebra*, pp. 206–15.

5.15. AND circuits, OR circuits, adders, and other elementary circuit devices: John S. Murphy, *Basics of Digital Computers* (New York: John F. Rider Publisher, 1958), 2.2–2.6, 2.46–2.47.

5.16. Powerful processors are built of large numbers of elementary switching devices: Ralston, *Encyclopedia*, pp. 1127–31; Herbert Hellerman, *Digital Computer System Principles* (New York: McGraw-Hill, 1967), pp. 165–66.

5.17. Electronic storage circuits: Helms, *McGraw-Hill Computer Handbook*, §7.3.

5.18. Advances in storage chip capacity: Davidson, *Amazing Race*, p. 107; "16 Meg—a Test Vehicle for Now," *Electronic News*, March 2, 1987, p. 36; P. S. Stone, "TI, Hitachi Join to Develop Chips," *Infoworld*, January 2, 1989, p. 3.

5.19. Processor storage as a collection of cells: Matthew Mandl, *Fundamentals*, p. 164; Anthony Ralston, *Encyclopedia*, pp. 944–45.

5.20. Difference between processor storage and long-term storage: see Helms, *McGraw-Hill Computer Handbook*, §2.4; Ralston, *Encyclopedia*, pp. 955–67, 1264–65; J. Hecht and D. Terisi, *Laser, Supertool of the 1980s* (New Haven: Ticknor & Fields, 1982), pp. 207–8.

5.21. Operating systems solve operational problems caused by differing device speeds: see Stanley Kurzban, Thomas Heines, and Anthony Sayers, *Operating System Principles* (New York: Petrocelli/Charter, 1975), pp. 93–107.

5.22. Forms of data that can serve as computer input: Ralston, *Encyclopedia*, pp. 736–38.

5.23. Common input devices. Ralston, *Encyclopedia*, pp. 739–66.

5.24. Computers as input devices: Ralston, *Encyclopedia*, p. 647; see also, Dimitris N. Charofas, *Personal Computers and Data Communications* (Rockville, Md.: Computer Science Press, 1986), p. 299.

5.25. Forms of computer output: Ralston, *Encyclopedia*, pp. 739–66.

5.26. Operating systems facilitate input and output to a computer: Kurzban, Heines, and Sayers, *Operating System Principles*, pp. 93–107.

5.27. Control of computer systems is the job of software authors: see Mandl, *Fundamentals*, p. 241.

5.28. Computers communicating over phone lines: Paul E. Green, Jr., ed., *Computer Network Architectures and Protocols* (New York: Plenum Press, 1982), p. 3.

5.29. Computer network applications to law and banking: see *West Publishing Co. v. Mead Data Central, Inc.*, 616 F. Supp. 1571 (D. Minn. 1985), *aff'd* 799 F.2d 1219 (8th Cir. 1986); William Stallings, *Data and Computer Communications* (New York: Macmillan Publishing Co., 1985), pp. 299–319.

5.30. Data communications networks versus local area networks: see Green, *Computer Network Architectures*, p. 148; Stallings, *Data*, pp. 189–92, 240–43.

5.31. Programs causing computers to behave like post offices or telephone exchanges: Uyless D. Black, *Data Communications and Distributed Processing* (Reston, Va.: Reston Publishing Co., 1983), pp. 121–35.

Chapter 6

6.1. The bases for the discussion of the *SAS* case in this chapter are the opinion in the case, *SAS Institute, Inc. v. S&H Computer Systems, Inc.*, 605 F. Supp. 816 (M.D. Tenn. 1985) and discussions with counsel for S&H.

6.2. History and description of the ENIAC: Stan Augarten, *Bit by Bit: An Illustrated History of Computers and Their Inventors* (New York: Ticknor & Fields, 1984), pp. 107–31; Goldstine, *The Computer*, pp. 149–84; Herman Lukoff, *From*

Dits to Bits: A Personal History of the Electronic Computer (Forest Grove, Ill.: Robotics Press, 1979), pp. 29–41; Nancy Stern, *From ENIAC to UNIVAC* (Bedford, Mass.: Digital Press, 1981), pp. 7–86.

6.3. Instruction set causes the processor to perform specified operations: Weik, *Standard Dictionary*, pp. 296, 315.

6.4. Elements of machine language programs: Marilyn Bohl, *Information Processing*, 4th ed. (Chicago: Science Research Associates, 1984), pp. 192–93.

6.5. Elements of assembly language programs: Bohl, *Information Processing.*

6.6. Comments as elements of assembler language programs: Helms, *McGraw-Hill Computer Handbook*, §11.3.

6.7. Computer ignores comments in a program: Suad Alagic and Michael A. Acbib, *The Design of Well-Structured and Correct Programs* (New York: Springer-Verlag, 1978), pp. 11, 17, 254.

6.8. Assembler language programs as translators: Bohl, *Information Processing*, p. 368.

6.9. Assembler language and machine language specify each elementary processor action: Bohl, *Information Processing*, pp. 365–68; Terrence W. Pratt, *Programming Languages: Design and Implementation*, 2d ed. (Englewood Cliffs: Prentice-Hall, 1984), p. 21.

6.10. High-level languages: Bohl, *Information Processing*, pp. 370–91; Richard L. Wexelblatt, ed., *History of Programming Languages Conference* (New York: Academic Press, 1981), pp. 25–41.

6.11. Compilers as translators of high-level languages: Pratt, *Design and Implementation*, p. 21; Sammet, *Programming Languages*, p. 9.

6.12. Voices crying out for repeal of the copyright law as applied to software: see, e.g., Pamela Samuelson, "Steering the Right Course"; Peter S. Menell, *Tailoring*; and the following papers submitted at the International Symposium on Legal Protection for Computer Software, Tokyo, Japan, October 28–30, 1987: S. Abe, "Treatment of Computer Programs"; A. Koch, "How to Protect New Technology and Creations."

Chapter 7

7.1. Good and bad programming style: Brian W. Kernighan and P. J. Plauger, *Elements of Programming Style*, 2d ed. (New York: McGraw-Hill, 1978).

7.2. Commentators who resist the notion that programs are literary works: see Goldstein, "Infringement;" Karjala, "Copyright"; Samuelson, "Steering the Right Course"; see also R. Kost, *Whelan v. Jaslow: Back to the Rough Ground*, 5 *Computer L. Rep.* 145 (1986); Kenneth A. Liebman, Salem M. Katch, and David D. Leitch, "Back to Basics: A Critique of the Emerging Judicial Analysis of the Outer Limits of Programming 'Expression,' " *Computer Law*, December 1, 1985.

7.3. Modules as elements of program structure: Ralston, *Encyclopedia*, p. 996; Dennie Van Tassel, *Programming Style, Design, Efficiency, Debugging and Testing* (Englewood Cliffs: Prentice-Hall, 1978), pp. 67–73.

7.4. Splitting a program development project into modules and submodules:

Joel D. Aron, *The Program Development Process* (Reading, Mass.: Addison-Wesley, 1974), pp. 99, 102.

7.5. Reusable block of code: see Philip Sherman, *Techniques in Computer Programming* (Englewood Cliffs: Prentice-Hall, 1970), pp. 100–102.

7.6. Techniques for reusing blocks of code: Philip Sherman, *Techniques;* Jeffrey Ullman, *Fundamental Concepts of Programming Systems* (Reading, Mass.: Addison-Wesley Publishing Co., 1976), pp. 133–40; 152–53.

7.7. The description of macros is taken from Ullman, *Fundamental Concepts,* pp. 133–34.

7.8. Macro definition as reflecting programmer's creativity and style: Edward Yourdon and Larry L. Constantine, *Structured Design* (New York: Yourdon Press, 1976), pp. 285–86.

7.9. Uses of macros: see Ralston, *Encyclopedia,* p. 904; A. Simpson, *Understanding dBase III* (Berkeley: Sybex, 1985), pp. 170–73.

7.10. Re nonreturning routines: see Weik, *Standard Dictionary,* p. 302.

7.11. Re subroutines: see Sherman, *Techniques,* pp. 110–15.

7.12. Re entry points: see Weik, *Standard Dictionary,* p. 261.

7.13. The nature of data structures is described in detail in the following works: A. T. Berztiss, *Data Structures,* 2d ed (New York: Academic Press, 1975); Roy S. Ellzey, *Data Structures for Computer Information Systems* (Chicago: Science Research Associates, 1982); Ivan Flores, *Data Structure and Management* (Englewood Cliffs: Prentice-Hall, 1970); C. C. Gottlieb and Leo R. Gottlieb, *Data Types and Structures* (Englewood Cliffs: Prentice-Hall, 1978).

7.14. Commonly occurring types of data structures: Ralston, *Encyclopedia,* pp. 497–501.

7.15. The nature of control blocks: David K. Hsiao, *Systems Programming: Concepts of Operating Data Base Systems* (Reading, Mass.: Addison-Wesley Publishing Co., 1975), pp. 79–81; Weik, *Standard Dictionary,* p. 44.

7.16. Control block fields and bits within fields: David K. Hsiao, *Systems Programming,* pp. 79–81; International Business Machines Corporation, *Systems Network Architecture Reference Manual: Architectural Logic,* 3d ed. (Raleigh, N.C.: International Business Machines Corporation, 1980), App. A p. A–23; A. D. Lister, *Fundamentals of Operating Systems,* 3d ed. (New York: Springer-Verlag 1984), p. 95.

7.17. How control blocks are defined: see, e.g., Henry M. Levy and Richard H. Eckhouse, Jr., *Computer Programming and Architecture—The VAX–77* (Bedford, Mass.: Digital Press, 1980), pp. 192–93; Harold Lorin and Harvey M. Deitel, *Operating Systems* (Reading, Mass.: Addison-Wesley Publishing Co., 1981), pp. 172–78.

7.18. Definition of data structures illustrative of the broad range of programming expression: Van Tassel, *Style, Design, Efficiency,* p. 52; Levy and Eckhouse, *The Vax-77,* pp. 192–93; see also Ben Schneiderman, *Software Psychology,* pp. 161–71; G. Weinberg, supra note 0.2 at p. 29; Yourdon and Constantine, *Structured Design,* pp. 223–27.

7.19. The discussion of the *Synercom* case is based on the court opinion, *Synercom Technology, Inc. v. University Computing Co.,* 462 F. Supp. 1003 (N.D. Tex. 1978).

7.20. *Williams v. Arndt,* 626 F. Supp. 571 (D. Mass. 1985).

Chapter 8

8.1. Flow of control from instruction to instruction: Matthew Hecht, *Flow Analysis of Computer Programs* (New York: North-Holland, 1977), p. 4; Mandl, *Fundamentals*, p. 241; Sherman, *Techniques*, p. 48.

8.2. Looping through a set of instructions: Flores, *Data Structures and Management*, pp. 139–71.

8.3. Flow of data is like gossip: Hecht, *Flow Analysis*, pp. 4–5.

8.4. Data items have names and roles: John M. Hartling, Larry E. Druffel, and F. Jack Hilbing, *Introduction to Computer Programming: A Problem-Solving Approach* (Bedford, Mass.: Digital Press, 1983), pp. 38–44.

8.5. Data flows out of data areas when its name is called: see Hartling, Druffel, and Hilbing, *Problem-Solving*, pp. 38–39.

8.6. Data flow patterns are a distinguishing feature of programs: Hecht, *Flow Analysis*, pp. 14–15.

Chapter 9

9.1. "Logic" may refer to abstractions unprotected by copyright: see United States Copyright Office, *Copyright Office Compendium II: Compendium of Copyright Office Practices* §325.02 (c) (Washington, D.C.: U.S. Government Printing Office, 1984).

9.2. Nimmer on the tyranny of labels: M. Nimmer, "Declaration Regarding the National Commission on New Technological Uses of Copyrighted Works (CONTU) Final Report," published in Anthony L. Clapes, Patrick Lynch, and Mark R. Steinberg, "Silicon Epics and Binary Bards: Determining the Proper Scope of Copyright Protection for Computer Programs," 34 *UCLA L. Rev.* 1493 at App. A, ¶25 (Winter 1987).

9.3. The need for logic in fiction: John Gardner, *The Art of Fiction* (New York: Alfred A. Knopf, 1983), pp. 53, 79.

9.4. The nature of detailed program logic: see J. Craig Cleaveland and Robert C. Uzgalis, *Grammars for Programming Languages* (Amsterdam: Elsevier Scientific Publishing Co., 1977); Glenford J. Myers, *Software Reliability: Principles and Practices* (New York: John Wiley, 1976), pp. 89–90.

9.5. Common elements of program logic expression: see, e.g., Pollack and Sterling, *A Guide to PL/1*, pp. 39–55, 313–27, 365; Moshe Augenstein and Aaron Tenenbaum, *Data Structures and PL/1 Programming* (Englewood Cliffs: Prentice-Hall, 1979), pp. 47–81, 97.

9.6. Logic, flow, and structure comprise design: see Van Tassel, *Style, Design, Efficiency*, pp. 41–112.

9.7. Detailed design is the essence of program authors' expression: see Phillip Bruce and Sam M. Pederson, *The Software Development Project: Planning and Management* (New York: John Wiley, 1982), pp. 85–86.

9.8. Naming conventions reflect the author's personality and experience: Weinberg, *Psychology*, pp. 223–24.

9.9. Preferable for naming conventions to convey the purpose of the thing named: Kernighan and Plauger, *Programming Style*, pp. 144–45; Van Tassel, *Style, Design, Efficiency*, pp. 11–18.

9.10. The categories of program comments: Van Tassel, *Style, Design, Efficiency*, pp. 4–7.

9.11. Comments can be anything the author wishes: Van Tassel, *Style, Design, Efficiency*, pp. 3–9; Kernighan and Plauger, *Programming Style*, pp. 141–44; Schneiderman, *Software Psychology*, pp. 66–70.

9.12. User interfaces: Alan Kay, "Computer Software," *Scientific American*, September 1984, pp. 53–59.

9.13. Each programmer develops a style: Weinberg, *Psychology*, passim.

9.14. Collective rather than individual style: see, T. Rullo ed., *Advances in Computer Programming Management*, Vol. 1 (Philadelphia: Heyden, 1980), pp. 135–51; Philip W. Metzger, *Managing a Programming Project*, 2d ed. (Englewood Cliffs: Prentice-Hall, 1981), pp. 86–91; Weinberg, *Psychology*, pp. 67–93.

9.15. How style is reflected in computer programs: Kernighan and Plauger, *Programming Style*, pp. 9–26, 59–78; Van Tassel, *Style, Design, Efficiency*, p. 52.

9.16. Elegant versus clumsy programming: see Kernighan and Plauger, *Programming Style*, passim.

9.17. Different programming objectives affect style: Weinberg, *Psychology*, pp. 19–20, 22–25.

Chapter 10

10.1. The bases for the analysis of the *Whelan* case are the opinions of the courts, *Whelan Associates, Inc. v. Jaslow Dental Laboratory, Inc.*, 609 F. Supp. 1307 (E.D. Pa. 1985), *aff'd* 797 F.2d 1222 (3d Cir. 1986), *cert. denied* 479 U.S. 1031 (1987), the author's review of trial exhibits and conversations with counsel for Whelan.

10.2. Commentators criticizing the trial court opinion in *Whelan*: see, e.g., Kost, "Rough Ground"; Liebman, Katch, and Leitch, "Back to Basics."

10.3. International interest in the Whelan appeal was evidenced by the attendance at and papers presented at the Conference on the International Legal Protection of Computer Software at Stanford Law School, July 24–26, 1986: see, e.g., W. R. Cornish, "Legal Protection of Computer Programs in the United Kingdom and Parts of the British Commonwealth"; Adolph Deitz, "Copyright Protection for Programs: Trojan Horse or Stimulus for the Future Copyright System" (Germany); Zentaro Kitagawa, "Legal Protection of Computer Programs—One Aspect of Technology Law in Japan."

10.4. President Ford's memoirs: *Harper & Row Publishers, Inc. v. Nation Enterprises*, 105 S. Ct. 2218 (1985).

Chapter 11

11.1. Literary works in which only a narrow range of expression is possible receive limited copyright protection: see, e.g., *Cooling Systems & Flexibles, Inc. v. Stuart Radiator, Inc.*, 777 F.2d 485 (9th Cir. 1985); *Rockford Map Publishers, Inc. v. Directory Services Co.*, 768 F.2d 145 (7th Cir. 1985); *Landsberg v. Scrabble Crossword Puzzle Game Players, Inc.*, 736 F.2d 485 (9th Cir. 1984); *Hoehling v. Universal City*

Studios, Inc., 618 F.2d 972 (2d Cir. 1980), *cert. denied*, 449 U.S. 841; *Brown Instrument Co. v. Warner*, 161 F.2d 910 (D.C. Cir. 1947), *cert. denied*, 322 U.S. 801; *Dow Jones & Co. v. Board of Trade*, 217 U.S.P.Q. 901 (S.D.N.Y. 1982). See generally Robert Gorman, "Fact or Fancy? The Implications for Copyright," 29 *J. Copyright Soc.* 560–610 (August 1982).

11.2. "Why is Programming Fun?" Frederick P. Brooks, *The Mythical Man-Month* (Reading, Mass.: Addison-Wesley, 1975), p. 7.

11.3. Carl Alsing's microcoding experience: Tracy Kidder, *The Soul of a New Machine* (Boston: Little, Brown & Co., 1981), pp. 101–2.

11.4. Decision to write a program is like the decision to write a novel or poem: J. F. Leathrum, *Foundations of Software Design* (Reston, Va.: Reston Publishing Co., 1983), p. 11.

11.5. CASE tools and techniques: see articles collected in "Product Spotlight: CASE Tools."

11.6. Social engineers: Thomas Paine, *Common Sense* (1776); Upton Sinclair, *The Jungle* (1906).

11.7. Herbie Hancock and Piérre Boulez use CASE-like techniques: John Rockwell, "Computer Music Is Very Much Alive," *New York Times*, September 22, 1985, Arts & Leisure Section p. 21.

11.8. Effects of CASE on programming style: see Vaughan Merlyn and Greg Boone, "Sorting Out the Tangle of Tool Types," *Computerworld*, March 27, 1989, p. 65.

11.9. Availability of alternate expression is the rule rather than the exception in programming: National Commission on New Technological Uses of Copyrighted Works, *Final Report*, p. 20 n. 106.

11.10. "At every level, the process is characterized by choice, often arbitrary. . . .": *SAS Inst., Inc. v. S&H Computer Sys.*, 605 F Supp. 816, 825 (M.D. Tenn. 1985).

11.11. "The possibility of two programmers creating identical programs without copying was compared . . . to the likelihood of a monkey sitting at a typewriter producing Shakespeare": *Apple Computer, Inc. v. Macintosh Computers, Ltd.*, No. T–1232–84, No. T–1235–84, slip op. at 3 (F.C. Can. April 29, 1986).

11.12. "Virtually unlimited number of sequences that would enable a programmer to construct a program": *M. Kramer Mfg. Co., Inc. v. Andrews*, 783 F.2d 421, 436 (4th Cir. 1986).

11.13. Irrelevance of compatibility strategy to idea-expression merger: *Apple Computer, Inc. v. Franklin Computer Corp.*, 714 F.2d 1240, 1253 (3d Cir. 1983).

Chapter 12

12.1. The discussion of NEC v. Intel is based on the opinion: *NEC Corporation v. Intel Corporation*, No.C–84–20799-WPG, slip op. (N.D. Cal. Feb. 7, 1989), and the author's review of trial exhibits and discussions with counsel for Intel.

12.2. Disappearance of "©": see Herbert Mitgang, "Old Copyright Treaty: New Shield for U.S. Artists," *New York Times*, March 10, 1989, section B, p. 7.

12.3. Fair use under the copyright law: 17 U.S.C. §106 (1976).

12.4. Competitive use is virtually never fair use: *Sony Corp. of America v. Universal City Studios, Inc.*, 464 U.S. 417, 451 (1984).

12.5. Similarities in an intermediate version of the accused work may be evidence of infringement: see *Miller v. Universal City Studios*, 650 F.2d 1365 (5th Cir. 1981).

12.6. Intermediate copying may itself be infringement. Compare *Miller v. Universal City Studios, Inc.* (intermediate copies may be infringement); *Telerate Systems, Inc. v. Caro*, 689 F. Supp. 1221 (S.D.N.Y. 1988) (not all things done in the name of reverse engineering are proper); *Hubco Data Products Corp. v. Management Assistance, Inc.*, 219 U.S.P.Q. (BNA) 450 (D.C.Ida. 1983) (use of reverse engineered code in a product is infringing); *E. F. Johnson Co. v. Uniden Corp. of America*, 623 F. Supp. 1485, 1501 (D.C. Minn. 1985) (no infringement); *Vault Corp. v. Quaid Software, Ltd.*, 847 F.2d 255 (5th Cir. 1988) (no infringement).

Chapter 13

13.1. *The Iliad of Homer*, trans. R. Lattimore (Chicago: University of Chicago Press, 1951).

13.2. The phases in a program-writing project: Metzger, *Managing*, pp. 86–91; G. F. Hice, W. S. Turner, and L. F. Coshwell, *System Development Methodology*, rev. ed. (Englewood Cliffs: Prentice-Hall, 1978).

13.3. Coding can be entrusted to a beginning programmer: see Richard C. Gunther, *Management Methodology for Software Product Engineering* (New York: John Wiley, 1978), p. 49.

13.4. The discussion of the *Frybarger* case is based on the court opinion, *Frybarger v. International Business Machines Corp.*, 812 F.2d 525 (9th Cir. 1987), the author's review of the trial exhibits, and discussions with counsel for IBM.

13.5. The karate game case: *Data East USA, Inc. v. Epyx, Inc.*, 862 F.2d 204 (9th Cir. 1988).

Chapter 14

14.1. Argument that there is a public interest in relatively free appropriation of software: Menell, "Tailoring"; Karjala, "New Protectionism."

14.2. Free appropriation arguments are being strenuously advanced in Japan: Dennis S. Karjala, "The Protection of Operating Software Under Japanese Copyright Law," 29 *Jurimetrics* 43 (Fall 1988).

14.3. Free appropriation arguments advanced in Jaslow's Petition for Certiorari: Petition for Certiorari, *Jaslow Dental Laboratory, Inc. v. Whelan Assoc., Inc.* 30 (No. 86–675), *cert. denied*, 107 S. Ct. 877 (1987).

14.4. Academic public interest arguments: see, e.g., "Note, Copyright Infringement of Computer Programs: A Modification of the Substantial Similarity Test," 68 *Minn. L. Rev.* 1264, 1291 (1984); "Note, Defining the Scope of Copyright Protection for Computer Software," 38 *Stan. L. Rev.* 497, 498, 518 (1989); cf. "Note, Copyright Protection of Computer Programs in Object Code," 96 *Harvard L. Rev.* 1723, 1739–42 (1983).

14.5. Argument that the purpose of copyright law is to promote dissemination: Pamela Samuelson, "CONTU Revisited: The Case Against Copyright Protection for Computer Programs in Machine-Readable Form," 1984 *Duke L.J.* 663, 705–53 (1984).

14.6. K. C. Munchkin jeopardized the investment in PAC-MAN: *Atari, Inc. v. North American Philips Consumer Electronics Corp.*, 672 F.2d 607, 620 (1982).

14.7. J. D. Salinger's unpublished letters: *Salinger v. Random House, Inc.*, 811 F.2d 90 (2d Cir. 1987).

14.8. Copyright Office deposit and registration procedures: United States Copyright Office, *Copyright Office Circular R61*, May 1983 at 1; *Copyright Office Circular R7d*, August 1982 at 2.

14.9. The discussion of the Broderbund case is drawn from the opinion: *Broderbund Software, Inc. v. Unison World, Inc.*, 648 F. Supp. 1127 (N.D. Cal. 1986), and from a review of trial exhibits.

14.10. Separate audiovisual display said to be necessary to protect screens: compare *Broderbund*; *Digital Communications Associates, Inc. v. Softklone Distributing Corp.*, 659 F. Supp. 449 (N.D. Ga. 1987); *Manufacturers Technologies, Inc. v. CAMS, Inc.*, No. N–85–253 (TFGD), *slip op.* (D.C. Conn. 1989).

14.11. Copyright Office refusal to accept separate registration of visual displays: 36 Pat. Trademark & Copyright J. (BNA) 155 (1988).

Chapter 15

15.1. Judge Orrick on freedom to copy ideas: *Broderbund*, at 1133.

15.2. Access will be presumed if the accused text is identical to the original: *R. Dakin & Co. v. Charles Offset Co., Inc.*, 441 F. Supp. 434, 438–39 (S.D.N.Y. 1977); see also *Midway Mfg. Co. v. Bandai-America, Inc.*, 546 F. Supp. 125, 146 (D. N.J. 1982).

15.3. Clean room procedures at Western Digital: Steve Cummings, "Bus Structures and BIOS: Where Do They Fit In?" *PC Week*, January 19, 1988, p. S5.

15.4. Cloning *Meet the Beatles*: Michael Miller, "Fujitsu Can Legally Clone IBM Software; The Question Now: Will It Be Able To?" *Wall Street Journal*, December 1, 1988, p. B1.

15.5. The argument that software is utilitarian, like a hammer: see, e.g., Gary Dukarich, "Patentability of Dedicated Information Processors and Infringement Protection of Inventions that Use Them," 29 *Jurimetrics* 135, 201 (Winter, 1989); Liebman, Katch, and Leitch, "Back to Basics," p. 7; Goldstein, "Infringement of Copyright," p. 1126; Karjala, "New Protectionism," p. 94.

15.6. The principal international compacts for copyright are the Berne Convention and the Universal Copyright Convention.

15.7. The analysis of *Plains Cotton* is based on the appellate court opinion in the case: 807 F.2d 1256 (5th Cir.), *cert. denied*, 108 S. Ct. 80 (1987).

15.8. Suggestion that Plains Cotton is inconsistent with Whelan: see, e.g., *Manufacturers Technologies, Inc. v. CAMS, Inc.*, at 11 n. 12.

Chapter 16

16.1. Argument that traditional copyright protection confers patent-like monopolies for software: Goldstein, "Infringement of Copyright," p. 1127; Dukarich, "Patentability," p. 201; T. Kline, "Requiring an Election of Protection for Patentable/Copyrightable Computer Programs," 67 *J. Pat. & Trademark Off. Soc.* 280, 297 (1985).

16.2. "The purpose of the Copyright Act is and always has been to grant a monopoly": *Apple Computer, Inc. v. Macintosh Computers, Ltd.* at 49.

16.3. Listing of the copyright owner's rights: 17 U.S.C. §106.

Chapter 17

17.1. This chapter consists of materials released by the American Arbitration Association on November 29, 1988, in *International Business Machines Corporation v. Fujitsu, Ltd.*, No. 13T–117–0636–85: Opinion, November 29, 1988; Opinion, September 15, 1987; Remarks of John L. Jones, November 29, 1988; Remarks of Robert F. Mnookan, November 29, 1988; Instructions Fact Sheet, November 29, 1988.

Chapter 18

18.1. ADAPSO's study of suppliers' interface practices: Association of Data Processing Service Organizations, *ADAPSO Guidebook on Software Product Assessment of Interface Openness*, November 28, 1988.

18.2. Formats and protocols: see, Hice, Turner, and Coshwell, *System Development Methodology*, pp. 144–49, 182–83.

18.3. Conversations with demons: J. Gardner, *Grendel* (New York: Alfred A. Knopf, 1971); Ann Rice, *Interview with the Vampire* (New York: Ballantine, 1986).

Chapter 19

19.1. Regarding aggressive compatibility strategies, see, *Whelan*, p. 1244; *Apple v. Franklin*, pp. 1250–52; *Broderbund*, pp. 1131–33; John M. Conley and Robert M. Bryan, "A Unifying Theory for Litigation of Computer Software Copyright Cases," 63 *N.C.L. Rev.* 563, 590–95 (1985).

19.2. The discussion of the mobile phone case is based on the court opinion: *E. F. Johnson Co. v. Uniden Corp.*, 623 F. Supp. 1485 (D. Minn. 1985).

Chapter 20

20.1. The source of the phrase "total concept and feel": *Roth Greeting Cards v. United Card Co.*, 429 F.2d 1106, 1110 (9th Cir. 1970).

20.2. Kay,"Computer Software," p. 59.

20.3. Clone suppliers say it is difficult to coax customers away from popular programs: see, Kathleen K. Weigner and John Heins, "Can Las Vegas Sue Atlantic City?" *Forbes*, March 6, 1989, p. 130; David Churbruck and Beth Freedman, "Suits Against 1–2–3 Imitators May Have Wide User Impact," *PC Week*, January 20, 1987, p. 1; see also, Frank G. Smith and Martin J. Elgison, "DCA v. Softklone: The Continuing Saga of Copyright, Computers and Clones," 4 *Computer L.* No. 4 at 13, 17 (Apr. 1987).

20.4. One thousand dollars in Lotus user training investment: Weigner and Heins, "Can Las Vegas Sue?"

20.5. Argument that protection of user interfaces will engender monopolies:

see Goldstein, "Infringement of Copyright"; Dukarich, "Patentability"; Kline, "Requiring an Election."

20.6. Professor Karjala's myopic view of competition: Karjala, "New Protectionism," pp. 57, 79.

20.7. What the academics are really worried about is program-to-program interfaces: see, Karjala, "New Protectionism," pp. 64–69 and authorities he cites p. 65 n. 112.

20.8. Argument that user interfaces should be standardized: see Menell, "Tailoring," p. 1345; Karjala, "New Protectionism," pp. 63–69.

Chapter 21

21.1. Oliver North's discovery that "erasing computer files does not make them disappear: see, Philip Elmer-DeWitt, "Can a System Keep a Secret?" *Time*, April 6, 1987, p. 68.

21.2. IBM's position in the computer industry: see, *Allen-Myland, Inc. v. International Business Machines Corp.*, 693 F. Supp. 262, 279–80 (E.D. Pa. 1988).

21.3. Monopoly power is the power to raise prices and exclude competition: *U.S. v. Grinnell Corp.*, 384 U.S. 563, 571 (1966); *U.S. v. duPont & Co.*, 351 U.S. 377, 391 (1956).

21.4. The nature of standardization activities in the computer industry: see, e.g., James Moulton, "Think or Swim: Systems Integrators and Open Systems Interconnect," *Mini-Micro Systems*, November 1988, p. 94; Richard Goering, "Standardization Effort Targets Data Management for CASE," *Computer Design*, October 1, 1988, p. 28; Wayne Fischer, "Real Time Computing Demands Standards," *Computer Design*, October 1, 1988, p. 79; D. Chambers, "To Standardize or Not to Standardize: Is That the Question?" *Computerworld*, September 12, 1988, p. 51; Fritz Dressler, "CASE Standards: A Grab Bag of Good Intentions," *PC Week*, August 29, 1988, p. 90; Daniel P. Stokesberry, "Interim Standards Could Ease the Migration to OSI," *Government Computer News*, July 22, 1988, p. 81.

21.5. Patent protection for software: *Diamond v. Diehr* 450 U.S. 175 (1981).

21.6. The process of obtaining a patent: see, P. Rosenberg, *Patent Law Fundamentals*, 2d ed. (New York: Clark Boardman Co., 1988), chs. 13, 15.

21.7. Blocking strategies using patents: see Dukarich, "Patentability," pp. 186–87; W. Bulkeley, "Will Software Patents Cramp Creativity?" *Wall Street Journal*, March 14, 1989, p. B1.

21.8. Trade secret is any information that is kept secret: *Restatement of Torts*, ¶ 757 Comment b. (1939); *Richardson v. Suzuki Motor Co.*, 9 U.S.P.Q. 1913 (Fed. Cir. 1989).

21.9. Reverse engineering: see, *Bonito Boats, Inc. v. Thunder Craft Boats, Inc.*, 109 S. Ct. 971 (1989).

21.10. Distributing programs in object code form to preserve trade secret: L. J. Kutten, "Software Developers Must Take Steps to Protect Own Secrets," *Computerworld*, August 25, 1986, p. 86.

21.11. European copyright directive: Commission of the European Communities, "Proposal for a Council Directive on the Legal Protection of Computer

Programs," *Official Journal of the European Communities* No. C 91/4, December 4, 1989, pp. 5, 7, 9, 13.

21.12. MITI legislative initiative on copyright: see "MITI Drops Plan to Limit Copyright," *Computerworld*, March 25, 1985, p. 14; Jake Kirchner, "Japan Buries Copyright Bill; U.S. Fears It May Resurface," *Computerworld*, April 23, 1984, p. 92.

21.13. New Japanese copyright law: see Y. Takaishi, "Intellectual Property Right and Its Protection in the Information Industry: A Criticism to a Theory Characterizing Programs as Special Copyrightable Works," 30 *Jouhou Kanri* [Information Management] 945 (1988) (in Japanese, but with summary in English); Gary Hoffman and Jon Grossman, "Software Ideas, Expression Need a Uniform System of Protection," *National Law Journal*, August 1, 1988, p. 27.

21.14. Fujitsu representative's view of copyright protection for software: Abe, "Treatment of Computer Programs," p. 3.

21.15. Education of the *Intel* judges: "Judge Ingram Discusses the Rigors of Educating the Court," *Computer Industry Litigation Reporter*, February 27, 1989, p. 9,060; L. Wirbel, "The Education of Judge Gray," *Electronic Engineering Times*, March 13, 1989, p. 49.

Index

ABOUT THE AUTHOR

ANTHONY L. CLAPES is a Senior Corporate Counsel at IBM and is presently responsible for managing IBM's intellectual property and antitrust litigation. For many years he has represented IBM in large and complex cases. Much of his recent casework has related to software copyrights. Mr. Clapes has lectured on copyright law as it applies to computer programs in numerous symposia, and he is the co-author of an influential law article on the subject: "Silicon Epics and Binary Bards: Determining the Proper Scope of Copyright Protection for Computer Programs," 34 UCLA L. Rev. 1493 (Winter 1987).